AF675117

6

States, Citizens and Outsiders

The Uprooted Peoples of South Asia

Edited by
Tapan K. Bose
Rita Manchanda

South Asia Forum for Human Rights
Kathmandu

South Asia Forum for Human Rights
G.P.O. Box 4906, Kathmandu, Nepal.
Phone: +977 1 420634, Fax: +977 1 418408
Email: south@safhr.wlink.com.np

Cover photographs: Usha Tiwari
Front cover picture shows Bhutanese refugees at the Beldangi Refugee Camp in Jhapa in East Nepal. Back cover picture shows food being brought from the store to distribute to the refugees.

Printed at: Union Press (Pvt.) Ltd, Putalisadak, Kathmandu-31, Nepal. Phone: 227624.

Contents

SECTION ONE

INTRODUCTION

State policies makes refugees. It is the leitmotif underpinning this collection of writings and shaping the ensuing recommendations for a South Asian Charter for the protection of refugees, migrants, internally displaced and stateless persons. The basic premise is that states should be held accountable for displacing their citizens. But where displaced people seek refuge across borders, the host state should receive refugees on humanitarian grounds and respect the principle of *non-refoulement.*

In the South Asian region, the modern state building process of the post-colonial states has been marked by the trails of divided communities and mutilated *mohallahs* (neighbourhoods) and the wails of rejected peoples. The history of these post-partition states of South Asia has been one of consolidating majoritarian elites producing persecuted minorities, of citizenship giving rise to statelessness, of borders resulting in illegal but not unnatural cross border movements and of development policies uprooting millions. It has made South Asia a region crowded with refugees and the displaced. South Asia has the fourth largest concentration of refugees in the world and this does not include the army of stateless migrants and the internally displaced.

Estimates of Political Refugees (1996)

Host Country	Origin	Number	Total
Bangladesh	Burma	24,000	24,000
India	Afghanistan	19,800	368,500
	Burma(Chin)	50,000	
	Bhutan	40,000	
	Chakma	43,000	
	Sri Lanka	96,000	
	Tibet	119,000	
	Others	700	
Pakistan	Afghanistan	1,300,000	1,302,500
	Iraq	1,200	
	Iran	300	
	Somalia	1,000	
Nepal	Bhutan	93,000	121,000
	Tibet	18,000	
			Total: 1,816,000

Sources: Annual reports of UNHCR- 1995-1996, Report of the US Committee on Refugees 1996. Appeal Movement Coordination Committee and Bhutan National Congress (Bhutan); Revolutionnary Association of Women of Afghanistan (Pakistan) ;Jana Samhati Samiti (CHT); Tibet information Centre (New Delhi); Chin Refugee Committee (New Delhi); The Other Media (New Delhi); National Peace Council (Colombo); newspapers - *The Rising Nepal,* and *The Kathmandu Post* (Nepal); *The Telegraph*, *The Asian Age* and *The Pioneer* (India); *The News* (Pakistan); *Holiday* (Bangladesh); and *Island Observer* (Sri Lanka).

It is a situation which calls for urgent action. For no South Asian state government has formulated a policy towards refugees or migrants. Responses to refugee influx are ad hoc and refugee status often arbitrarily determined at the local level, especially where the refugees have no political profile in the receiving country. South Asian governments have declined to accede to what is the magna carta of international refugee protection law, the 1951 International Convention for the Protection of Refugees and the 1967 Protocol. All the governments insist that the principle of *non-refoulement* is upheld and there is no push back policy, however the record is an ambiguous one of imposed repatriation in many cases.

The United Nations High Commissioner for Refugees (UNHCR) has been allowed to extend its protection mandate for refugees only on a case by case basis. Access to local and international NGOs is discretionary and withdrawn at will.

Moreover, the peculiarities of the situation of refugees and people in refugee like situations in South Asia can only be partially addressed by the existing international protection regime. The restrictive 1951 definition does not provide protection to those who have been forced to flee because of ethnic strife, civil disturbance, breakdown of law and order, denial of human rights and insecurity of food, land and water caused by forces beyond their control.

There have been efforts at the regional level in Africa in the 1969 OAU Convention and in Central America in the 1984 Cartagena Declaration, to expand the scope of the definition of refugees. The time has come for South Asia to develop a regional framework for the protection of refugees and migrants which responds to the peculiar South Asian reality of fractured communities. No South Asian state feels confident enough to unilaterally commit itself to a framework of refugee protection given the level of suspicion and tension in the region. Moreover refugees are trans-national issues which cannot be addressed unilaterally.

In November 1996, South Asia Forum for Human Rights in collaboration with the Faculty of Law, Tribhuvan University undertook the initiative to bring together in Kathmandu, politicians, former bureaucrats, academics, professionals, human rights activists and media persons to review the situation of refugees and the displaced. The five-day seminar was organised with the support and cooperation of Friedrich-Naumann-Stiftung.

This collection of writings is based on that seminar. The perspective reflects the concern to humanise the response to the situation of refugees by integrating an academic with an activist approach. The analysis of the country situation is by an academic and the detailed look into the specifics of a particular refugee situation is by and large by an activist.

Refugees are not faceless people. They are not just numbers that create a security problem for the host state. Much of the debate on the refugee and displaced person issue has been dominated by a statist perspective that views refugees and migratory movements as disruptive of state order. This collection of writings seeks to widen the perspective and to restore human dignity back to the refugee and migrant. It frontally takes on the issue of migrants which most academic analyses have avoided as abutting on to the illegal. In South Asia the distinction between refugees and migrants is a blurred one and the usage of the term refugee in the book reflects this blurred distinction.

More by accident than design, the geographic axis of South Asia in the book is an eastern one, with Pakistan regrettably not getting its due share of attention. The geopolitical canvas of the refugee map of South Asia, however, has been expanded to take in the refugee influx from Afghanistan in the west and Myanmar in the east.

The historian Barun De, in an encyclopedic mapping of the history of population movements, sets out the themes, which are picked up in the writings in this collection. His peoples history of indigenous popular geopolitics goes beyond the boundaries drawn by Eurocentric cartographers to trace the long and deep tracks of traditional migratory routes resulting in the cultural bonding of peoples of the region. The history of traditional South Asian cultural interaction is a record of settlements but also of movements, as legitimate or illegitimate as today's non-resident Indian bound for Canada or the migrant disguised as a sailor who drowns in the Ionian sea, says Barun De.

The building of the nation-state has drawn in blood, boundaries which have divided communities and disrupted traditional migratory routes. Transplanted by the post-colonial elite in South Asia, the state building process has been violent, militarising the state structure.

Tapan Bose develops this linkage between state formation and refugee flows. Drawing upon Hannah Arendt's study, he walks us past the persecution, violence and hunger which drove thousands of refugees and migrants out of the territorial nation-states of Europe. International refugee protection instruments were evolved to meet the European situation and later the cold war. But they are inadequate to meet the demands of mass population displacements following the emergence of the post-colonial nation-states.

In South Asian states, national identity has been articulated through the symbolism of majority ethnicity, all others became minorities competing for political space, often through violent means in the face of a militaristic state. In his analytical construct of the refugee-migrant problem in South Asia, Bose delves into the way cross-border migration has got mired in the national security complex of the dominant elite and projected as threatening national integrity. Rejecting the knee jerk response of fencing borders, Bose argues that the reality of the South Asian political economies and the historic practice of labour migration demands that a mechanism be developed to regulate what is a de facto integrated regional labour market.

Bose emphasises that a uniform refugee law with humane provisions will have to be promoted regionally for given the mutual mistrust among states of the region no single state can be expected to enact such a law. Moreover, institutionalising the rights of refugees and the displaced in national legal systems, is the first step but refugees are a trans-national issue, and demand more than national and bilateral efforts.

What a civil rights agenda for the protection of refugees and migrants should be is explored by Ranabir Samaddar. It should be linked to a campaign of peace which stresses not peace-keeping and safe havens but people's rights and consensus, for it is human rights abuses which produce refugee movements. And these include denial of food, land and water security.

Samaddar questions the distinction made between political and economic refugees or voluntary migrants. While the pull factor may operate in response to what is an informal integrated labour market, there is the complication of the traditional patterns of centuries of seasonal migration which 50 years of border making have disrupted. Drawing upon his study of border communities along the porous Indo-Bangladesh border, Samaddar brings out the contradictions between the nation-state building project which must glorify the border as the symbol of the state and the unreality of the border for the people who live the reality of trans-border flows.

The neatness of the pull factor in separating refugees from migrants is further blurred by the fact that the migrant communities are often victims of political persecution or deliberately denied development aid. They are unwanted people at home as well as in the host country where they are seen as threatening scarce resources and fragile demographic balances. Later essays on the Chin-Burmese refugees in Mizoram, the Rohingyas in Bangladesh and the Chakmas in Tripura examine the inadequacy of the conventional political versus economic categorisation.

Also, four facets of migration are probed in companion pieces. Dr. Haroon Ahmed looks at the one million Bangladeshi migrants hidden in the lanes of Karachi. If the police were to stop taking bribes, a million people would be exposed as stateless for Bangladesh refuses to recognise that they are its citizens. Gautam Navlakha picks on the security driven obsession to view migration as a numbers game which ends up mystifying it and serving xenophobic politics. Sadeq Khan turns the perspective round to that of a country which produces migrants — Bangladesh — arguing that where the land-people ratio is adverse, people will migrate. Shifting from illegal to legal migration and from porous to legally open borders, Basanta Thapa casts a worried look at the dangers of Nepal, a small country being overwhelmed by mass migration from its huge neighbour, India.

The theme that all cross-border population movement is in a sense involuntary runs through many of the writings and shaped the final recommendation that while the distinction between refugees and migrants should be maintained, migrants too should be recognised as Persons of Concern deserving of some kind of protection. Given the South Asian reality, migration driven by the pull-push factor will not stop. To ignore it is to leave completely vulnerable a growing army of stateless people.

A sharp critique of the existing level of refugee protection in South Asia is made by Ravi Nair who asserts that all categories of refugees in the region face serious problems from forcible repatriation to starvation. As none of the governments of South Asia have formulated a refugee policy, treatment of refugees is ad hoc and arbitrary. And while all claim to respect the fundamental principle of refugee law — *non-refoulement*, Nair demonstrates that in the case of India and Nepal, both have repatriated refugees under duress. UNHCR is hauled up for not arming itself with its international mandate to protect refugees and not pushing the Indian government. UNHCR's avowed objective in India is to promote a legal framework, but it should not be used as an excuse to shirk its protection role. Nair singles out for particular criticism the UNHCR's far from humane treatment of the urban refugees in Delhi, the Afghans or the Burmese. It has resulted in a piquant situation where the UNHCR office needs security against an attack by refugees whom it should be protecting.

The difficult relationship between governments and UNHCR is brought out in Meghna Guhathakurta's country paper on Bangladesh, in the case of the forcible repatriation of the Rohingya refugees to Myanmar. When UNHCR protested, it was denied access to the camps however even under the revised MoU between UNHCR and the government, what was left ambiguous was the crucial issue of whether repatriation should be promoted only when there is an appreciable improvement in the home situation and the safety of the returnees can be assured. Anxiety about imposed repatriation dominates the discussion about other refugees like the Sri Lankan Tamil and Chakma refugees.

Guhathakurta focuses on population movements in Bangladesh caused by the politics of the nation-state and environmental and economic pressures. Denial of food, land and water security, exacerbated by population pressure, inadequate planning and the desertification effect of the Farraka barrage has generated a westward movement of millions of landless labourers into India, Pakistan and outside the region. The government has encouraged migration.

Refugee outflows caused by the politics of the nation-state, like that of the Biharis and the Chakmas are further looked at. Muhammad Nur Khan details the plight of the Biharis, stranded Pakistanis in Bangladesh, the victims of the partitioned states of South Asia not once but twice over. Disowned by Pakistan and unwanted in Bangladesh, the plight of the Biharis huddled in refugee camps in Bangladesh for over 25 years highlights the responsibility of states not to arbitrarily disenfranchise their citizens or impose restrictions in re-acquiring citizenship.

The Buddhist tribal Jumma refugees from the Chittagong Hill Tracts of Bangladesh fled violence at the hands of a Muslim majority state.Chakma refugees crossed the border because of political discrimination and developmental policies which destroyed their livelihood. Insurgency in the CHT since the early 70s has claimed nearly 20,000 lives. The signing of the peace accord between the Bangladesh government and Parbottya Chattogram Jana Samhati Samiti on December 2 1997 will hopefully end the two-decade-old fighting in the CHT.

Shifting the perspective away from refugee generating states to that of the host state, Partha Ghosh focuses on India and the interface between refugee flows and domestic politics. Ghosh, in a sense, dives back to the security perspective which has dominated the refugee debate. There is the security issue of the involvement of the migrants in local politics. But more threatening to the elite is the ethnic and communal character of many of the migratory flows, especially as in its trail come notions of sub-national identity and in some cases the gun culture. Ghosh however rejects responses like barricades or forcible eviction as just unworkable. The paradox is that the political rhetoric of expulsion of illegal immigrants has increased in direct proportion to the inability of states to control their movement. Ghosh questions the politically manipulated assumption that local labour regards migrants as threatening, suggesting that migration does not invoke a nativist reaction unless it is projected as a racial, communal or ethnic threat.

Rita Manchand's report on the Chin-Burmese refugees in Mizoram in India brings out the way in which, they have become victims of a xenophobic campaign whipped up by local politicians. The federal government in New Delhi is tacitly colluding in a policy of push back of refugees across the border often into the hands of the waiting Myanmar military. The Christian ethnic Chins are regarded simply as economic refugees, but they demonstrate the problem of blurred categories as the Chins are fleeing generalised violence, human rights abuses and the discriminatory policies of a Buddhist Burman majority state which has kept Chin state underdeveloped.

In the case of the Sri Lankan Tamils, the Indian government did recognise them as refugees however, as Fr. C. Amal Raj demonstrates for asylum or protection to have meaning a minimum standard has to be maintained in the refugee camps. The trend is to let conditions in the camp deteriorate to such an extent that the refugee is forced to get assimilated or return. India's forcible repatriation of the refugees, its denial of information about the ground reality to the returning refugees is exposed. Many of the returnees, unable to go back home have joined Sri Lanka's army of internally displaced people kept from crossing the international border regardless of how unsafe it is.

The forcibly displaced whether internally or those who cross international borders to become refugees are the victims of political persecution or generalised violence. Involuntary displacement is also caused by environmental devastation both natural and man-made. Malika Basu analyses the involuntary displacement of millions in India as a result of the planned development policies of the state. Sometimes termed as environmental refugees, the development displaced and refugees have in common the fact that they are victims of events over which they have no control. Basu warns against the sliding process whereby inhabitants become oustees and then refugees because of the failure of resettlement policies.

State obligation to protect the right of citizens to remain in their habitat and to be held accountable for the displacement of citizens both within the country and outside, finds strong expression in the recommendations of the Kathmandu group. States have arbitrarily changed their citizenship laws creating thousands of stateless peoples like the Bhutanese refugees. Nepal, a hill state with a very limited carrying capacity has had to shoulder the burden of Bhutanese and Tibetan refugees as Hari Phouyal examines.

Rakesh Chetri and Ratan Gazmer in complementary articles on Bhutanese refugees detail the background of the making of a stateless people. The UNHCR has played a major role in keeping intact the identity of the Bhutanese people of Nepali origin in the refugee camps who otherwise would have been forced to melt into the South Asian night. Gazmer describes the abortive campaign of the Bhutanese peace marchers to assert their right to return to Bhutan. Chetri however cautions against local or regional integration of the refugees as it legitimises the right of South Asian states to disenfranchise its citizens.

Angela Dietrich delves into the condition of the Tibetan refugees in Nepal, in many ways a model refugee resettlement situation made possible because of the politics of the cold war. However, Nepal is now in a bind, faced with fresh influx of refugees, it has to balance the sensitivities of its big neighbour China on Tibet and pressure from the West including aid donor countries not to push back Tibetan refugees.

While *non-refoulement* is the bedrock of refugee protection, Darini Rajasingham makes a plea for the internally displaced in Sri Lanka to have the right to remain. War between the Sri Lankan government and the LTTE has created a new ethno-national border dividing the LTTE-controlled areas in the north and the government controlled Sinhala dominated areas in the south. A tenth of the population of the country has been displaced. When bargains for peace are struck and given the system of proportional representation, will the cynical necessity of the democratic electoral process force the displaced to return? Rajasingham questions the domination of concepts like imagined communities which for the internally displaced in Sri Lanka mean a prolongation of the crisis.

In a companion piece Ajith Rupasinghe picks up the recurring theme of the book which is the accountability of the Sri Lankan state structure for pursuing the politics of ethnic discrimination which led to the crisis. The refugee population both within and outside Sri Lanka has no voice or effective political power. It is the human face of the situation of the internally displaced which is mapped by Joe William. While UNHCR has extended its mandate to cover the internally displaced, i.e. would be refugees, there is no legal framework of protection. The dilemma is how to ensure humanitarian aid and respect for human rights of the displaced in a hostile domestic environment where the state is an active perpetrator of violence.

This collection of writings is an effort to look at the complexity of the situation in South Asia of refugees, migrants, internally displaced and stateless persons, with a view to shaping the debate on a regional framework of protection. The situation of refugees and displaced persons in South Asia has evolved to a point where it demands special attention and action. The recommendations of the Kathmandu group show the way forward.

We appreciate the efforts made by all the contributors to revise and update their papers. We gratefully acknowledge the support of our partner in this venture, Friedrich-Naumann-Stiftung. Finally, we thank our colleagues in SAFHR — Som Prasad Niroula who kept track of all the papers and the various revised versions, Pragya Ojha who typed the entire manuscript, Manesh Shrestha who diligently read the entire volume several times and corrected the factual errors and other mistakes, Pierre-Etienne Beaulieu who came to Kathmandu from Montreal, Canada to assist SAFHR in setting up a "home page" on the internet and ended up designing the publication and B. R. Sastha who looked after the administrative and financial aspects of this project. Their enthusiasm and commitment has made this book possible.

- Editors

Kathmandu,
November 1997

Moving Beyond Boundaries

Contradictions between people and territory

Barun De

Relevant to all of us in South Asia is the question of what has been called 'mega-diversity', probably the principal cultural bonding which exists among us in the countries of Nepal, Bhutan, Bangladesh, Sri Lanka, Maldives, Pakistan, India and other peoples on the periphery of South Asia such as in Afghanistan, Tajikistan, the Xinjiang and Tibet regions of China and in Myanmar. I do not claim to expertise, but just to a share in the common problems of humanity concerning the process of flowing beyond boundaries.

May I begin by invoking a passage which moved me several years ago when I first read it. It explicates the contradictions between people and territorial boundaries.

An Indian scholar from Darjeeling Dr Kumar Pradhan has written, for the Sahitya Akademi of India, a history of Nepali literature, also focusing on Nepali literature in India. He quotes and translates into English, the Nepali poet Vijay Malla's, *Chhorilai Manchitra Parhauda* (While Teaching Map Reading to a Daughter).

"Rato ragatle korieko Saadh Chha
khetma dil lae jhai
hera, harek rashtrako fatma,
yo ho Bharat yo ho Pakistan
Hindu Musalmanko ragatla muchieko
Yahi ho rekha mahan,
Jata hera Rato ragatle taeko chha ghera
Parevalai ganjakma banda gare jhai
Manis chha bandi yas khorma"

[Drawn by red blood are these boundaries
like enclosures in every field
Look, to delimit nation each
This is India, this is Pakistan
this is a line bold, kneaded with the blood of Hindus and Muslamans
Wherever you look drawn are the lines by red blood
Like the pigeon encaged
Men are closed in their traps.] [1]

I am reminded of a poem my wife heard after the Partition when she was a girl of seven or eight. It is written by the Indian Civil Servant and literatteur, Annada Shankar Ray. One of the lines in this jingle runs as follows:

"Teler shishi bhanglo bole, khukhur pare raag karo !
tomra joto burho khoka, bharat bhenge bhag karo !
Tar bela !"

[Because a little child breaks a bottle of oil, you get angry with it. You infantile old dodderers - you break up Bharat and divide it.
What then?]

This is the keynote we must emphasise. When one talks of states, one is talking of these sorts of policies. When one talks of history as being dominated by states, one is talking of the history of these sorts of policies. But there is another history that is now being discovered. A generation other than mine is writing it. It is called the history of popular culture.

In the history of the popular culture of South Asia, the basic concepts are not necessarily those of ephemeral empires, which the British taught those of us who were born in British India and their dependencies, to believe were the essential elements in our subcontinent's history. Let us consider certain examples.

Myth of permanence: Empires in South Asia

The Asokan Empire was obviously the Indian government's beau ideal for the Indian state form. Adopting the symbol of the *Asoka Chakra* or the Asokan Lion capital, the Nehruvian Indian state harked back to Asokan ideas of *satyameva jayate* and *dhammavijaya* as examples of syncretism and non-aligned diplomacy. Yet, historical data tells us that the Mauryan empire hardly lasted more than a hundred years.

The shadowy Gupta Empire, which we presume from the historical evidence of the *Harisena prasasti* of Samudragupta on an Asokan pillar in Allahabad Fort, as well as from scattered sources such as that of the Chinese traveller Fa Hsien and some Sanskrit texts, is after all only a representation of a political empire, seen as the forebear of the Mughals, whose emperor Jahangir inscribed the date of his ascension, on the Allahabad Fort Pillar. Pre-British "imperial" India is an intellectual construct meant to validate the national integrationism of British India and the Indian state to which *inter alia* it transferred power.[2]

The Mughal Empire, as a politically stable entity is supposed even by its greatest contemporary scholars to have lasted not more than a hundred and fifty years — from Akbar to Aurangzeb. The Indian composite culture was concretised at times by integrationist consolidation. But historically, its content and style has always been more coalitional and federative than purely unitary: as much "diversity in unity" as "unity in diversity". This is not to deny the fact that a strong authority ruling the bulk of the subcontinent was definitely an element of stability and authority to build a certain measure of prosperity for Indian elites. But to emphasise only this, is to ignore regional and sub-regional realities.

The positive record of imperialism in South Asia as the heritage appropriated by British imperialism, the record of all South Asian imperialism as the heritage appropriated by contemporary nation-states, is not high. British imperialism may have been invoked by American neo-colonialism as well as some sub-imperial elements in the South Asian bureaucracy since 1947 or in the army and Inter-Services Intelligence of Pakistan in its 1947-1971 phase. It has been challenged by the democratic spirit of many of those who fought in the Indian freedom struggle.

Obscured by the Leviathanic imperial tradition which in the Asokan, Gupta, Mughal, and British cases, rose from or collapsed into smaller principalities or state structures, there are at least two thousand years of political history of small principalities. The records that have been translated or interpreted are indeed often of political domination. But if one goes even into those records — the inscriptions, the manuscripts, the religious and ethical *Sastraic* and *Puranic* texts which have been quarried for political information, one can find a great deal more information about what an eminent historian of ancient India, in Jawaharlal Nehru University, Brajadulal Chattopadhayaya has called "autonomous spaces" in ancient and early medieval India. Below the Rajas were groups of people whose consensus was equal to that of classical state power. They regulated their own lives, they led cooperative lives, they led competitive lives, often autonomous of the Raja's control or even authority, provided of course they yielded up to his state and court the often large share of the surplus on which the latter maintained its regulative systems and occasionally appealed to him/her for legitimation of sanctions.[3] Not till the Mughal period, which is only about four to five hundred years ago, did the Indian state radically intensify its direct impingement on the life of the common people. Even then, it was like a matted lattice work, or a canopy, open on all sides, suspended over the affairs of rural or inner-city quotidian life.

The state in South Asia, as we define it in European terms, in the English language, the only language in which all of us seem to communicate with each other, or in French terms or in Dutch or German, is not even more than four or five hundred years old as we now know it. What then were the other realities of traditional South Asian cultural interaction? In strict historical terms, it was a record of settlement, but also of movements.

Popular diaspora in historical perspective

Even in the standard histories of our subcontinent, there are records of large-scale agricultural movements. The Vedic peoples were called Aryan by European historians of the past. Aryan was a term popularised by the highly statist Germans. Today it is fairly well-known that the people who spoke and then wrote the Vedas, and their Eurasian affines, spoke certain languages called Aryan, but which should on the contrary, be studied in terms of different stages of social, cultural and material development. The Vedic peoples were a moving community, stretching all the way from southern Central Asia from Soghdiana and Bactria, called in Muslim literature *Mawar-an-Nahar* (across the river), i.e. the Oxus or Amu Darya, today the border along Turkmenstan, Uzbekistan, Tajikstan and Afghanistan. And they moved all that way across to Bihar, Madhya Pradesh and the northern Deccan.

They expanded herding, grazing and agriculture. As they moved, they employed different forms of agriculture — slash-and-burn, hoe-farming, dibbling, plough-cultivation and a range of other activities including pastoralism.

The Vedic peoples were succeeded by other movements of settlements. British historians tended to emphasis only movements from the north-west into the south-east across the Khyber and the Bolan Passes. But there were movements of the Mongoloid as well as Eastern Turkic peoples across the Karakoram into the high Himalayan ranges, south of the Karakorams, in what is today Chitral, Gilgit, Hunza, Ladakh, Kashmir and Zanskar.

There were movements later on of people from the upper Gangetic plains to western Nepal, from Tirhut into *Mades* Nepal, and from Yunnan in China, and Laos into what is today called Assam, what they themselves call Asom. Their descendants were people who call themselves Ahom. Even today in Ahom religious functions, a language is invoked which only their priests understand. This is *Tai Ahom*, the language somewhat similar to that of the people of the Shan principalities in eastern Burma, of Chiangmai in north Thailand and of Laos and northern Vietnam. In fact some Australian scholars in the University of Canberra researching the early history of Indo-China had looked for linguistic parallels in Thailand, the Shan states and upper Assam. On the other hand there are legends among the Karen people of deltaic Burma, that have been interpreted as reflecting their migration in the far past from as far north of Asia as Mongolia.

Today, there is talk of an economic and cultural region which extends from eastern Nepal and upper Bihar all the way through north Bengal, Bangladesh and north-east India to Yunnan and Burma. In a broader regional perspective, there are common problems of development and prosperity from eastern U.P. to Upper Burma. In Bangladesh the commonalities of culture and economy in this region have been encapsulated in the *SAENE* concept which stands for South Asia's East and North East. Similarly there are economic and cultural commonalities between Jammu and Kashmir, eastern Xinjiang, the Badakshan regions of Afghanistan and Tajikistan, and the Balkh and Surkhan Darya/Kashka Darya regions of Afghanistan and southern Uzbekistan. These have not crystallized after late medieval times due to the exigencies of fragmented territoriality and non-existent communication. On the other hand, land highways such as the Arniko Rajpath from Tibet to Nepal, built by the Chinese and the Karakoram Highway from western Tibet into Pakistan, have recreated old links.

Population movements existed within India too, but these have been greatly ignored. The Ramayana, for instance, is one of the greatest epics about popular transfers within our subcontinent. To me, it is a sacred text of culture since it talks of the ways, cultural, peaceful, as well as violent, indeed dialectical in all aspects, of movements from north to south. It is one of the elements in the record of domination and subordination in Indian history. One ideologically disapproves of domination and its consequences, but as a historian one has to look at this in all its social and economic aspects. One can get the best record of this in the two great epics of South Asia, the earlier, *Kshatriya*-glorifying Mahabharata and the later, *Brahman*-worshipping Ramayana. Both talk about population movements. The Mahabharata is the more violent epic. The Ramayana is more dialectically rich with a variety of cultural and ethical themes across India, of groups struggling with others to establish their own ideologies and identities in which the epic gives pride of place to the *Bharata* lineage.

I am not of course being original. I am just repeating the ideas of one of the great cultural historians of Hindu India in his 1913 first Benaras, and then Calcutta University lectures. Dr. Radha Kumud Mukherjee, in his book called *The Fundamental Unity of India* traces this fundamental unity to the domination of the concept of Bharatic lineage as kings of Ayodhya over the whole of India. He argued that the pilgrimage centres in India are interlinked in this encompassing myth. For instance, there was the idea of the 108 parts of the body of *Sati*, the spouse of *Pashupati Siva*, which fell all over India leading to temple shrines springing up.[4] There is one such shrine in Kathmandu itself in Guheswari near the ancient sanctum of Pasupatinath, another one in Kamakshya in Guwahati in Assam and another one in my own city — Kalighat in Calcutta. There are others all over India. Hindu politics of ideological domination is splayed out in locational terms. I am not arguing that this is what traditionalist historians would call, "true history" because I do not believe in the idealist concept of truth in history. History after all is a construct which has to be seen in relative terms, in terms of the construction of peoples' varied concepts about what they thought was a particular history of the past.

The point is to identify ways in which the popular consciousness acquired ideological forms. They are based on movements of people for a variety of agricultural shifts, a variety of forms of labour mobility and a variety of transformation of power relations. Take the emblem of the hero *Bajrangbali* or *Hanuman*, so popular nowadays among many people, including the intelligentsia. Surely, Ram, the mythological north Indian hero, did not have central Indian monkeys fighting for him. It has been argued that they were really totem-worshipping warriors with a monkey as their emblem or even a mask for ritual purposes. Again I am not saying anything new. This was said slightly before R. K. Mukherjee, around 1910-11 by Rabindra Nath Tagore in his *Bharat Varshe Itihasher Dhara*, (The Course of History in India). These totemic people, Tagore hypothesised were people who fought for the dominating groups. Tagore believed that there was some sort of symbiosis between the Brahmin and Kshatriya, the typical caste-dominating combine of India. Tribal people worshipping totems, fought for the upper caste combine in their conquests.[5]

We may now turn to the idea of labour mobility. In my own state of West Bengal a tradition still persists in the areas between the hills and the plains, i.e. in the lower upland of Rarh in south-west Bengal (between the Chota Nagpur plateau and the Hooghly river) of *Namal* labour. *Namal* means *jara ba ja neechey namey* (those or that, who or which, come down). They are normally Santhal, Ho or Munda tribes who have been subordinated and kept backward over the years, tribes on whom Bengalis, Biharis and Oriyas generally established their usurious control as moneylenders. In the 19th century this led to occasional revolts which was recorded by the British and later appropriated by the leftist intelligentsia. In late 19th and early 20th century these groups were in cultural subordination. Among them are people who come down from the plateau edges, when the crop-cutting season comes. I myself saw them some twenty years ago in the then backward *thanas* of Arambagh sub-division of Hooghly District in West Bengal, coming single file, as if they were walking down a hill track, along ridges between low-lying paddies with baskets on their heads. They come, they do the crop-cutting and are allowed to take the gleaning and leavings from the fields. They are given a certain daily wage — increasing in the recent years — and they go back to their villages in the uplands to eke out their subsistence for the rest of the year.

If you have the *Namal* in West Bengal, you also have the *Powinda* merchants and petty usurers who came from southern Afghanistan, the region where today the Taliban movement completely dominates, that is, Ghazni, Kandahar and Herat from where the Taliban burst out towards Maimana and Balkh in their northward thrust against General Dostam in September 1996. Powindas would work in their upland pastures in the southern Afghan hills but every year they would come down the Bolan, Sibi and Gomal passes into Baluchistan and then spread out to South Asia.[6] In Calcutta people like them are still called *Kabuliwallah*, because Afghanistan is only known as Kabul to us. In Bengal they would be peddling moneylenders who used, till recently, to nomadically carry money slung over their shoulders, lent at usurious rates to local labour. They would also sell housewives dates, raisins or figs, imported, they once used to boast, from Bukhara and Samarkand. But they had, historically, also acted as mercenaries in north India. There were the famous Rohilla fighters (originally from Ruh, the southern Afghan mountains) who built up the principalities of Rampur, Shahjehanpur, Bareilly or Ferrukhabad in 18th century India, leaving their name even today as Rohilkhand. Some Afghan migrants would settle on the plains, others would go back every year.

A Pakistani geopolitician, Mahnaz Ispahani, describes the impact made by roads through Afghanistan built by the Soviets and Americans during the cold war. Americans built in southern Afghanistan, Soviets in the north, from Kushka in Turkmenstan to Herat, from Termez in Uzbekistan to Mazar-i-Sharif to Kabul through Pul-i-Khumri and the now famous Salang Tunnel where Uzbeks and Tajiks of north Afghanistan and the mullahs of the Taliban are embattled. These roads transformed the economic pattern of Afghanistan, leading Pakistan (even before the fall of the Afghan royal dynasty) to close the boundary of the Durand Line which stopped Powindas moving south. So in the last 15 to 20 years the Powinda tribes exerted pressure on the soil and became victims of economic disorder. They were unable to move across into the Pakistani border or splay out.[7]

Any Bengali will know that in the last twenty years Kabuliwallahs have been scarce in West Bengal. I remember meeting an Afghan ex-ambassador to India at a UNU Kyoto seminar in 1979, who said to me he used to have a big problem in the 60s dealing with Kabuliwallahs involved in disputes with local clients in Calcutta. Now one hardly sees recent migrant Afghans in eastern India. They have stopped moving to South Asia from Central and Northwest Asia in the way the Bengali middle class nowadays seem to be moving inexorably to England and America. And they were moving with as much of legitimacy, or illegitimacy and validity or lack of legal authority, as our present non-resident Indians move, not just to Oxford or Essex or New Jersey or Calgary in Canada but also to rocky inlets on the coasts of Greece and south Italy *en route* to a globalised and often criminally lumpenised European labour market. The question of moral judgement on such movements hardly arises. If there are any judgements, these are to be made on the pressure of consumerism which is the allure of the economy, on the fringes of which they flit. Those pressures and those market forces express themselves in open entry at certain times and in restrictive practices at other times.

One could go on multiplying examples of such professional movements. In the period of the late Mughal empire the *Peshwas* of Poona particularly from the time of Balaji Baji Rao down to Madhav Rao Narain in the middle of the 18th century, dominated Gujarat, eastern Rajasthan, Malwa, Gondwana as well as present-day Andhra, and Karnataka to the east of Maharashtra, northern Tamil Nadu, Orissa and the southwestern tip of Bengal. The Brahmans who found very few jobs in the arid hills of the western Ghats, since one subcaste, the *Chitpavan* Brahmins, dominated that region, felt the *Chitpavan* competition very unfair in Maharashtra. Most notably these were the *Deshastha* and the *Karhade* Brahmans many of whom migrated across the Deccan into the east Godavari basin. This was administered through the 19th century by *Deshastha* Brahmins who used the Maharashtrian surname, Rao. A book was published thirty years ago about local administration in Guntur showing Maratha migrants of a century or more migratory standing as the local elites of Guntur. There were similar migrations of Tamil Brahmins from Tamil Nadu and the east of south India to the Palghat region in the west of deep south India. A large number of Tamil Brahmans became landlords in Palghat in Kerala and even *dalawais* or *dewans* in its 18th century Nair principalities.[8] But then there were so many of this ethnic sub-community by the mid-20th century that they could not get jobs in South India, so having learnt English some became stenographers in Delhi or Calcutta. Pandit Jawaharlal Nehru's stenographers, the best in India, were a succession of Palghat Tamils. Of course now, Palghat Tamils are part of the general "non-resident" diaspora of the consumerist Indian middle class in Europe and North America.

In West Bengal we have a great name like Sakharam Ganesh Deuskar, a nationalist Bengali writer, who wrote one of the first patriotic popular tracts in Bengali — *Desher Katha*.[9] He spoke Bengali, but his mother tongue was Marathi. He was settled in Deoghar, the Santhal Parganas, where his father had come as a Marathi, working with Bengali clerks and moneylenders among the Santhal population. We had a minister in West Bengal called Phadikar, which sounds like the Marathi Phadkar. But Shri Prabhas Phadikar lived in Daspur in Medinipur, whose folklore noted in O'Nalley's "Midnapur Gazetteer" of the early 20th century still had remnant memories of Maratha brigands of the 18th century such as *Sheo Bhat Sathe* who came to loot and stayed back to become Bengalis.

A final element of these normal movements are what I have referred to as pilgrimage routes. There is much research still to be done on the social flows and consequences of pilgrimages in South Asia. Bangladeshis who came to India, immediately after the independence of Bangladesh, would often make a pilgrimage, not to any centre in West Bengal, not to *Furfura-Sharief*, for instance but would go all the way to *Ajmer Sharief*, the Mazar of Sheikh Moinuddin Chisti in Ajmer, in faraway Rajasthan.

There is a tremendous novel and film in Bengali about Bengalis, among other Indians, on pilgrimage to a place in the far off deserts of the Khanate of Kalat in Baluchistan, now in Pakistan, called Hinglaj, where there is one of the 108 shrines to which I have referred to as *Avadhuta's*

Marutirtha Hinglaj (the Desert Pilgrimage to Hinglaj). This was a way of cultural bonding. In my very first article written about forty years ago, I referred to the point that Hindu, Muslim, Jain, Buddhist, Parsee, Sikh and Christian bonded themselves in what we used to call "India before 1947" by that sort of cultural diversity in unity — the diversity of common pilgrimages.

In the article entitled "A Note on the Nature of the Problem of Indian Unity" in the *Economic Weekly* in 1958, I differed from Radha Kumud Mukherjee as well as later sociologists and ethno-methodologists in the USA, like M.N. Srinivas, B. Subba Rao, Mckim Marriot and Bernard Cohn, who said that India was bonded by Hindu pilgrimages. India was indeed bonded by sacred pilgrimages but they comprised a composite variety of faiths. They could be Jain. There are Jain shrines in Karnataka. The present Chairman of the Indian Council of Historical Research, Prof S. Settar has written a book called *Inviting Death* about rocks opposite the Gomatesvara image in Sravana Belagola in Karnataka where Jains go to die[10] in a way that the Hindu widows are supposed to go to Kashi or Nepalis of piety are taken to Pasupathinath Ghat to die. Sikhs have shrines in Patna and in Assam, where one of the Gurus travelled and they also have a shrine incidentally in Baghdad where Guru Nanak is supposed to have gone.[11]

Endemic wars, fuzzy borders and refugee

We may look at another element of the general problem. Normal lines of bonding are disrupted by refugee flows created by wars and violence or chauvinistic repression. The problem in general as created by wars and violence in the 19th and 20th centuries has been greatly intensified by Eurocentric concepts of refugees and uprooted peoples.

In the last hundred or hundred and fifty years Europe has been under the sway of the concept of the nation-state, described in, for instance, Benedict Anderson's simplistic *Imagined Communities*, Ernest Gellner's more sophisticated book on nationalism or Eric Hobsbawm's superb and thought-provoking survey. European imperialism ignited the concept in the shape of anti-colonial nationalism in the southern hemisphere first, as Creole independence in Latin America, in the two great Latin American Wars of Independence 1812-1813 and 1825-1829, when Latin American states were formed, from Mexico in Mesoamerica down to the southern cone of Argentina and Chile. These ideas indigenously developed in Asia and in different formations in Africa and were also exogenously sparked by European changes. They were explicated by emulative indigenous elites, the new nationalists of anti-colonialism and then they were replicated by the compradore groups which set up the Europeanised state system imposed on the masscs "from above". It is this system which is now fragile and breaking down, for instance in, the erstwhile Yugoslavia, in Europe, in Rwanda and Brundi in Africa or in Afghanistan in Asia.[12]

This concept of the nation-state brought new forms of principality or nationality, each with a boundary "drawn by red blood", through a whole series of wars. The great cataclysms through the middle and the early modern ages in European imperial history — the Hundred Years War which led to the origins of early international law, the wars of Bourbon and Habsburg succession, the later war over North American Independence and the Napoleonic Wars, where there was a megalomaniac state seeking to dominate the whole of Europe — show that Chengiz Khan and Amir Timur in Inner Asia were not aberrations but part of a pre-modern system of *imperium*, which fascism in long-range terms still seeks to revive. In between these spurts of wars, from the time of the building of the Han, Maurya, Sassanid or Roman Empires down to campaigns of the 1980s around Iraq, there may have been only interludes when such endemic warfare did not take place.

Europeans of course had recorded delimitation of territorial boundaries for many centuries before the nineteenth century. Asians, Africans and Latin Americans have been less precise for the purposes of historical record. Inferences from inscriptions or coins or dubious textual reconstruction have made the matter of historical frontiers very foggy. If one looks at the history of frontier making in the late 19th and 20th centuries in Central, Inner and North-West Asia, one can see how uncharted terrain was being drawn into Eurocentric cartography.

For instance, mountains here were given heights only in late 18th and 19th century maps. I keep on nagging about this to anybody who has the misfortune of being with me in a car when we go north along Wood Street in my home city of Calcutta as the Survey of India building looms up on the right side, where Radhanath Sikdar, a Bengali compradore, calculated that Sagarmatha was the highest peak in the world. The credit was given to his boss Sir George Everest, the Surveyor General. It was named Mount Everest by Europeans. A popular but scholarly biography of Sir Aurel Stein, the Hungarian scholar who settled in Kashmir, naturalised himself a Briton and died in Afghanistan, describes how he would take Indian surveyors Ram Singh and Lal Singh to survey Xinjiang, Kansu and Ningsia — the vast Inner Asian tracts of China. The reputation of this mapping of Central Asia and later of southern Iran, went to men like Stein or Sir Thomas Holdich. Ram Singh went blind as a result of his tribulations and was pensioned off with a few hundred rupees annually.[13] No one knows what happened to Lal Singh and it is only recently that the far more famous "pundits" of the Rawat family of Milam in Uttarakhand trained to survey the upper courses of the Indus and the Tsanpo-Brahmaputra, by British spies have been popularised by a "British Raj" buff Charles Allan.[14] Whether done by Indian surveyors or organised by European explorers, what did happen was that Inner Asia was mapped in border lines — the Durand Line between Pakistan and Afghanistan which the Afghans still do not accept, the Macmahon Line between India and China along watersheds most of which had not then been seen or walked along by Europeans or Chinese, about which the Chinese had, and still have, great doubt. Indeed in one part of it the Chinese have arbitrarily built a road through the Karakorams; thus infringing upon territory claimed by Jammu and Kashmir, even before it became part of British India creating claims of succession by the Government of India. This border delimitation has been done in the interests of imperial, national, or socialist security states.

The security states of Asia were those among which the British, with a characteristic brutal joviality said a "Great Game" was going on. As if the espionage, treachery and intrigue between Britain and Russia through the 19th and the early 20th centuries was a "game" of cricket or even the more ferocious rugby football. Today South Asian writers, talking about rivalries in Central Asia and Afghanistan slavishly mimic North Atlantic geopoliticians in calling it a "New Great Game" although Afghans, Pathans, Tajiks, Uzbeks and Hazaras are killing each other.

There is as yet no rigorous historical record of how peoples of the locality look at this border delimitation. In the Aurel Stein biography there is a brief account of the way in which the first Kuomintang government in China, after it came to power saw to it that Sir Aurel and his British Indian surveyors did not step on Chinese soil. The Kuomintang's new intelligentsia was keen to protect the endogenous Buddhist remains in Dun Hwang Monastery on the eastern edge of the Gobi Desert (which Stein was purloining for the British Museum's collections and also for the National Museum in New Delhi) from being taken to London in the way that the Elgin Marbles had been looted from the Parthenon in Athens and taken to form the great prizes of the British Museum. The attitude of the peoples of the locality is reflected in the way, Afghan rulers resisted Aurel Stein's entry into Afghanistan which he visited only in his eighties to die in Kabul in 1943 during the Second World War[15] or the way in which Iranians, Kurds, Turks, Arabs resisted imperialist attempts at border delimitation in the interest of the old imperial and cultural trophy exhibition order.

It is interesting that Europeans themselves now are working on this theme with their access to funds, fieldwork, and linguistic and repository resources. In South and northwest Asia we need to work on the indigenous popular geopolitics of how border delimitation changed and transformed the scope of population transfers. Mahnaz Ispahani has talked of the ways in which the Powindas were choked up in Afghanistan. We need a similar description of the ways in which the Tajiks have, since the late 19th century, been divided into two, leaving what is known as Lower Badakshan in the Afghan hands of Ahmad Shah Masood, the Lion of Panjshir, and High Badakshan and Gorno Badakshan (Gorno means hilly in Russian) in what is Tajikistan. After the 1924 Soviet Nationality Delimitation Law, many plains Tajiks of the north and west (past Khojent and Kurgan Tyube) were made nationals of the Soviet Republic of Uzbekistan and today are treated as Uzbeks. Yet a submerged Tajik dissidence problem persists in these southern parts of Uzbekistan.[16] It could be compounded if the Taliban push into Afghanistan upto the Amu Darya, driving Afghan Uzbeks and Afghan Tajik refugees into Amu Darya-Syr Darya doab. Hutu refugees from Ruanda-Brundi have created similar problems in the Congo leading to the successful overthrow of President Mobutu.

Today refugee movements between the Tajiks in Afghanistan and Gorno Badakstan are fairly well-known to the United Nations High Commission for Refugees. In 1995 summer, I talked to Olivier Roy, the eminent historian of Islamic Resistance in Afghanistan,[17] who had been the UNHCR representatives in Dushanbe in Tajikistan, about instability in the region. We now hear that Shi'ite schismatic Ismailiyas in Gorno Badakstan are seeking full autonomy from plains Kuliabis and Khojentis who are mainly Sunni. In Afghanistan today the attack by the Taliban on the Tajiks of the Panjshir and Faizabad means that again there is the sort of bottling up process that we have described with regard to the Powindas of the south. Pakistan's "deep defence" strategy means considerable misery for the tribal people to Pakistan's west.

So these boundaries have brought a new heritage of war, disturbance and violence as the social structure of imperial and post-imperial state communist as well as capitalist concretises.

There is no reason for us to be sentimental and deny that "actually existing socialism" in the Soviet Union was not an "internally colonialist structure". It did mean a lot more popular benefits in the shape of universal literacy and women's upliftment, than under Tsarism, but it certainly was a post-imperial structure. It, too, has cracked with considerable fissures on the borders of Central Asia. This has led to refugee problems and ethnic stress.

Communalism, militarism and globalisation

All this forms an element in the development of communalism in South Asia. Partition of British India under imperialist aegis led to the growth of the national security state. In the 30s and 40s communalism existed in a symbiotic relationship with imperialism and the most feudal forms of Muslim sentiment in the Indus plains, called the Punjab School or Frontier-style authoritarianism, a landlord-cum-chieftain style authoritarianism which still prevails in junker-capitalist fashion all over Pakistan. It was also to be found, in a totally contradictory manner, in the populist petty landowner *Chaudhrai* and rural cleric, *mullahs* and *pirs* who dominated parts of East Bengal and Sylhet, then in Assam. An equally obnoxious Hindu variant of nationalist historiography, racial thinking and neo-populist rhetoric in inland Deccan and Central India, grew up under the influence of the Hindu Mahasabha, and the Rashtriya Swayam Sewak Sangh, and spread at the end of the Second World War. After partition and a brief interlude of a type of democracy in India as well as Pakistan which amalgamated Weimar liberalism and remnants of junkerdom,[18] these authoritarian contradictions and communalist interrelationships led to the growth of military oligarchy in Pakistan, the traumas of Bangladesh, and the highly authoritarian tendencies as well as the corruption of democracy which have engulfed India from the 70s.

A consequence of this has been in South Asia's east and north-east where for instance, the disregard of the local and ethnic character of the Chittagong Hill Tracts has led to the Chakma or as some militants call it, the Jumma problem. Another aspect of the problem is the cynical way in which Indian ruling cliques gave arms and training to Bodo militants in the jungles south and east of Bhutan[19] and to Eelam militants operating against the Sri Lankan regimes. Then there is the ineptitude with which the genuine grievances of the Punjab were allowed to be co-opted by Sikh religious politics and Khalistani fanaticism. There have also been developments related to the *holding on to Kashmir* and the incapacity of the Pakistan and Indian regimes to think in terms of any magnanimous solution to the problems of the Kashmir Valley. These have created the milieu in which rose the demand, right or wrong, for *Azaadi* which are voiced not only by the *Hurriyat*, but also by other groups in the Valley and its western hill ramparts.

The transition after Indian independence was mishandled in Nagaland, Manipur as well as Mizoram. In Burma, a similar transition led to the Shan, Karen and Kachin problems in Upper Burma, sandwiched as they are between Yunnan and Assam with only tenuous linkages with the people of the Brahmaputra Valley or lower Myanmar.[20] Ba-ma, i.e. Burma, means union of peoples who comprise the old kingdom, dominated ultimately by the Myan, the people indigenous to the plains. They dominated the Kachin and the Shan of the northern and eastern hills, the Karen a separate ethnic group in the plains and the hills, and the Rohingyas of Arakan and other small groups in the hills. Myanmar as a name signifies majoritarian control by the plains of the hills. The Kachin, the Karen and the Shan problems are part of a meaningful silence, if one sentimentalises rather than rationally considers the democratic implications of Aung San Suu Kyi's tribulations. When we rightly rhapsodise about Daw Suu Kyi's stand, we do not necessarily think of the problems of the hill peasantry of Upper Burma, or the Christian Karen subaltern groups of lower Burma. They were actually Burmese subalterns, i.e. low level officers of the British imperialists, resisting the democratisation of the Burmese nationalists till the end of the Second War, beleagured by the mafia and the warlords, as much as by the SLORC, drawn into opium cultivation and thus into the international structures of drug cartelisation. This is a type of warlordism which exists also in southern and eastern Afghanistan, where poppy cultivation accounts for the bulk of cash crop income.

Problems have grown and the state, in our case the South Asian regimes, have sought to solve them, by militarising themselves, that is, by more and more use of para-military formations and by the direct use of the Army. A senior officer in Fort William in Calcutta at a private dinner gathering addressed by the Indian Home Minister and the Indian Commander-in-Chief said in response to some comments made by me, "Thank you for saying what I could hardly have, the Army does not like killing its brethren in the North-East. It would much rather be concerned with training for actual war." One doubts if the army should like training for war as distinct from frontier defence either. Whatever that may be, granted that when there is no war the army would prefer to train in their cantonments rather than be sent to the villages of Bodoland, to fight civilians in the name of encounters and missions. At Sitabaldi Fort in Nagpur about six or sever years ago, just after Prime Minister V. P. Singh had pulled the Indian troops out of Sri Lanka, I heard the same view from a non-commissioned officer, a real Indian subaltern, who was showing us round the site of a Anglo-Maratha battle fought in 1818. He had been in Jaffna. He said that he hated the business of what he called "flushing out the terrorists". He hated it absolutely and thought it a messy business unworthy of a self-respecting soldier, meant to fight in an honourable and declared war.

What people really think, probably does not matter. In the last resort, national security considerations are what people *en masse* allow to predominate. And this has led to authoritarianism and the entire paraphernalia of border control by means of militarisation of state power, particularly in peripheral areas of insurgency.

At the same time, as authoritarianism and diplomatic bargaining grows, so also does globalisation of society, economy and political culture. Globalisation breaks down these petty diplomatic bargains and petty authoritiarnisms in the same way as capitalism destroyed the indigenous societies of Asia in the nineteenth century or Chinese walls as Karl Marx figuratively called them in his articles on the China War and the East India Company's politics in the 1850s. He said in 1853 about "the future results of British rule" that whatever happens, indigenous societies will crumble before the "juggernaut wheels" of capitalism.

If globalisation is not to be a battering ram but a facilitator of mass progress, if we have to indigenise it and popularly benefit from it in our own culture, then we have to think in terms of co-operative, but also enforceable, processes, by means of which the popular will can become the general will.

Notes

1. Kumar Pradhan, *A History of Nepali Literature*, Delhi, 1984, pp 1-2.
2. References on the 20th century construction of

imperialism and counter imperialism of the colonial and nationalist ruling elite will be found in Barun De, "Unity/Diversity : An Aspect of the Construction of National Identity" in D.N. Jha, ed. *Society and Ideology in India. Essays in Honour of Professor R. S. Sharma*, pp 399-412.

3. Brajadulal Chattopadhyay, "Autonomous Spaces and the Authority of the State : The Contradiction and its Resolution in Theory and Practice in Early India" I. Modelle in B. Kolver ed. *Recht, Staat Und Verwaltung in Klassischen Indian,* Munchen, 1977. For earlier examples of his thinking about political plurality in Indian traditional culture, see chapter 5 and 6 of Brajadulal Chattopadhyay *The Making of Early Medieval India,* New Delhi, 1994.
4. Radha Kumud Mukherjee, *Fundamental Unity of India,* Calcutta, 1914.
5. Rabindranath Tagore "Bharatabarshe Itihasher Dhara" reprinted in *Itihasa*, Calcutta, 1362, B.S. reprint of 1395 B.S. 19 , in particular, pp. 33-34 where Tagore referred to the now common dichotomy between early text of Rama mythology where the hero is shown as a friend of Chandalas like Guhaka and late texts like the Uttararamacharit where he orders the execution of Sudra ascetics and forsakes his wife to maintain social stability. "That a social revolution was implicit in the Ramacharita was sought to be wiped out by newer social ideals to which that earlier history was subordinated ... Yet India could not forget that he was the companion of Chandalas, worshipped by monkeys, and friend of Bibhishana. His glory was not that he destroyed enemies but that he made them his allies. He built bridges of amity between Aryas and non-Aryas. Studying sociology we find that among barbarian tribes, many worship a particular animal. Often they call themselves descendants of those animals. They call themselves by the names of those animals. Serpent dynasties are found in India in this way. The non-Aryas, whom Ramachandra subjected in Kiskindhya too were known as monkeys, indubitably for this reason. Not only

monkeys but also bears were found in Ram's companies. There would be no sense in bears if monkeys were only a term of personal abuse.

6. Mahnaz Ispahani, *Roads and Rivals: The Politics of Access in the Borderlands of Asia*, London, 1988, pp 113-14,119.
7. ibid.
8. R.E. Frykenberg, Guntur District, 1788-1848.*A History of Local Influence and Central Authority in South Asia*, Oxford, 1965. Ashin Dasgupta, *Malabar in Asian Trade, 1748-1800*, Cambridge, 1967 pp. 52-53.
9. Sakharam Ganesh Deuskar, *Desher Katha* ed. by Mahadevprasad Saha, Calcutta, new edition, 1377 B.S..
10. S. Settar, *Inviting Death: Historical Experiments on Sepulchral Hill*, Dharwad, 1986.
11. A.C. Banerjee, *The Sikh Gurus and the Sikh Religions*, Calcutta, 1983.
12. Benedict Anderson, *Imagined Communities Reflections on the Origin and Spread of Nationalism*, London, 1983. Ernest Gellner, *Nations and Nationalism*, London, 1983. Eric Hobsbawm, *Nations and Nationalism Since 1780s: Programme, Myth and Reality*, Cambridge, 1990.
13. Annabel Walker, *Aurel Stein : Pioneer of Silk Road*, London, 1995.
14. Charles Allen, *A Mountain in Tibet : The Search for Mount Kailas and the Sources of the Great Rivers of India* London, 1983. Indra Singh Rawat, *Indian Explorers in the Nineteenth Century*, Calcutta,1973.
15. Walker, op.cit: vide chapters 12 and 15 entitled "The Chinese Debacle" and "Death in Some Far-off Country".
16. An interesting Tajik version of problems created by the 1924 Soviet Nationality Law has been found in a English translated version of Rakhim Masov's Russian tract published from Dushanbe, 1991, entitled in translation, *The History of the Axe - Type Division*. It alleges "great Uzbek" discrimination of Tajiks in southern and eastern Uzbekistan.

17. Olivier Roy, *Islam and Resistance in Afghanistan*, Cambridge, 1990.
18. The analgamation of Junker/Wiener as the dominant theme of South Asian democracy en route towards upper-caste fascism has been pointed out to me by my son, Bikramjit De.
19. Sanjoy Hazarika, *Strangers of the Mist : Tales of War and Peace from India's North-East*, New Delhi 1994, pp 158-9 describes Bodo and Rajbangshi masses, north of the Brahmaputra, being trained, since India's 1962 border debacle, in weapons technology by India's Special Security Bureau at Chakrata and at Mahabaleshwar in covert operations; against East Pakistan and later in struggles to gain autonomy within the Indian Union.
20. Bertil Lintner, *Burma in Revolt, Opium and Insurgency Since 1948*, Bangkok, 1994.

The Changing Nature of Refugee Crisis

Tapan K. Bose

I

State formation and refugees

Movement of population is an age old phenomenon but the practice of forcing people to move from their known habitat began with the birth of the territorial "nation-state". Nationalism emerged in fourteenth century Europe, as a challenge to the supremacy of the Holy Roman Empire. Over a period of about four hundred years, the map of Europe was drawn and re-drawn as the secular concepts of "commonwealth", "nation" and "national territory" became the basis for reorganisation of territories. However, as the new rulers established their control over the newly emergent nation-states, "nationalism" became the new religion. The rulers invoked it to lay claim to the highest loyalties of their citizens as was once claimed by the medieval Christian church from the laity. The nation-states established absolute power over their territories and the people. In order to create a "nation", out of the disparate groups of peoples within the fold of the nation-state, the ruling elite created a homogenous "national identity" by imposing the language, religion and culture of the dominant group on all the people. Those who refused to conform to the ideological or religious identity of the dominant group became the "minorities". They were persecuted, exploited and often pushed out by the "nation-states". Hannah Arendt in her study of totalitarianism in Europe establishes the link between state formation and flow of refugees.[1] Zolberg and Tarzi estimate that between the 15th and 17th centuries about a million people were displaced in Europe, an enormous number in the view of the population of Europe at that time.[2]

In the 17th century, religious persecution in France forced about 250,000 Huguenots Protestants to flee to England, Holland and Switzerland. Spanish Muslims and Austrian Jews also faced a similar fate. After subjugation of Ireland in the 17th century, the British evicted thousands of Irish peasants to make way for absentee landlords. Thousands of Scots were similarly expelled from the highlands in the 18th century. The great waves of Irish migration of mid-19th century were caused by a mix of political and economic factors. The famine of 1840 was perhaps the worst of a series of famines that visited Ireland under British rule.[3]

The process of mass expulsion continued. In the wake of colonial expansion during the 19th and early 20th centuries about fifty million Europeans migrated to the so-called "new world" and populated the settler states like the United States of America and Australia. The European settlers uprooted millions of indigenous peoples who were forcibly confined to "reservations for native peoples" which were invariably set up in remote and unproductive areas. Condemned to these reservations, the bulk of the native populations died of disease and starvation.

During the period between the 15th and the 19th centuries, when the minorities and the poor of Europe were being pushed out of their habitat, it is estimated that European slave traders abducted about 10 million black people from Africa who were sold as slaves to the rich white people of Europe and the "New World" colonies.

The legal "definition" and European bias

The doctrine of national sovereignty established absolute power of the states over their territories. It also established the principle that only the people of the same national origin were entitled to enjoy the full protection of the legal institutions of that state. Non-nationals therefore, had no rights. In the first half of this century, the growth of nationalist sentiment caused mass killing and widespread population transfer. During the first World War about 1.5 million Armenians were killed by Turkish forces and another 320,000 fled to other countries in search of safety. About 1.3 million Greeks were repatriated to Greece from Turkey, while about 400,000 Turks were sent back. The Russian revolution expelled nearly 2 million Russians from the Union of Soviet Socialist Republics. In the words of Eric Hobsbawm, "the world accustomed itself to compulsory expulsion and killing on an astronomical scale, phenomena so unfamiliar that the new words had to be invented for them: stateless or genocide".[4] After the First World War, faced with the problem of millions of stateless persons, the European governments devised a new document, the so-called Nansen Passport of the League of Nations. Under the auspices of the League of Nations, between 1922 and 1938 a series of international treaties were concluded which recognised the "refugees" as persons of international concern and provided for their protection and rehabilitation by the governments of host countries. Those who were recognised as refugees were issued identity certificates or the Nansen Passport for the purpose of travel and resettlement in countries which were willing to accept them.

These treaties also created a legal definition of refugees as, "persons who were (a) outside the country of their origin and (b) without the protection of the government of that state." For example in 1926, a Russian refugee was defined as a "person of Russian origin who does not enjoy or who no longer enjoys the protection of the government of the Union of Soviet Socialist Republics and who has not acquired another nationality".[5] In the "Provisional Arrangement Concerning Status of Refugees Coming from Germany" signed by seven European states in 1936, initially, all persons fleeing Germany were defined as refugees. However, as the flow of German refugees increased, the states became more selective in "recognising" refugees. In the 1938 "Convention Concerning the Status of Refugees Coming from Germany" a distinction was made between "voluntary" and "involuntary" asylum seekers. Article 1(2) of the Convention excluded from the definition of refugees persons "who left Germany for reasons purely of personal convenience". This distinction in the legal definition became an important factor in deciding entitlement of support from the international community. [6]

During the Second World War, more than 40 million people were displaced in Europe. The War and its aftermath uprooted almost a similar number of people outside Europe. In West Asia, the state of Israel was created as a homeland for Jews as a reward for their participation in the Second World War. The newborn state of Israel accepted 1.2 million Jews from Europe. As the Jews occupied the land and the homes of the Palestinian Muslims, nearly 1.3 million

Palestinians became refugees. The decolonisation of India in 1947 displaced about 15 million people on the subcontinent while, the Korean war, an extension of the Second World War, created about five million refugees.

In the decades following the Second World War, mass expulsion of people became a regular feature of world politics. Despite their condemnation of Hitler's policy of mass expulsion of non-Germans from Germany and settlement of "ethnic Germans" in the annexed territories, the victorious allies themselves were party to several compulsory population transfers in Eastern Europe. The process of decolonisation in the 60s and 70s led to the establishment of a large number new territorial nation-states in Asia, Africa and Latin America. These were the decades of liberation struggles, revolutions, coups and counter-coups which caused large scale movement of populations within and across the borders of these newly independent countries. Readjustment of old colonial boundaries rekindled old rivalries, unleashed ethnic and religious conflicts. Entire communities and groups of peoples were rejected and disenfranchised by the dominant ruling elite of these countries.

In recognition of the need for an international structure for refugee protection, the United Nations in 1946 created the International Refugee Organisation (IRO). The principal objective of IRO was "to bring about a rapid and positive solution of the problem of bona fide refugees and displaced persons". IRO was to seek an early return of the refugees and displaced persons to their countries of origin. But the UN was primarily concerned about the refugees in Europe. As a result, IRO remained a Eurocentric agency authorised to assist chiefly the victims of the Nazi, Fascist or Quisling regimes and such persons who were considered as refugees before the outbreak of the Second World War for reasons of race, religion, nationality or political opinion.[7]

The Statute of the United Nations High Commissioner for Refugees (UNHCR) was adopted by the UN General Assembly on December 14, 1950. The Statute brought within UNHCR's competence all refugees covered by various earlier treaties and instruments, empowered UNHCR to review decisions of IRO regarding eligibility and finally extended UNHCR's competence to, "any other person who is outside the country of his nationality, or if he has no nationality, the country of his former habitual residence, because he has or had well-founded fear of persecution by reason of his race, religion, nationality or political opinion and is unable or, because of such fear, is unwilling to avail himself of the protection of the government of the country of his nationality, or, if he has no nationality, to return to the country of his former habitual residence."[8]

This was followed by the creation of several other international instruments and mechanisms for the protection of refugees all over the world. In 1951, the General Assembly adopted the UN Convention Relating to the Status of Refugees. The Convention established the principle of *non-refoulement* and created an obligation on the contracting states to accord to the refugees within their territories, "treatment at least as favourable as that accorded to their nationals" in all spheres of life. In January 1967 the UN General Assembly adopted the Protocol Relating to the Status of Refugees to deal with the new refugee situation which had arisen since the adoption of the 1951 Convention. In the month of December 1967 the General Assembly adopted a Declaration on Territorial Asylum which established that, " the grant of asylum by a State to persons entitled to invoke article 14 of the Universal Declaration of Human Rights is a peaceful and humanitarian act and that, as such, it can not be regarded as unfriendly by any other State."[9]

While appreciating the rights conferred on the refugees by these international instruments, many non-Western jurists and scholars have pointed out that the Covenant and the Protocol were mainly used by the Western powers initially for the victims of Nazi persecution in Europe and later to protect refugees from Eastern Europe who had become targets of persecution by the communist governments.[10] Moreover, as the definition of the refugee in these instruments was essentially individualistic, requiring a case by case examination of the subjective and objective elements. While this approach was suitable for dealing with refugees from East European countries, it was unable to respond to the escalation in refugee crisis in the Third World where masses of people were being uprooted.

Between the two World Wars mass movement of refugees was mainly restricted to the western hemisphere. The beginning of the cold war generated a movement of refugees from East to West—from the Socialist block to the so-called Free World. For obvious ideological reasons in the 60s and 70s the Western nation states encouraged the flow of refugees from Eastern Europe to the West by offering them asylum. The era of mass movement of refugees across Europe was over. In the context of cold war the "category" approach to the definition of refugees was not relevant. This approach of the western nations was responsible for undermining the credibility of UNHCR in the eyes of many Third World intellectuals.

The definition of refugees as incorporated in 1951 Convention and the 1967 Protocol is being increasingly questioned today by social scientists and human rights activists especially as it does not take into account the emergence of non-military sources of instability in the economic, social, humanitarian and ecological fields. During the last three decades, masses of people have been displaced by man-made environmental disasters, natural calamities and by the highly elitist and capital intensive "modern" development policies adopted by the governments of the Third World countries. This rather complex model of development on one hand has put the "unskilled" masses of the poorer countries at a disadvantage and on the other have destroyed the traditional sources of livelihood of the people. While the majority of the flow of people across borders was within the countries of the South, for the first time there began a flow of refugees from the South to the North, from the poor to the rich countries. What begun as a trickle in the 60s, became an exodus by the 80s and 90s. They were classified as "migrants" or "economic refugees" by the governments and international agencies.

Regional instruments expand the definition

In an attempt to respond to the changing refugee situation in the the Afro-Asian region, in 1966, the Asian African Legal Consultative Committee tried to formulate a set of principles to regulate the rights and obligations of the refugees in the region. Unfortunately, despite attempts by Iraq, Pakistan and the United Arab Republic to expand the scope of the definition of refugee, the Bangkok Declaration of 1966, issued by the Consultative Committee ended up re-adopting the definition incorporated in the 1951 UN Convention. However, at a later date regional instruments adopted by the Organisation of African Unity and the Central American Governments provided a wider meaning to the concept of refugee.

For example, the OAU Convention Governing the Specific Aspects of Refugee Problem in Africa (1969) while retaining the definition of refugees contained in the 1951 UN Convention , expanded it by adding,

> "… the term refugee shall also apply to every person or persons who, owing to external aggression, occupation, foreign domination or events seriously disturbing public order in either part or the whole of his/their country of origin or nationality is/are compelled to leave his/their place of habitual residence."

The Cartagena Declaration on refugees adopted by the Central American Governments in 1984 further expanded the definition of refugees to include,

> "… persons who have fled their country because their lives, safety or freedom have been threatened by generalised violence, foreign aggression, internal conflicts, massive violation of human rights or other circumstances which have seriously disturbed public order."

Economic refugees/migrants

It has been argued that migrants cross international borders attracted by the "pull" of better economic opportunities and that unlike political refugees are not "pushed" out as a result of widespread human rights abuses or by racial and communal riots. Migration is said to be encouraged by transborder social, religious and ethnic linkages, especially in situations where the same community enjoys majority status in one country and that of an oppressed minority in another. "Migration", therefore, is interpreted as essentially a voluntary action. As a result, states argue that migrants can not be treated at par with refugees who are persecuted in their home states for reasons of religion, race or political opinion.

However, studies have shown that an overwhelming majority of the displaced persons in the Third World, who are generally classified as "migrants" by host governments and international agencies, belong to the minorities and economically backward sections of the society. For example between 1950 and 1990 about 21 million people were displaced in India by projects like big dams, mines, industries and wildlife reserves. Of these, nearly 40 percent were tribal/indigenous peoples who constitute 7.6 percent of India's population .[11] As these persons did not cross any international border they remained displaced within India.

In the mid-60s more than a hundred thousand Chakma tribal people were displaced by the Kaptai dam built in the Chittagong Hill Tracts of then East Pakistan, now Bangladesh. Nearly 52,000 of these displaced people belonging to the Chakma and Hajong tribes crossed over to India. About 30,000 person were displaced from the Mirpur district of Pakistan-controlled Kashmir by the Mangla Dam constructed with World Bank assistance. Most of then ended up swelling the ranks of Pakistani immigrants in the UK.

Need for reconseptualisation

Clearly there is an urgent need to reconceptualise the definition of refugees. It is not being argued that those who have been forced to flee their home and hearth because of political persecution and direct threat to their life should be equated with those who have been forced to move by loss of livelihood, man-made disasters and natural calamities. At the same time we can no longer ignore the fact that certain policies of the governments of developing countries have impoverished vast masses of their peoples, particularly those belonging to minority communities and economically backward sections. Studies have shown that some of the "development" projects implemented with international support have had an adverse impact on the economy and livelihood of people within the country and at times even across the border, uprooting them from their houses. They have become the "rejected peoples and unwanted migrants". Academics and NGOs today prefer to use such terms as "environmental refugees" and "refugees of development projects" to distinguish between certain types of displaced persons and voluntary migrants. The international community needs to apply its mind to this type of forced displacement. As a recent UNEP report has predicted, that day is not far when wars would be fought between communities and states over basic resources like water.

The existing definition of refugees, displaced persons and migrants is rather narrow and one-dimensional. It has to be considered also whether the accepted distinction between the forced and willed or political refugees and economic migrants are relevant today. These need to be reviewed and reformulated in order to accommodate the existing reality. New and effective international instruments and national laws need to be created to protect the rights of these hapless millions who have no legal existence in most countries of the world today.

II

Decolonisation and refugee flow from South to North

With the emergence of post colonial nation states in the Third World began another process of refugee movements. These movements have been variously called movements of "refugees, migrants and displaced persons". The period of decolonisation was also the period when the Third World was drawn into cold war politics. During the 70s and throughout the 80s the superpowers continued to destabilise "unfriendly regimes" and "revolutionary" governments in the Third World contributing to the flow of refugees in this region. The conditions of abject poverty, natural calamities and man-made environmental disasters also encouraged a large number of people to migrate and seek asylum in the developed countries of the West.

As the number of migrants and asylum seekers increased, the North changed its policy and initiated steps to contain and stop such flows. However, it should be noted that in the last three decades the largest flow of refugees and asylum seekers has been from one country in the South to another. Out of a world total of 15.33 million external refugees (those who have crossed international borders) in 1995, only 2.7 million were in Canada, Europe and United States of America.[12] Africa had the largest number of refugees, followed closely by West Asia. These are also regions experiencing intense conflicts.

The policy of *non-entree*

Mass population displacements are on the increase. It was hoped that the end of the cold war and the final victory of liberalism would usher in an era of peace. Speedy integration of the national markets in a global economy would bring economic prosperity to all and the problems of the world would be solved. This hope seems to have collapsed in the face of tidal waves of refugees unleashed by political violence and civil war in the former Socialist block of countries, the escalation of ethnic war in parts of South America, Africa and Asia and environmental and social disasters.

Conflicts within states have increased enormously. New notions of security have emerged on the basis of demography, resources and territory. Proxy wars between states and internal wars between rival communities are being fought over scarce resources. The neo-liberal world order is facing its greatest challenge from the population movements unleased by ethnic unrest, environmental degradation and technological change.

Faced with this new challenge, most northern states have implemented "non-entree" mechanisms, including visa requirements for nationals of refugee-producing states, burden-shifting arrangements like "carrier" sanction and even the forcible interdiction of refugees at frontiers and in international waters. The December 1996 tragedy in which about 300 job seekers or economic refugees from South Asian countries met their death in the icy waters of the Inoian Sea, off Malta, is a direct result of such policies. The policy is to contain the refugees within their homelands. It is being promoted as the "right to remain". A new category has been added to the growing body of international legal definitions - the internally displaced persons (IDPs).

Internally displaced persons

These are people who have been displaced within their countries as a result of internal conflicts, ethnic strife, forced relocation and gross violations of human rights. In 1992 the UN Human Rights Commission had estimated that there were close to 24 million IDPs all over the world. According to a report released by the Refugee Policy Group of Washington D.C., USA, by 1995, the world total of IDPs had risen to 30 million. Of these about 12 million were in Africa, 8 million in Asia, 6.5 million in Europe, about 1 million in North America while the rest were scattered over South America and Oceania. In June 1994, the UN High Commissioner for Refugees, Sadako Ogata, in her address to the World Bank said that internal conflicts force about 10,000 persons every day to flee their homes and either cross international borders or become displaced in their own countries. The reluctance of the North to admit large numbers of refugees or even to finance their stay in a third country has forced these persons at risk to remain displaced in their own countries. In other words these refugees have been denied the option to flee and the right to search for a more secure haven abroad.

Internally displaced persons, unlike refugees, live under the control of their national governments. They normally live under adverse conditions of a hostile domestic environment. Their rights are often abused by the law enforcement agencies of the states. No "Rules of War" of the Geneva Conventions are applied to internal conflicts. The doctrine of national sovereignty prevents international organisations like the UNHCR from extending its protection mandate to the IDPs. Under the pressure of the North the Secretary General of UN in 1993 asked UNHCR to be involved in situations of internal displacement. The UN High Commissioner for Refugees has called for a redefinition of refugees and its protection mandate to focus on "preparedness, prevention and solution".[13] However, in the absence of an international commitment to deliver dependable military and humanitarian interventions which attack the root causes of refugee flow—a necessary precondition for the meaningful exercise of the "right to remain"—the expansion of UNHCR's mandate to protect IDPs remains a hollow exercise.

As the experience of UN interventions in Iraqi Kurdistan, Somalia, Liberia, Angola Mozambique, Rwanda, Burundi and former Yugoslavia show, the international community's approach to these conflicts which displaced thousands of persons, was essentially reactive and without reference to any coherent doctrine. The management of conflicts in these areas was marked by inconsistency. There was a serious gap between what needed to be done on the ground and the resources available for doing it, despite enormous sums that were spent. The humanitarian interventions were not planned and there was no coordination between the military wing and the humanitarian agencies of the UN. It would appear that they were done, mainly to stop a large scale flow of refugees towards the developed countries. In reality it meant closing the borders and holding the displaced persons in camps within the zone of conflict.

Imposed repatriation

Since 1994 UNHCR has changed its approach towards "voluntary repatriation". Earlier individual refugees were interviewed and informed about the developments in the country of origin by UNHCR officials, as the Guidelines on Voluntary Repatriation emphasised that the return of the refugee must be on the basis of an individually and freely expressed wish. Since July 1994, UNHCR has adopted a new procedure in repatriation operations. Individual interviews are not being held any more. Instead, the camp refugees are being encouraged to register enmasse to return. The manner in which about 60,000 ethnic Rohingya refugees were repatriated to Myanmar in 1994-95 shows that UNHCR is no longer averse to the idea of sending refugees back to their home countries even when the situation may not have improved.[14]

The UN High Commissioner of Refugees in her statement on the programme of Voluntary Repatriation to the 46th session of Ex-Com meeting in 1995 admitted that, "in none of these instances is a return likely to be under ideal conditions. In many, it will be dogged by political insecurity and economic uncertainty." She argued that," New dimensions to our protection responsibilities have led us to interpret our mandate for solutions in a protection oriented and proactive manner. ... we can no longer passively wait for conditions to change so that the refugees can volunteer".

The return of the refugee is the most desired solution. However as experience shows, the return of the refugee should not be taken for granted as a "natural" and a "problem free" process. In fact it is undoubtedly one of the most misleading myths surrounding the process of repatriation. The new policy of UNHCR which has been criticised as "imposed repatriation" leaves several important questions unanswered. Under what circumstances can refugees be returned to a conflict zone? Who should determine whether it is safe for the refugees to return? Under what circumstances can people be forced to repatriate in "organised" repatriation? What is the relationship between the length of exile, shortage of funds and mass repatriation? Under what conditions should UNHCR withdraw services to refugee settlements in order to induce mass repatriation. What levels of information do refugees have or need to have in order to determine whether the return is voluntary? What sort of pre-departure and post-departure services should returnees be provided ?

III

South Asia: An overview

No ethnic or religious communal conflict in recent times has caused so much bloodshed and destruction as was caused by the Partition of the subcontinent by the British Raj in 1947. Nearly a million people belonging to the minorities of each country were killed in the Hindu-Muslim riots that followed Partition. Though the two governments did not force their minorities to leave, they failed to stop the carnage. An estimated 15 million people had to migrate as a result. Pakistan granted citizenship to all Indian Muslims who chose to move to Pakistan. Similarly India accepted Hindus and Sikhs who did not wish to live in Pakistan.

Then there are the "rejected people". These are people who were forced to leave the country of their residence by the governments. Decolonisation of South Asia witnessed similar instances of rejection of people by newly emerged independent states. After Burma's independence in 1948 nearly 500,000 Indians who have been living in Burma since the early part of this century, had to leave in the wake of the policy of Burmanization. Sri Lanka, after her independence created approximately 900,000 stateless persons. These were the Tamil estate workers who were taken to the island country in 1830 from south India by British planters.[15]

South Asia has the fourth largest concentration of refugees in the world. This does not include the millions of displaced persons who have been forced to move from their home by generalised violence, environmental devastation and ethnic strife. In Nepal, there are 75,000 southern Bhutanese of Nepali origin who fled ethnic persecution. A million people of Bangladeshi origin have got lost in the by-lanes of Karachi. There were about 3 million Afghan refugees in Pakistan. About 238,000 unwanted Biharis are "stateless" in Bangladesh and as 47,000 Rohingya-Burmese refugees in Bangladesh await "imposed repatriation" while again are fleeing Myanmar. In Sri Lanka a million or more are internally displaced. In India there are 51,000 Chakma and 56,000 Sri Lankan refugees. Thousands of Tibetan, Bhutanese and Burmese refugees have come to India along with millions of "migrants" because of natural and man-made environmental disasters.

Nation building and the rise of ethno-nationalism

The model of the "nation state" that the elite of South Asia adopted was that of a territorial "national society" within a sovereign state. It was to derive its "legitimacy and stability" from the idea of "national unity". The enterprise of nation-building rested on a two-pronged strategy: i) modernisation of a traditional society and ii) large-scale mobilisation of human and material resources.

The process of "modernisation" (which actually meant the infiltration of market forces) was expected to integrate all the "people" into the national society. However, given the colonial policy of divide and rule which had effectively dismantled the traditional institutions of social authority and destroyed the harmonious inter-community relationships, it came as no surprise that the "national identities" of the respective South Asian states were articulated through the symbolism of majority ethnicity.

The other ethnic communities in these states simply became "minorities" especially since they did not in addition, speak the lingua franca which each newly emergent nation had adopted, namely, Hindi in India's case, Sinhala in the case of Sri Lanka and Urdu in that of Pakistan. They soon realised that they had to fight for their "due share" of the national bounty. Thus, the process of "nation building" which was to create integrated nation-states in South Asia created the opposite. It politicised all the ethno-linguistic, ethno-religious and tribal groups. Each was forced to compete with the other at one level, and at another level, against the state to achieve political autonomy.

South Asia has already become an arena of considerable ethnic unrest—Sri Lankan Tamils and Sinhalese in Sri Lanka, Assamese, Bodo, Meities and Nagas in the North-East of India, Chakma and other tribal people in Bangladesh, Sikhs in India, Kashmiris in the disputed Kashmir region, Sindhis, Mohajirs, Baluchis and Pushtoons in Pakistan. South Asian governments in their negotiations with all the dissenting ethnic groups adopted the "carrot and stick policy"—sending the army and the security forces in to beat up the "hardliners", while offering a package of economic incentives coupled with a few minor political reforms to the "moderates" among the dissenters.

Communal violence and ethnic strife

Ethnic conflicts often involves more than just conflict between the ethnic groups and the states. Sometimes there are conflicts between different ethnic groups and at times there are conflicts between factions within each group. In Sri Lanka, the Sinhala Tamil conflict led to assassinations and riots between political factions in both groups and violence against the Muslims in Sri Lanka. In India's North-East, the rivalry between two dominant factions of Naga insurgents have resulted in the death of many Naga civilians. Threatened by the Kaphlang faction of the Naga insurgents, hundreds of Tangkul Nagas, a sub-group of the Naga tribe, suspected to be the supporters of Issac-Muiva faction of the Naga independence movement, had to flee from Nagaland. The armed wings of Bodo and Kuki tribes of North-East India have forced thousands non-tribal people as well as people belonging to other minority tribes to flee from the areas under their control. Recent ethnic unrest in India's Mizoram district has displaced nearly 12,000 people belonging to Reang.

Pakistan's unity and integrity is being challenged by the rising tide of ethno-nationalism. Pakistan is a land of four nationalities. Punbajis comprise 66 percent, Sindhis 13 percent, Pusthuns 9.5 percent and Baluchis 2.5 percent. The

Mohajirs (refugees from India) who constitute about 7.6 percent of Pakistan's population claim the status of the fifth nationality or at least, of a subnationality. Punjabi domination is a fact of Pakistan's politics. While Pakistani bureaucracy is Punjabi dominated, the army is almost totally Punjabi.

The Mohajirs who are largely Urdu speakers have become a powerful political force in the Sindh province of Pakistan. They control the city of Karachi, the capital city of Sindh, where only 6.3 percent of the population speak Sindhi. In rural Sindh on the other hand about 78 percent of the population are Sindhi speaking. As Sindhi Muslims were mainly illiterate peasants at the time of Partition, the Mohajirs were able to corner most of the coveted public sector jobs and private business in the province. Mohajir domination in Karachi and Punjabi domination of the political life of Pakistan gave birth to Sindhi ethnic consciousness, erupting into militancy and a separatist demand. The Sindhis are caught between Punjabi domination and the demands of the Mohajirs. The problem is further compounded by the increasing number of Bihari Muslims, repatriated from Bangladesh.

Violence has become a way of life in Karachi and other cities of Sindh. In the cities of Sindh, followers of MQM battle with various Sindhi nationalist groups. In the countryside, Sindhi frustration is expressed through the pervasive Kalashnikov culture which spread in Pakistan after the Afghan war. Banditry, kidnapping and extortions are every day affairs. In 1992 the Pakistan army had to be deployed by the federal government in a massive operation against the Sindhi nationalists and the MQM. Pakistan's human rights groups have reported about serious violations of human rights of the ordinary citizens of Sindh by the army.

Communal violence is another refugee generating factor. Protection of minorities is impossible given the way South Asian states are developing politically and economically. These are states in the process of building a nation. Such states of necessity will go on producing majorities and minorities. Communal disturbances in the Indian cities of Mumbai, Surat and Ahmedabad a few years ago caused the exodus of Bengali Muslims from these places to the relative safety of West Bengal. Anti-Hindu riots in Bangladesh have also caused displacements. Riots in Sindh and Karachi have resulted in a similar displacement of a large number of people. Recently there were reports that many Bangladeshi settlers from Karachi have returned to Bangladesh.

After mass killing of Sikhs in 1984, several thousand Sikh families moved back to Punjab from different cities of India. As a result of the conflict in Kashmir about 98,000 Kashmiri Pundits (Hindus) and nearly 70,000 Kashmiri Muslims fled the valley and are now living in the camps for "migrants" in Jammu and other parts of India. According to reports about 10,000 Kashmiri Muslim were forced to cross the Line of Control and are being housed in 11 refugee camps in the Pakistan-controlled Kashmir.

National security perspective

The last fifty years' experience shows that the South Asian states are essentially clannish, dynastic and dictatorial in character and thus, highly dependent on the armed forces, despite the fact that some of them have been able to maintain a facade of democracy. Almost every political, economic and human issue, be it internal or external, is examined through the prism of national security. The issue of cross-border migration has been deliberately projected by governments and the elite as threatening national security and national integrity. Across the porous borders of these post-colonial nation-states in the making, people slip over into neighbouring states to escape political persecution, generalised violence or the denial of basic human rights, including the right to food, water and shelter. The existence of cross border ethnic communities which are in a minority in one country and a majority in another, further entraps the refugee into a national security complex, especially where host governments use refugees (warrior refugees) to further security or foreign policy goals.

In the bubbling cauldron of inter-state tension in South Asia, the cross border movement of peoples gets mired in suspicion. The dominant line of tension in South Asia is the Indo-Pakistan conflict. The problem of Kashmir, allegations of interference in Punjab and Sindh and suspicions about incitement of minorities, form the national security subtext of cross border flows.

Then there is the inter-dynamics of big brother politics and the nation-state identity complex in the case of India and the neighbours. With Bangladesh there is the river waters dispute, the tribal insurgency in the Chittagong Hill Tracts and the destablising effect on the border areas of migrants. In the case of India and Nepal, there is deep resentment over the feared destabilising economic and demographic effect of the open border policy. Inevitably it has got entangled in the politics of insecurity, a spillover from the interdependence of two unequal neighbours. With Sri Lanka, India is pulled into the vortex of the Tamil-Sinhala ethnic conflict.

South Asia is also criss crossed by minor lines of tension, between Nepal and Bhutan and Pakistan and Bangladesh. Bhutan has expelled thousands of people of Nepali origin who were pushed into Nepal by India. Between Pakistan and Bangladesh is the unfinished legacy of the division of 1971: the repatriation of the Biharis to Pakistan.

The backdrop of inter state tensions in South Asia has legitimised a militarised response to cross border movements of peoples over and beyond the general militarization of civil society in the region.

Migrants, the unwanted people

South Asian governments have basically ignored the issue of the rights of migrants, refugees and stateless persons. Given the hostile relations between the states of South Asia, it is natural that the host countries have tried to use refugees and migrants for political leverage and often for interfering in the internal affairs of neighbours. In some cases these helpless persons have been used as a buffer population by the host country. Chakma refugees were settled in the then remote North Eastern Frontier Agency (NEFA) of India, bordering China as a protection against Chinese incursions in that area after the Sino-Indian war.

Illegal immigrants are usually tolerated till they become a focus of political controversy. As these people survive through "sweat labour" in the industrial and commercial centres of the host countries, they are exploited by all kinds of vested interests. South Asian countries do not have a system of granting resident permits or job licenses. The fear of detection and of being thrown out, forces them to search for "protectors". Political parties who are also in search of reliable vote banks often get these people included in voters' lists through unfair means. When opposition parties or local people agitate against these "illegal voters", the government start talking about expelling these people.

India claims that there are six to seven million Bangladeshi illegal immigrants living in India, who are classified as economic refugees. The larger concentration of Bangladeshi migrants are in the Indian states of Tripura and Assam. In Tripura they are now in a majority outnumbering the local tribal population. In 1983, during the anti-foreigner violence in Assam, thousands of immigrants settled in Assam had to flee. About 5,000 were killed. In 1985, the government of India adopted the policy of the forced expulsion of illegal immigrants.

While India wants to push back the immigrants, Bangladesh claims that they are Indian citizens who possess Indian ration cards and have voted in Indian elections. Of the 12 million Bangladeshis who had taken shelter in India during Bangladesh's war of independence, not all returned. Most Hindus from then East Pakistan, had stayed back. The BJP, the Hindu nationalist party which is spearheading the campaign to "push back Bangladeshi immigrants" for reasons of its own, makes a distinction between Hindu and Muslim immigrants from Bangladesh. They only wish to expel the Muslims.

The second largest cross border migration in South Asia was out of Nepal. Nepal's average annual population increase is about 500,000. Their outward migration has already reduced several indigenous people of the Himalayan region into a minority in their own habitat. Nepali migration to Sikkim reduced the Lepchas and Bhutias into a minority in that state. It is difficult to say whether the Nepalis in Sikkim had come from Nepal or from Kalimpong and Darjeeling of West Bengal in India which have a substantial ethnic Nepali population. However the Nepali migration to Bhutan is an old fact.

Although half-hearted attempts have been made to resolve some of these problems at bilateral level, it is clear that this problem can not be resolved through bilateral efforts.

Given the resources, no one nation alone can be expected to guarantee the rights of the migrants and refugees. The dominant ethnic majorities of the South Asian states will always treat the migrants as a threat to their political hegemony. The migrants will be blamed for bringing down wage levels, high rates of crime and the proliferation of dirty slums.

Conclusion

We can not continue to ignore the rights of refugees, migrants and displaced persons in the region. During the last five decades, millions of people have been uprooted from their homes in this region by a combination of political, military, economic, ethnic, communal and environmental factors. The efforts of the South Asian elite to build majoritarian nation-states of the European kind ignoring the region's 5000- year-old social, economic and cultural links and the attempts to glorify the territorial borders crafted by the departed colonial rulers have not only destroyed the social and cultural harmony of the region but also generated mistrust and suspicion among common the people. It has fuelled ethnic and communal passions, unleashing mindless violence in its wake often with transborder repercussion. Traditional trade routes and markets have been destroyed. Established patterns of labour migration have been disrupted, forcing people to give up their age-old professions. Almost all the governments of the region are guilty of forced eviction. The model of "modern" development adopted by them has led to the collapse of food security, land security and environmental security compelling millions to seek alternative sources of livelihood. The majority of them have crossed over to neighbouring countries. Transborder population flux is the symptom. The cause lies imbedded in the internal and external policies of the states.

Knee-jerk response, which has become the hallmark of South Asian policy making, is visible in the pathetic attempt by some of the states to stop transborder population movements by erecting barbed wire fences along the borders. While a section of the region's political parties and the media have been whipping up xenophobia, almost all the governments of South Asia have imposed severe visa restrictions on the citizens of their neighbours. But the transborder population flux continues unabated. It is obvious that the massive flow of uprooted people can not be stopped by such measures. This is a regional problem and it requires a regional approach.

Institutionalisation of the rights of refugees, migrants and the displaced persons within the national legal systems is the first essential step that needs to be taken. Given the prevailing atmosphere of mutual mistrust among states of the region, no single state can be expected to enact such a law. For obvious reasons, a uniform refugee law with humane provisions shall have to be promoted regionally so that it is adopted by all the countries of the region. UNHCR has been promoting this idea informally in its dialogue with governments of the region, most of whom are current members of UNHCR's Executive Committee. Four informal consultations on "Refugee and Migratory Movements" were held during the last three years where a select group of eminent jurists, academics and human rights activists have tried to develop comprehensive strategies to contain involuntary population movements in the region. The most comprehensive document produced by the consultations is a "Draft Model National Law on Refugees". (Appendix A)

In the proposed Draft Model National Law on Refugees, the scope of the definition of refugee has been considerably expanded. While retaining the original definition of the 1951

UN Convention, it has incorporated the expanded version of the OAU Convention and the Cartagena Declaration on Refugees. The proposed definition of refugee therefore, includes "any person who owing to external aggression, occupation, foreign domination, serious violation of human rights or other events seriously disrupting public order in either whole or part of his or her country of origin, is compelled to leave his or her place of habitual residence in order to seek refuge in another place outside his or her country of origin." The draft model law integrates the principle of *non-refoulement* and provides for setting up an independent refugee committee at the national level as an appellate authority. The draft model law while laying down refugee status determination procedures, incorporates a provision for dealing with situations of mass influx. It has also proposed a set of rights and duties of refugees. When adopted by the governments of the region, this law will remove the most serious lacuna in the protection of the rights of the refugees and displaced persons of the region. It will also strengthen the cause of peace and democracy in the region as the process of protecting the rights of the immigrant population will lead to ensuring justice beyond national frontiers.

The states of South Asia need to look beyond their narrow national security perspectives. In a region where land security, water security, food security and environment security are collapsing, building up gigantic military establishments is a criminal activity. It is clear that the states of the region will soon have to come closer and work together to resolve the problem of forced displacement of people. To achieve this, they must begin to deal with the causes rather than the symptoms of mass displacement. This will entail reorientation of current foreign and economic policies. This will not come about simply as a result of moral exhortation.

Nor can it be achieved by the rhetoric of regional cooperation which is routinely dispensed by the heads of states at every SAARC summit. Decision makers in South Asian capitals must be convinced of the pragmatic benefits to be gained from regional cooperation and the peaceful settlement of disputes. Regional cooperation should not be restricted to free flow of capital and goods only. In view of the reality of the South Asian labour situation and the historic practice of labour migrations across the subcontinent, a mechanism for a regulated flow of services and labour across the borders shall have to be developed. The objective should be to create an integrated regional labour market.

In November 1996, at the invitation of South Asia Forum for Human Rights, 42 academics, media persons, former state ministers, diplomats, bureaucrats and human rights activist met in Kathmandu to review the situation of the refugees and displaced persons in the region. The Kathmandu group concluded that South Asia needs to develop a regional mechanism for the protection of the rights of the refugees, migrants and displaced persons, whether in Bangladesh, Bhutan, India, Nepal, Pakistan or Sri Lanka. At the end of a five-day workshop, where country situations were reviewed in depth, the participants called on the states of the region to create a regional protocol for the determination of the status of refugees and displaced persons. They also recommended that the South Asian states create a charter of rights for the refugees and displaced persons in the region. The Kathmandu group felt that the regional instrument should incorporate provisions for cost sharing on a regional basis as it will be rather difficult for some of the smaller countries to carry the burden of a massive influx of population. Under the regional instrument an independent body should be set up for monitoring and early warning.

There should be provisions for humanitarian intervention by the regional body in specific situations. The recommendations of the Kathmandu seminar was presented to the heads of states, members of parliaments and leaders of political parties of all the South Asian countries (Appendix B).

NOTES

1. Hannah Arendt, *The Origins of Totalitarianism,* HBJ, New York, 1993.
2. Shah M. Tarzi, "The Nation-state, Victim Groups & Refugees," Ethnic & Racial Studies, Vol. 14, No. 4, October 1991 and Aristide Zolberg, "The Formation of Nation-states as a Refugee Generating Process," *The Annals*, Vol.467.
3. Aristide R. Zolberg, Astri Sukrke and Sergio Aguaya, *Escape from Violence - Conflict & Refugee Crisis in the Developing World*, OUP, New York, 1989.
4. E. Hobsbawm, *Age of Extremes*, London 1994. p. 50
5. League of Nations Treaty Series, 12 May 1926: LNTS no. 2004. The same definition was later extended to Armenian, Assyrian, Assyro-Chaldean and assimilated refugees. The important aspect is that the League Nations adopted a group or category approach to the definition of refugees. This was changed to an individual approach by the UNHCR under the influence of the Western powers during the cold war.
6. Guy S. Godwin-Gill, *The Refugee in International Law*, Clarendon Press, Oxford, 1987.
7. For the complete text of the definition of refugees see Part I of Annex I of the Constitution of IRO in *Collection of International Instruments and other Legal Texts Concerning Refugees and Displaced Persons,* Vol. 1, pub. Division of International Protection, UNHCR, Geneva, 1995. p 59-61.

8. ibid. p. 7.
9. ibid p. 73.
10. Justice Dorab Patel, Refugee Problem of Pakistan, paper presented at the UNHCR sponsored Regional Consultation on Refugees and Migratory Movements, Colombo, Sri Lanka, 25-27 September 1995. Pub. S.S.Wijeratne, Coordinator of Consultation, UNHCR, Geneva. p 32
11. Walter Fernandes, *Development, Displacement and Rehabilitation in Tribal Areas of Eastern India*, Indian Social Institute, 1994.
12. *World Refugee Survey 1996*, U.S. Committee for Refugees, Washington, DC.
13. Report of the UN High Commissioner for Refugees, UN Doc.E/1995/52, April 25, 1995.
14. *Awareness Survey: Rohingya Refugee Camps*, March 1995, Medicines Sans Frontiers, MFS/F, 1995, New York.
15. Myron Weiner, *Rejected Peoples and Unwanted Migrants*, Centre for International Studies, MIT, Massachusetts, 1991.

Understanding Migratory Flows in South Asia
A humanitarian agenda

Ranabir Samaddar*

Large-scale population movements of "refugees, migrants and internally displaced persons" across borders have become one of the defining characteristics of the post-Second World War global order. Mass population displacements are on the increase. The phenomenon seemingly remains unconcerned with end of cold war, the end of history, rise of regionalism and a resurgence of local nationalisms. If anything, those who had predicted the final victory of liberalism backed by a benign state, economic prosperity and economic integration, are now terrified by the "coming anarchy", which according to people like Robert D. Kaplan, Zbignew Brzezinsky and Paul Kennedy, will be signified by the "break-up of nations under the tidal flow of refugees from environmental and social disasters". "Wars (will be) fought over scarce resources, especially water, and war itself (will become) continuous with crime, as armed bands of stateless marauders clash with the private security forces of the elites."[1] In other words, transborder population flux is being increasingly viewed as a challenge to the neo-liberal world order — a challenge that originates from a combination of technological change, environmental degradation, ethnic unrest and demographic growth.

The intensity of the phenomenon has given rise to debates within the international community on how to respond to these population movements. The magnitude of the refugee phenomena can be guaged from the following facts. The total number of refugees and "other persons of concern" by UNHCR estimates reached a figure of 22,729,000 in 1997. Of this, refugees were 13,200,000 returnees 3,311,000; others of concern 1,365,000 and internally displaced 4,854,000. Africa accounted for, 80,91,000 peoples. Next was Asia with 7,925,000; then Europe, 5,749,000. Latin America 169,000, North America 720,000 and Oceania 75,000.[2]

States are increasingly taking steps to obstruct the arrival of asylum seekers, to push back and contain displaced people within their homeland, and to return refugees against their will to their country of origin. This is because today, population displacement is not simply a consequence of some occasional conflict, but an explicit objective of warring parties and a continuous product of the present global order. The threat of superpower confrontation has receded, but new notions of security are emerging on the basis of demography, resources, and territory. Therefore refugee problems are by definition transnational problems. Given the security perceptions of the states, these problems cannot be resolved by means of uncoordinated activities in separate countries. An alternative consensus or paradigm is thus required and also possibly emerging in view of the situation. Such an alternative view has to be based on new definitions, pro-active policies, a holistic attitude and the need to recognise the integral link between population flux and patterns of global-regional economy and social-political order.

Today's human rights abuses are tomorrow's refugee movements. Major population displacements in the present decade have occurred in the context of war, ethnic strife, partition, minority persecution, new state formations and environmental disaster. When people abandon their homes and land, they do so because of the threat of violence, more accurately speaking, perpetual threats of perpetual violence. Therefore the guarantee of human rights is a guarantee for a minimum of stability which discourages population movements. But there is one other aspect to this linkage. Human rights abuse also occurs when such fleeing people are denied shelter and sustenance often because of the security perspective of the states and the absence of various international and regional refugee protection regimes. Ironically, human rights abuses are compounded when it is overlooked that population flux is not always forced or violence-driven. Such population flux has often featured in world economic history. If we can have free movement of goods, why can we not have free movement of labour and services ?

This brings us to the question of the rights of refugees, particularly of women, children and the aged. Such rights are rarely or almost never recognized, because it is generally assumed that refugees or displaced persons will never return. It is an assumption of exile. Therefore, they have to be given citizenship and helped to get integrated legally and economically. This is known as the strategy of "local settlement", an exile-oriented approach. The history of refugee-management has shown, that such a strategy has failed in the current situation of heavy population flux.

A policy more responsive to the changing nature of mass refugee movements is one which recognizes the rights of the refugees, impels the home state to encourage the refugees to return in conditions of safety and security and the guarantee of proprietorial rights. It encourages international human rights monitoring, improves the condition and security of refugee settlements and progressively ensures freedom so that the skills of the displaced persons are gainfully employed and utilized in the host country as well. In other words, the concept of protection for refugees and displaced persons, is inseparable from the notion of human rights. Refugee women and girls, in particular, have to survive violence and neglect. As experience shows, while the use of rape as weapon of persecution and war has found its way into the media headlines, "the protection problems of displaced females are found in less dramatic conditions of day to day struggles for survival". Therefore, economic and social rights and relevant institutional arrangements and relationships are very important. Institutional arrangements mean in the first place, establishing and/or reforming an international presence. International safeguards are unlikely to succeed in preventing population displacements, if a state based on majoritarianism is determined to violate the rights of the people. While citizenship is an indicator of certain rights, the concept of citizenship creates the category of "non-state persons", who are without any recognizable right to social and political existence. In many countries today, stateless persons remain a testimony to the ironies of the nationalist discourse of "citizenship".

A civil rights agenda of protection of refugees, migrants and internally displaced persons is, above all, linked to a campaign for peace. Traditional peace-keeping methods have failed, partly because, they are outdated and because they are now the instrument of great power hegemonism and aggression. New directions in a peace campaign have to be different from "peace-keeping". This means an emphasis on a range of peoples rights, on consensus and consent, new legal instruments, anti-militarism, clarity of roles and objectives and reconciliation. Humanitarian assistance is often regarded as having political consequences and is therefore manipulated by states who are parties to a conflict for their own ends. This cynicism has increased as states know that with the end of cold war, the great powers have a significantly reduced interest in impoverished nations and regions. With international migration growing and becoming more complex, states are placing more curbs on migrants. This adversely affects the situation of the refugee and internally displaced persons. A campaign for peace and reconciliation, which provides for protection of minority rights, rights of migrants, and free movement of labour will help the formulation of polices that are not just confined to "peace-keeping" and creating "safe areas".

Partition and porous borders

With these generalities shaping our perspective, we can take a brief look at the peculiarities of the South Asian situation. The carving up of South Asia into modern nation-states through partitioned independence has made the problem of population displacement and population movement more acute. Nationalism in South Asia has become reflexive. India is nationalist with reference to Pakistan or Bangladesh and not so much with reference to the USA or the United Kingdom. Bangladesh defines its nationalism against India and Pakistan and not Japan or the UK. Reflexive nationalism in South Asia is a gross caricature of its predecessor, anti-colonial nationalism. It makes ethnic suppression and suffering in the wake of forced migration, tolerable to the ethics of a nation. And while political parties often give calls for sealing the country's borders to check migration, their "porous border" argument based on the fears of the native population, remains ignorant of the historically established patterns of migration of peoples in South Asia. It is a phenomenon now laden and valorized with the history and the politics of Partition.

It will be worthwhile to remember that moments and epochs of economic and political restructuring have been accompanied by demographic flexing, subcontinentally, through group migrations. This is in addition to the traditional seasonal mobility, across mountains and widespread swamp areas, of communities like the Chakma, M'to Mizo or Kuki peoples in the Patkoi ranges on either side of the India-Myanmar-Bangladesh trijunction. In the 19th and early 20th centuries, indentured labour, mostly landless and poor peasants, who had already been moving from hills to plains and from one area to another in eastern and central India, were shipped from Calcutta to sugar and coffee plantations, to build railways and work the mines in the Indian Ocean islands, the South Pacific, the Caribbean Sea, Guyana in the Amazon Delta and to East and South Africa. This kind of labour exodus became obsolete with British decolonization. However, new industrial opportunities in the West and the growing west European demand for restructuring of their economies in the 1950s and 1960s led to the next phase of labour outflow from the subcontinent with another generation of the Indian poor and the dissatisfied middle classes seeping into England, France, the Low Countries, Germany and even into the erstwhile socialist countries of Europe and of course into the USA. Most of them became members of the menial or service layers of the underclass of Atlantic capitalism.

The large-scale cross border mobility of population in South Asia, continued in the political conditions perpetuated by Partition and the economic condition of petty production.

Sudden dramatic displacements were to produce periodic spurts in industrialization of people across borders. Political consolidation of the nation-state and periodic spurts in industrialization cannot be fully explained without taking into account the far reaching effects of transformations often termed as "globalization". Ancillarization and decentralization of certain industries which make small production units viable, growing trade linkages between the countries, off shore assembly, subcontracting and the export processing centres and zones, have made sweat labour, ironically, a necessity in the modern production system in Asia, and particularly post-Partition South Asia.

Low-wage workers from a neighbouring country in South Asia sometimes compete with low-wage workers of the host country, but often they fill the void created by an expansion of the labour market due to developments stated above. The employment of non-national labour in South Asia, mostly of illegal immigrants, seen in this context, has emerged as a component of the restructured international division of labour. The example of migrant South Asian workers in the Gulf and elsewhere in the region of South Asia itself shows how with or without formal arrangements between states on contract workers, states and employers do acquiesce to clandestine migrations to meet the requirements of capital, particularly in semi-skilled and unskilled categories.

The migrant worker in South Asia makes minimal demands on the social expenditure of the host country, and since the worker is usually an illegal immigrant, the country sending labour has little or no say in determining the wages of the emigrant, his/her conditions of work, duration of stay and social benefits. The situation is, thus, at times close to slavery. They are often branded as a threat to 'national security, public order and public morals'. Their alienation and disenfranchisement from the social collective is extreme. Even when they are not "refugees", they have to live the ghettoized life of the refugees.

Given the background of globalization, its companion regionalization and the partitioned nature of the region of South Asia, the existing social theory of migration is called into closer scrutiny. The argument of neo-classical political economy has been around "push" and "pull", i.e., gains to be won by movement from areas of relatively low productivity to areas of high productivity, which motivate migration. But push factors which include such circumstances as overpopulation, unemployment, scarcity of land, low wages and natural calamities and pull factors which attract people to new locations such as employment, high wages, educational and cultural facilities, do not operate in their neoclassical neatness in South Asia. There may be an integrated labour market, however imperfect. But then again, people may migrate to sweat labour jobs because of minority persecution, violence, ethnic ties, general lack of confidence in a nation's stability or even a historically established tradition of seasonal migration, typical of the peasantry in South Asia. All these defy the conceptual neatness of the push and pull theory of neo-classical political economy regarding migration. Community networks, not unnaturally, have revived in this condition.

Nation-state or state-nation

Protection of minorities has become a catchword for the liberal agenda in South Asia. And there is the tendency to ignore its complexities. Protection of minorities is impossible given the way the states of South Asia are developing both politically and economically and assuming the form of "nationalising states", i.e., states which are not sufficiently nations and must develop into nations to gain legitimacy. Such states, therefore, go on producing, of necessity, majorities and minorities, for they can survive only on the basis of a continuing and permanent agenda of building an "ethnic core" and thereby marginalising others. Riots therefore continue to occur seasonally, giving clarity to the agenda of nation building. Migrants become the marker of the "minority niche" in a country, and thus the target of attack, insults, torture, killings and riots. They are not citizens. Hence they die an ignoble and unnoticed death.

There is no doubt that migrants and refugees will continue to be treated as unwanted guests by the ethnic core of the nation-states in South Asia which remain perpetually involved in the process of defining themselves through exclusionary practices. Citizens will be told that migrant labour brings down wage levels by competing with local wage workers, that they put pressure on the social security provisions of the country, accentuate the trend towards lumpenization and criminalization, that they have no loyalty to the country which provides succour and hence they deserve periodic beatings, killings, warnings and sometimes expulsion. The tragedy of these refugees and migrants is double because their home country, too, does not want them, treats their emigration as "good riddance", indeed, an occasion for consolidation of the "nationalist core". Migration therefore has become an issue linked to the emergence of the New Right, the increasing fascization of the polity of both countries, emigrating and immigrating. Migration has becomes the elaborate defence of persistent inequalities.

Thus, migrants and refugees will remain always on the margins of the post-partition state system in South Asia. They are there to be ignored and to be eternally peripheralized. But they are required to define the system, to define the core and the periphery of the nations in South Asia. The "illegal" migration system makes possible a mode of political and economic management which exploits the difference between legality and illegalities. Migrant labour therefore becomes one of the principal forms of investing national boundaries with power.

The history of the past fifty years of this region has managed to appear so absolute that in spite of the long history of population mobility in the subcontinent, transborder and transnational migration is the source of enormous political controversy and passion. Possibly, at no time in the history of our region has, migration been so linked to the issue of power, security and the destiny of a state. Herein lies the characteristic of the post-partition situation of the subcontinent. Migration is not simply an issue of demography or labour economics, it is now perceived as an issue concerning or threatening a nation's survival and consolidation. To the migrant also, moving to another place is not just an economic choice, but a political decision. To the leaders of the states and keepers of the conscience of the nations, the exodus is an embarrassment, to be philosophized, explained or glossed over in silence. The greater the distance from the metropolis of the regions, the more the urge to move. Migration has become the most emphatic question mark on the career of political nationhood embarked upon by the core elites of South Asia both on the nation which the moving population leaves and on the nation which it enters.

Nationalizing states produce "reasons of state", that is, a rationale for producing refugees, "illegal" migrants, and the internally displaced persons. The states in South Asia have reasons to be disturbed over the flux given their permanent agenda of nationalization. Reasons of state, therefore, are linked very much with such an agenda. Whatever may be the actual figures of migrations across the borders, the reality of transborder human flow is so perennial and persistent and hence so overwhelming and real that states succumb to it. Laws and legal practices bow down before this reality. The state realizes that this is not only the territorial border, but the margin of the nation too. The nation cannot be imposed on the population on the border. Either the glorious nation in these areas is today a thing of the past, or this is a border village, *thana*, subdivision, district and a province which does not respect the nation. In the eyes of the state, the border thus threateningly shrinks inward.

The state discovers that people of the 'border' do not respect security officers, they do not salute the flag flying near the security camps in border villages. Out of this 'discovery' has come a reluctant acknowledgment that people on the border cannot be prevented from interacting with each other, trade will continue, that brutal methods of treating the migrants will incur the severe displeasure of people on the border. Hence some other method than mere policing the border has to be found. The state has been inclined to pursue not one policy, but three combined policies : the total demarcation of border, issuance of photo-identity cards to villagers near the border and border fencing.

This characteristic state response to trans-border migration creates an extreme anxiety regarding the "number" of immigrants. So paramount, pervasive and anxious becomes the enquiry of those in power about the number of migrants coming over from across the border, that all other questions about migration vanish or get subsumed in the quest for numbers. This obsession with quantity inhibits any meaningful understanding. Ironically, it ends up mystifying migration, so much so that crucial questions about linkages of political, geographic, economic, and sociological nature remain suppressed under the debris of numerical exercises, i.e., the "numbers game". Meaningful dialogue between the states on migrants and refugees is consequently ruled out. The diplomatic game of mutual admission and non-admission is not without meaning. It is to keep alive the script of a nationalist dramaturgy in which the scriptwriter knows that nation is marginal to those coming over and to those who are tolerating them "on the border."

In such a situation, legality produces illegality; reality produces nationalist lament; quantitative search produces mystery; welfare measures produce even more migration; border produces subversion and partition perpetuates its illegitimacy. Pitted against popular perceptions built on 'accessibility from both sides' and 'the psychology of a free border', states decide on fencing, i.e., enclaving and colonizing a place. The question is, is fencing a mere psychological ploy or the final solution to stop migration ? Seemingly it is now a mix of both, only the history of fenced territoriality in South Asia can tell us what it will turn out to be. The outcome could be no less full of tension, conflict and as bloody as guarding the territory has become today. Fences will go up, but will that stop the return of the native? Will it not add all the more to the mythology of migration — a myth which is already impenetrable ?

Blurred categories

We have already noted the inadequacies of prevalent definitions in the context of the general situation. We shall see now how definitions and categories regarding migration are even more inadequate. Indeed, they are "blurred categories". The International Encyclopaedia of the Social

Sciences presents "migration" and "refugees" as wholly different subjects.[3] Migration indicates population movements, according to William Petersen who wrote the entry. Petersen assets that the 1953 UN definition of migration was arbitrary and misleading, as it deliberately excluded refugees who constitute a large portion of total international population movements.

The conventional view of migration takes an "externalist" view. Factors external to the origin of migration are considered crucial in the decision to migrate. The "internalist" view dominates refugee literature, that is, the crucial factors determining a refugees decision to cross the border are internal to the state of origin. Apart from the fact that internals and externals are hard to strictly differentiate and distinguish, the internalist conceptualization remains because international law is founded on the notion that the world is divided into a finite set of states with mutually exclusive jurisdiction over segments of territory and clusters of population and therefore social causation can be located within or among particular states. There is thus the need for a reconceptualization, as the typology of "migrant" and "refugee" has been found wanting.

Some observers argue that the migrant is an "environmental refugee". Jacques Vernant had observed in 1953 that "a refugee is someone who has been compelled to abandon his home." [4] Thus refugees may be victims of earthquake, flood, war or persecution. The emphasis is thus on victimization by events for which as an individual, the refugee cannot be held responsible. If that is so, is not the "illegal migrant" also similarly compelled to move and abandon his/her home? Religious persecution, political unrest, ethnic conflicts, weak state, weak economy, natural disaster, environmental catastrophe and finally fear of violence — all these have provoked human movements on a large scale. The "victim" here is both a migrant and a refugee. One can only say that the refugee movement is climactic, while migration is endemic.

In post-partition South Asia, therefore, the equation : voluntary economic = migrants, and involuntary political = refugees, is suspect. In fact this kind of schematic equation is clearly problematic since it refers ultimately to some doctrine of rights. Which rights are we to accord primacy to? Similarly, the other dichotomy, economic versus political is problematic as well. For behind apparent political reasons, we may find in many cases economic imperatives. The great waves of Irish migration from 1840 to 1854 were the result of a mix of both political and economic causes. The Hunger of 1840s was only the worst of numerous famines. But in contrast with England and Scotland, Ireland had no system of public relief. In bad times the only alternative to starvation is emigration. Viewed in this light, the response of the South Asian states to their population fleeing famine conditions is reminiscent of the attitude of English landlords and British authorities which amounted to an opportunistic deportation policy.

"Violence" also cannot effectively distinguish a refugee from a migrant. For if refugees are escapees from violence, what about migrants like women sex workers from Nepal or Bangladesh or women workers engaged in various forms of sweat labour who leave their countries for fear of "endemic violence" by husbands or other males and from the unorganised garment industry, the village and society as a whole? These realities thus make the traditional distinctions between a migrant and a refugee, between economic reason and political reason, or between volition and compulsion, largely irrelevant. It also makes irrelevant the notion that the migrant "opts out", while the refugee is "pushed out". On the other hand, the refugee/migrant becomes a pawn in the low key wars in South Asia, where states show what Gill Gilloescher and John Scanlan have termed a "calculated kindness" to refugees/migrants pouring in.

Violence has blurred the distinctions between phases and incidents of migration. Thus, today's realities of South Asia remain laden with bitter memories of the past. The massive migration of the late 40s, associated with large scale violence following Partition, has become the subject of collective memory an event of national memory. Its shadow overhangs ongoing population movements in the subcontinent. Though the two short conventional wars between India and Pakistan in 1948 and 1965 did not produce a refugee flow, before the outbreak of the third war (1971), the refugee flow acquired enormous dimensions. Once again violence was the chief feature of the event. Though the legitimizing framework of some liberal democratic institutions of the 'host' country may have acted as an attraction for incoming people across the border, violence continued to be associated with population movements both at the point of origin and resettlement.

If we take a brief look into twelve important flows of rejected peoples and unwanted migrants in South Asia, we shall see that violence was the chief characteristic of the process. These twelve population flows are: i) India-Pakistan refugee flows, 1947-48, involving nearly 15 million Hindus and Muslims; ii) exodus of Burmese Indians numbering about 1 million, 1948-65; iii) exodus of about a million Sri Lankan Indians and Sri Lankan Tamils from 1954 and still continuing; iv) flight of Bangladeshis to India, 1971 about 10 million; v) "stranded Pakistanis" in Bangladesh numbering nearly 300,000; vi) flight of some 200,000 Burmese Muslims to

Bangladesh in 1976; vii) flight of about 100,000 Chakmas to India in 1981; viii) nearly three million Afghans from Afghanistan to Pakistan, 1978-93, of whom an estimated two million have returned; ix) flight of 100,000 Tibetans to India, 1958-63, x) exodus of nearly 90,000 Bhutanese of Nepali origin to Nepal in 1990-91; and the two controversial and "unwanted" population flows, xi) from Bangladesh to Assam in India and xii) the two-way flow between Nepal and India. Certainly the last two cases are different and distinct, but violence remains the common marker.

Besides violence, other factors, too, blur categories of population flux. It is important to remember this phenomenon of the blurring of the categories, because part of the failure of a refugee management policy in South Asia has to do with rigid attitudes and policies of all concerned institutions the state, the UNHCR, political parties and the NGOs. Violence is certainly a catalyst, but it works only in the perspective of other given factors like land availability, agricultural seasonality, village location, communications and information network, persistence of traditional ties, economic linkages and the overall "mentality of living". The correlation of ecology, demography, ethnicity, democracy, insecurity and economic links is a crucial point in understanding the dynamics of population flux in South Asia.

Need for a regional arrangement

Any regional arrangement on protection of refugees, unwanted migrants, and internally displaced persons must first of all confront the valorisation of borders in South Asia. No doubt, it is a product of national struggle and the territorial vivisection of the subcontinent by post colonial 'national' elites, but this valorisation has now become a stumbling block to any meaningful cooperation. Border is a cartographic representation of nationalism, it effaces alternative identities and replaces them by one based on the modern sovereign nation state — that of the citizen. Thus, steps like mutual guarantee for protection of minorities, liberalization of visa regimes, border trade, introduction of work permits, bilateral and multilateral agreements, a more active role for the UN bodies and other such steps will go a long way towards protection of the refugees and unwanted migrants.

A South Asian regional arrangement is therefore an imperative. A SAARC agreement, an active UN role, a public supervisory body, a commission for minorities in South Asia, a recognition of labour rights, and a refugee watch body, should become elements of a new refugee policy for the region.

Notes

1. Robert D. Kaplan, *Atlantic Monthly* Feb. 1994; Zbignew Brzezinsky, *Out of Control Global Turmoil on the Eve of the Twenty-first Century;* Scribner New York 1993. Paul Kennedy, *Preparing for the 21st Century;* Random House.
2. UNHCR by Numbers 1997.
3. *International Encyclopedia of the Social Sciences*, vol. 10, New York, Macmillan, 1968.
4. Jacques Vernant, *The Refugee in the Post War-World*, London Allen and Unwin, 1953.

Refugee Protection in South Asia

Ravi Nair

Refugee protection has international dimensions and requires global cooperation. This was acknowledged as far back as 1921, after the First World War. However, the real movement to protect refugees got its impetus only with the Universal Declaration of Human Rights which proclaims basic rights for all human beings irrespective of their nationality or citizenship. This declaration was an important first step as refugees present a unique problem in the human rights area. Therefore, it is the international community's responsibility to protect the rights of refugees in countries of origin and countries of asylum.

Applicable laws

A myriad of specialized regional human rights instruments have sprung up from the foundation of the International Bill of Human Rights. The non-derogable rights enshrined in Article 6 of the International Covenant on Civil and Political Rights (ICCPR) are also applicable to refugees. The juridical basis of the international obligation to protect refugees, namely, *non-refoulement* including non-rejection at the frontier, non-return, non-expulsion or non-extradition can be traced to international conventions and customary laws. *Non-refoulement* is the magna carta of any refugee law.

The principle of *non-refoulement* has been applied wherever there has been fear of torture or violation of right to life of the refugee. The foremost authority on refugee law is the 1951 Convention Relating to the Status of Refugees, known simply as the Refugee Convention. It codified a very precise definition of a refugee[1], as someone who, "owing to a well-founded fear of being persecuted for reasons of race, religion, nationality, membership of a particular social group or political opinion, is outside the country of his nationality."[2]

More contemporary legal instruments have advanced beyond this limited and legalistic definition by acknowledging civil disturbances and human rights abuses as valid claims for refugee status.

None of the South Asian countries are a party to the 1951 Convention Relating to the Status of Refugees which has been ratified by 134 nations. This may reflect the unwillingness of South Asian governments to submit themselves to international scrutiny.

In South Asia, all categories of refugees face serious problems, from forcible repatriation to starvation. South Asian refugees find themselves living on the edge, clawing for mere survival. There is an urgent necessity for legislation to protect refugees and asylum seekers in South Asia to prevent political ad hocism and forcible repatriation.

India's refugee policy

For centuries, the territory known as India has provided shelter to refugees. Political upheaval in countries bordering India, often forced citizens to seek refuge across the border. Additionally, ethnic and religious persecution forced minorities to join similar peoples in India's multi-ethnic and multi-lingual society. Better opportunities to start life afresh in India also contributed to the influx of peoples from across the border.

India is not a party to the 1951 Refugee Convention. However, as the general principle prohibiting forcible repatriation or *non-refoulement,* has risen to the status of customary law, it binds even non-signatories. In India's federal Constitution, the matter of entry and regulation of aliens falls under the Union List [3] and it is the central government which is empowered to deal with refugees. Traditionally, the Union Cabinet has made reactive decisions as regards each refugee influx, often taking action only when a particular refugee influx went beyond the control of its Border Security Force and became a political issue.

India thus lacks a cohesive national policy for handling refugee inflows. The lack of a national policy limits the ability of state governments and the Border Security Force to deal with refugees, often resulting in mass rejections at the frontier or non-recognition of refugees sneaking into Indian territory.

As India has not acceded to the international protection regime for refugees, its legal obligation to protect refugees rests on customary international law. An examination of this aspect, raises the basic question of the relationship between international law and Indian municipal law.

The Constitution of India contains just a few provisions on the status of international law in India. Leading among them is Article 51 (c), which states: "the State (India) shall endeavor to foster respect for international law and treaty obligations in the dealing of organized peoples with one another."

This provision differentiates between international law and treaty obligations. It is, however, interpreted and understood that "international law" represents international customary law and "treaty obligations" represent international conventional law.[4] It directs India to foster respect for its international obligations arising under international law for its economic and social progress. Article 51 (c) is placed under the Directive Principles of State Policy in Part IV of the Indian constitution, which means it is not an enforceable provision. Since the principle laid down in Article 51 is non-enforceable and India has merely to endeavour to foster respect for international law, this Article would mean *prima facie* that international law is not incorporated into Indian municipal law which is binding and enforceable. However, when Article 51(c) is read in the light of other Articles, judicial opinion and Indian foreign policy statements, it suggests otherwise.

Before India became independent, the Indian courts administered the English Common Law. Under English Common Law doctrine, the rules of international law in general were not accepted as part of municipal law. If, however, there was no conflict between these rules and the rules of municipal law, international law was accepted in municipal law without any incorporation.

English Common Law principles are still applicable to India even after its independence, by virtue of Article 372 of the Constitution, which says, "all the laws in force in the territory of India immediately before the commencement of this Constitution shall continue in force therein until altered or repealed or amended by a competent legislature or other competent authority."[5]

This common law practice has been followed by the Indian executive, legislature and judiciary even after the independence of India. For instance, until specific legislation was adopted India observed the international customary rules regarding immunity from domestic jurisdiction and the law of the sea, particularly with regard to the high seas, maritime belt and innocent passage.

Confirming the common law principle relating to the specific incorporation of certain treaties, Article 253 provides that "Parliament has power to make any law for the whole or any part of the territory of India for implementing any treaty, agreement or convention with any other country or countries or any decision made at any international conference, association or other body."

The judicial opinion is that rules of international law and municipal law should be construed harmoniously, and only when there is an inevitable conflict between these two laws the municipal law should prevail over international law.

Against this backdrop when one examines the binding force of international refugee law on India and its relations with Indian municipal law, one can conclude that as long as international refugee law does not come in conflict with Indian legislation or policies on the protection of refugees, international refugee law is a part of the municipal law.

From this conclusion, let us examine whether international refugee law is in conflict with Indian legislation or in the absence of such legislation, with Indian attitudes and policies on refugees.

India does not have a clear policy on determining refugee status. In 1949, when the question of adoption of the Convention and the establishment of an agency for the international protection of refugees came up for discussion in the Third Committee of the UN General Assembly, the Indian delegation was of the opinion that the already existing International Organisation for Refugees should be maintained and that attention should be focused on the drafting of a Convention for the legal protection of refugees. India also made clear that it would have voted for the establishment of a High Commissioner's Office, if it had been convinced that there was need to set up an elaborate international organization whose sole responsibility would be to give refugees legal protection.[6] At a time when India was hard pressed to cope with thousands of refugees after the Partition, the government of India felt obliged to vote against all the resolutions submitted at the UN. However, it hoped that its stand would not be misinterpreted.

After the 1951 Convention was adopted India did not accede to it. The reasons for not doing so have never been clearly explicated. Much later, the then External Affairs Minister, B R Bhagat told the Indian Parliament that the government had come up against certain difficulties as regards the implications of it acceding to the Convention.[7] In other words, India was reviewing its earlier support.

On the question of admission and *non-refoulement,* India's attitude has not been particularly sympathetic. Although India accepted the principle of *non-refoulement* as including non-rejection at the frontier under the "Bangkok Principles 1966", in practice, it has not observed the principle. Ignoring the fact that refugees leave their homes suddenly due to threats to life and liberty and that by the very nature of their flight, the refugees are unable to secure the necessary travel documents from their home states, India tends to apply the same rules to them as to other foreigners who voluntarily leave their homes, enter and stay on in India.

The chief legislation for the regulation of foreigners in India is the Foreigners Act, 1946 which deals with the "entry of foreigners in India, their presence therein and their departure therefrom". Paragraph 3(1) of the Foreigners Order, 1948 lays down the power to grant or refuse permission to a foreigners to enter India, in the following terms :

> "No foreigner shall enter India
> (a) otherwise than at such port or other place of entry on the borders of India as a Registration Officer having Jurisdiction at that port or policy may appoint in this behalf either for foreigners generally or any specified class or description of foreigners, or
> (b) without leave of the civil authorities having jurisdiction at such port or place."

This provision lays down a general obligation that no foreigner should enter India without the authorization of the authority having jurisdiction over such entry points. It is mainly intended to deal with illegal entrants and infiltrators. In case of persons who do not fulfil certain conditions of entry, the sub-para 2 of the para 3 of the Order authorizes the civil authority to refuse leave to enter India. The main condition is that unless exempted, every foreigner should be in possession of a valid passport or visa to enter India.

As observed earlier, if refugees contravene any of these provisions, they too, are liable to prosecution and deportation. However, when the Indian courts were approached by Afghan, Iranian and Burmese refugees, against whom the government of India had initiated deportation proceedings under Sections 3 and 14 of the Foreigners Act, 1946 for illegal entry into India, the courts responded positively by accepting the plea that if they were returned they would face threats to their life and liberty. The courts, on several occasions, have stayed deportation proceedings.[8]

As for the minimum standard of treatment of refugees, India has undertaken an obligation by ratifying the International Convenant on Civil and Political Rights and the International Convenant on Economic, Social and Cultural Rights. It obliges India to accord equal treatment to all citizens and non-citizens, wherever possible. Moreover, India is presently a member of the Executive Committee of the UNHCR and it entails the responsibility to abide by international standards on the treatment of refugees.

As early as 1953, the Prime Minister of India, Jawaharlal Nehru informed parliament that India would abide by international standards governing asylum by adopting similar non-binding domestic policies. The right of asylum was affirmed on humanitarian grounds. Based on this policy, the Tibetans and Sri Lankan Tamils were granted asylum and refugee status. The 1971 refugees from then East Pakistan were called "evacuees" but in effect, treated as refugees requiring temporary asylum. No other community or group in India has been recognised as refugees

India claims to observe the principle of *non-refoulement* and that no refugee has been expelled whose life and liberty was under threat in the country of origin. However, human rights groups in India point to specific cases of forcible repatriation, based on the testimony of refugees.

Refugee categories

The condition of refugees in India generally depends upon the extent of protection they receive from either the Indian government or the UNHCR. Three primary categories of refugees can be identified:

i. Refugees who receive full protection as per standards set by the government of India.

ii. Refugees whose presence in Indian territory is acknowledged only by the UNHCR. They are protected under the principle of *non-refoulement*.

iii. Refugees who entered India and have been assimilated into communities. Their presence is not acknowledged by either the Indian government or the UNHCR.

Category I Refugees

Tamil refugees

The Sri Lankan Tamil refugees have come to India in successive waves. When the conflict in Sri Lanka between the Sinhala majority community and the Tamil minority took a violent turn in 1983, the Tamils fled to India in tiny boats from the northern peninsula of Sri Lanka. During the first wave, from 1983 to 1987, some 134,053 Tamil refugees crossed over to India.[9] Following the 1987 accord between the governments of Sri Lanka and the India, 25,885 Tamil refugees were repatriated between 1987 to 1989. India had to stop the repatriation program in 1989 when its shores were flooded by another refugee influx fleeing Sri Lankan violence.

During the second phase of Tamil flight in search of security, between 1989 and 1991, 122,037 Tamil refugees reportedly reached India. 113,298 of them are held in 298 camps along the coastal Indian states of Tamil Nadu and Orissa. Once again, the Indian government repatriated a large number of Tamil refugees with the cooperation of the UNHCR. About 31,000 refugees were returned to Sri Lanka between 1992-1995. As a result only half of the original 110,000 refugees are still in Tamil Nadu. However, with the breakdown of the peace talks and the resumption of hostilities between LTTE and the Sri Lankan government in 1996, fresh waves of refugees are fleeing violence.

Originally, though the refugees were made welcome in Tamil Nadu, the assassination of former Prime Minister Rajiv Gandhi in May 1991 by a suicide bomber suspected to be a member of the LTTE, turned public sentiment and government authorities against the Tamil refugees. Soon after Rajiv Gandhi's death, India began a programme of "voluntary" repatriation, under which more than 23,000 refugees were repatriated without international supervision. It is now apparent that most of those refugees were coerced to leave the refugee camps in Tamil Nadu.

The Tamil refugees who are still in camps in India, suffer from poor living conditions. The situation varies from district to district, depending on the sympathies of local officials. The camps closest to Madras are better maintained, while in Pooluvapatti camp near Coimbatore 4,700 refugees use eight latrines. Accumulated waste, cramped quarters, lack of electricity and poor sanitation all contribute to the miserable state of the camps.

Additionally, the health of the refugees has deteriorated significantly since NGOs were banned from entering the camps. Previously, NGOs had been allowed to provide primary health care and supplement the meagre monthly stipends and food rations such as rice, sugar and kerosene provided by the government of Tamil Nadu. Now, the refugees must spend what little money they have on expensive open market food because payment of the stipend rarely coincides with the arrival of subsidized rations. Also camp officials are known to use the stipend and rations as bargaining chips, that is, in return for the refugees agreeing to leave the country.[10]

The movement of the Tamil refugees in Tamil Nadu is also restricted. Members of the police and the notorious "Q" branch of the state intelligence agency are stationed at the gates of many of the camps, including the camps in Coimbatore and other places in Tamil Nadu. A government official claimed that the police are there to protect the refugees, but the Tamils believe that the guards are more concerned with controlling their movement. Camp authorities deploy indirect measures to restrain the Tamils. For example, refugees in Pooluvapatti and other Tamil Nadu camps were told by the village administration official that they could leave the camp to visit other areas if they wanted to, but their daily allowances would be cut if they did.[11] Obtaining permission to leave the camp often depends on the vagaries of the camp authorities. Travel restrictions make visits to the offices of the UNHCR or the Sri Lankan Deputy High Commissioner in Madras, virtually impossible for refugees confined to outlying camps.

In addition to the regular refugee camps, the state government has converted jails into so-called Special Camps to hold Tamils with suspected terrorist links. Since 1990, hundreds of refugees have been detained in these facilities. The South Asia Human Rights Documentation Centre (SAHRDC) and the National Human Rights Commission (NHRC) of India have compiled numerous reports of non-militant refugees, particularly young Tamil males, being arrested and detained under the Foreigners Act. Many of these individuals have been languishing in detention facilities for more than three years. In most cases they are unaware of the reasons for their detention. The government justifies these Special Camps as necessary to deal with alleged LTTE terrorists.

As regards Tamil refugees repatriated to Sri Lanka, the UNHCR claims that from 1992 to 1995, 54,059 persons have benefited from the UNHCR's special programme to provide support for the returnees in Sri Lanka. As of April 30,1996, 7,464 persons were still staying in government centres, while the rest had returned to their home areas. A total of 10,013 persons were repatriated in the first quarter of 1995. The UNHCR's claims of voluntary repatriation of refugees from India are not supported by empirical evidence. The UNHCR has allegedly connived with the government of India to hastily repatriate the Tamil refugees. Many of the repatriated refugees who have not been able to return to their native villages and live in refugee camps in Sri Lanka, are fleeing back to India. By October 1996, 2,000 more, had fled to Tamil Nadu for refuge.

As part of its protection mandate, the UNHCR is expected to share with the Tamil refugees, information about the conflict situation in the country of origin. It has failed to do so for the last five years. Instead, it had assured the refugees that "certain liberated zones" were available for the refugees to return to. However, the repatriated Tamil refugees, once back in Sri Lanka, found they could not return to their native places and languished in the UNHCR transit camps in Pesalai till 1996 when conflict broke out there. Many of them have returned to India.

At present, there are some 56,000 Sri Lankan refugees accommodated in camps in India and another 45,000 who reportedly reside outside the camps. A court order forced the Indian government to halt the repatriation programme and gave the UNHCR the right to interview the returnees. However, the UNHCR is not allowed access to the camps and cannot speak to the refugees until they have already consented to leave India. It is clear that the token presence of the UNHCR in Madras only provides respectability to what is essentially a programme of involuntary repatriation.

Following reports of forced repatriation and deplorable conditions in the Tamil refugee camps in Tamil Nadu, a SAHRDC researcher visited the camps in July 1996 and documented systematic violations of Tamil refugee rights. The findings of SAHRDC are that the Indian government appears determined to allow conditions in the camps to deteriorate to the point where refugees would rather return to a situation of violence in Sri Lanka rather than stay on in the camps.

As the Indian government has not acceded to the 1951 Refugee Convention which establishes a basic protection regime for refugees, treatment of the Tamil refugees is subject to the whims of the political party in power. The state government of Tamil Nadu, though originally sympathetic to the plight of the refugees, has failed to maintain the refugee camps in accordance with well-recognized international standards. If the Indian government is serious about maintaining acceptable standards in the camps, it should allow NGOs to resume their former role. Moreover, the UNHCR which is accustomed to treading lightly in India as it is not an officially recognized UN agency, should arm itself with the international conventions to which it owes its creation and take a more pro-active role in the protection of the Sri Lankan Tamil refugees.

Jumma refugees

The Jumma peoples from the Chittagong Hill Tracts of Bangladesh are another example of Category I refugees. The Buddhist Jumma peoples have been fleeing religious harassment in the Muslim majority Bangladesh. In a country with scarce arable land, the Bangladesh government has been trying to re-settle plains people in the tribal lands of the Chittagong Hill Tracts (CHT).

Since 1978, the Indian government has provided temporary shelter for the Jumma peoples in the neighbouring Indian states of Mizoram and Tripura. Following a series of massacres by Bangladesh security forces in 1986, nearly 70,000 Jumma refugees sought shelter in six camps established by the Indian government in Tripura. Their presence in India has been a source of embarrassment for the Bangladesh government.

As relations with Bangladesh improved from 1992, the

Indian government has been pressurising the Jumma refugees to return to CHT . In other words, shifting the status of these refugees from Category I to Category II. Geo-political and economic considerations have made for a shift in the Indian government's attitude towards the refugees. The government is encouraging "voluntary" repatriation of the Jumma refugees by making living conditions in the Tripura camps untenable.[12] Food rations to the Jumma refugees sheltered in camps in Tripura have been erratic since mid-1992. In an effort to keep up the pressure on the refugees, the supply of rice and salt was discontinued for a while from November 21, 1995. Food provisions are given in 10-day cycles but the quantity given normally suffices for only eight days. Often, even these meagre rations are delayed.[13] A delay of two days means that indigent tribal refugee families must go hungry.

The state government of Tripura also denies education facilities to Jumma refugees. A SAHRDC study on camp conditions in 1993 and 1994 revealed that the Jumma refugees have been systematically denied access to education. This is part of India's policy to pressurise the refugees who want their children to be educated, to return to the CHT.

Following bilateral discussions between India and Bangladesh in 1994 about 5,000 Jumma refugees returned "under duress" to the CHT.[14] Although the government of Bangladesh promised to return them to their lands, many of those repatriated are still dislocated. After the return of the first refugee group, the Jumma Refugee Welfare Association, visited the CHT in March 1994 and found that 103 families had not been able to reclaim the land they had left.[15]

SAHRDC filed a complaint with the NHRC about the involuntary repatriation of the Jumma refugees in 1994. Two years after the complaint was filed, an investigation team sent by NHRC to the Jumma refugee camps in May 1996 reported shortage of water, inadequacy of accommodation and woefully inadequate medical facilities. The report also pointed out that the scale of rations was meagre and its supply often suspended. The team also found that many of the tubewells were out of order. The camps were unclean and bore signs of neglect. The report noted that refugee children were suffering from malnutrition, water-borne diseases and malaria.[16] It "attributed the problems faced by the refugees, to the callousness and hostility of the officials towards the refugees, accumulated over the years, as they are not keen to go back".

Despite the complaint about involuntary repatriation of the Jumma refugees in 1994 pending before the NHRC, the government of India has decided to repatriate another 6,172 Jumma refugees without consulting the NHRC. Again SAHRDC drew the attention of NHRC on 7 March, 1997 about the undue duress being brought to bear upon the refugees to return. But the NHRC has failed to take any positive action to ensure voluntary repatriation exposing its ineffectiveness on human rights issues which have a geo-political dimension.

Category II Refugees

In addition to the refugees under the care of the government of India, there are about 20,800 Category II refugees under the care of the UNHCR. They include Afghan, Iranian, Somali, Sudanese and Burmese refugees. As of January 1, 1996, there are 19,900 Afghan refugees, 200 Iranian refugees, 300 Somali refugees, 300 Burmese refugees and 100 Sudanese refugees.[17] Their presence in India is acknowledged and protected under the principle of *non-refoulement* by the UNHCR. However, the condition of these refugees who receive protection and a subsistence allowance from the UNHCR is no better than that of Category I refugees who receive protection from the government of India.

There have been complaints that the UNHCR in Delhi has been arbitrary in its cancellation of refugee status and allowances. SAHRDC has conducted a study of the conditions of the refugees protected by the UNHCR in Delhi. In its May 1995 report, "The Status of Refugees under the Protection of the UNHCR in New Delhi",[18] SAHRDC investigated the services offered to refugees by the UNHCR in New Delhi including emergency aid, health care facilities, subsistence allowance, lumpsum payment in lieu of the refugee subsistence allowance, accommodation, employment, vocational training, education, legal aid, travel documents and resettlement. In particular, on the issue of the UNHCR's accessibility to refugee needs, SAHRDC found that its New Delhi office has become a fortress. The refugees view the UNHCR officials with suspicion and do not believe that they care about their plight. UNHCR officials, explain that the global policies of its organization have led to a virtual freeze on the refugee subsistence allowance in India. This has exacerbated resentment and tension in the refugee community.

In a callous attempt at reducing its refugee "case load", UNHCR, has arbitrarily terminated the subsistence allowance of over 2,000 refugees. Destitution has allegedly led to two suicides in the refugee community. SAHRDC has documented specific cases of human rights abuses perpetrated on asylum seekers, ranging from arbitrariness in determination of refugee status, suspension of subsistence allowance to beatings by UNHCR security guards.

Though the UNHCR is only as effective as the government permits it to be these actions indicate a general disregard for the plight of the refugees.

Category III Refugees

The Indian government does not formally recognise the presence of this category of refugees. It includes from Myanmar, ethnic Chin refugees from Chin State, Nagas and Rakhain refugees from Arakan State, and ethnic Nepalis of Bhutanese nationality. The largest among these refugees groups is the Chins, numbering about 40,000. While the Burmese Nagas have sought refuge in the state of Nagaland, the Chins and Rakhains have sought refuge in Mizoram.

Neither the government of India nor the UNHCR recognizes the presence of these refugees. Despite their large numbers, the Chins do not receive any state assistance or international assistance because of their ambiguous status. A large number of Chin refugees have been forcibly returned to Myanmar by the Mizoram state government since 1994.[19]

In situations where government of India denies access to the UNHCR and other foreign humanitarian agencies, domestic NGOs can play a most crucial role in providing "protection" to refugees. The Oslo Declaration on Partnership-in-Action (PARinAC) between the NGOs and the UNHCR provides the basis for cooperation between UNHCR and NGOs. But, UNHCR's present implementing partners (NGOs) neither have a track record of working with the refugees nor anything to do with "protection" of refugees.

Role of UNHCR

The UNHCR report to the 47th session of its Executive Committee is oblivious to the plight of the refugees looked after by the government of India. Refugees face numerous difficulties in India from denial of food to restrictions on the freedom of movement. The UNHCR objective in India is to create "public awareness of refugee situations and issues in India and promote a legal framework for the protection of refugees".[20] The creation of awareness and promotion of a legal framework as envisaged by the UNHCR is important to create an institutional framework to protect the refugee rights. However, it should not be an excuse for the UNHCR to shirk its responsibilities to provide "protection" to the refugees. Denial of access to the UNHCR by the government of India can not be used as an excuse, especially when the government of India allows the UNHCR to work with various NGOs in India.

The fundamental issue is that in a situation where the government of India repatriates refugees under duress and the UNHCR makes living conditions untenable for the urban refugees it looks after in the name of "rationalization of the care and maintenance", a legal framework will have little meaning.

While it is possible to bring the government of India under the scrutiny of the quasi-judicial bodies like the NHRC and the judiciary, there is no such mechanism to scrutinise the functioning of the UNHCR in New Delhi. "Official rules and procedures" have become an excuse to raise the "veil of secrecy". It has come to the point where the UNHCR's New Delhi office requires security protection fearing attacks from the refugees rather than UNHCR providing protection to the refugees.

In India, the lack of a legal framework is a basic flaw in providing protection for refugees. But the courts in India have awarded excellent judgements which uphold international principles on refugee protection including *non-refoulement.* However, the cardinal problem arises when both the UNHCR and the government of India violate their own standards and principles. The ratification of 1951 Convention Relating to the Status of Refugees is a statement of intent unless it is enforceable in domestic courts.

Nepal

In eastern Nepal, Bhutanese refugees are entering their seventh year of exile with no solution in sight. The Nepali and Bhutanese governments have attempted to resolve the matter through diplomatic negotiations, but after four years, the talks have reached a stalemate. Meanwhile, aid agencies which have been maintaining the camps are facing budgetary cuts imposed by UNHCR.[21]

The eight camps operated by the UNHCR and the Nepali government currently house 86,000 ethnic Nepalis who left Bhutan after the Bhutanese government initiated a campaign in 1990 to suppress Nepali cultural expression, revocation of citizenship, intimidation, arrest and even torture.

SAHRDC has been concerned about recent reports that international agencies, currently providing assistance to the Bhutanese refugees, plan to scale back relief programmes and even to withdraw entirely from the camps. There are indications that the international community is beginning to favour the option of refugee integration, that is, if the refugees can not return to Bhutan, a decrease in assistance will force them to integrate into neighbouring communities in Nepal and India.

Aid agencies fear that donor countries may soon tire of funding refugee relief, though there is as yet no clear evidence that they are actually planning to withdraw. Several agencies have made slight reductions in their budgets and the number of personnel, but only one, Oxfam, has announced that it will be ending its operations entirely. Some organisations, while continuing to give funds, seem to be gradually transferring the operation of their programmes to other authorities. In the case of the World Food Program, most of the responsibility for project administration has been given over to the refugee camp committees. UNHCR has progressively transferred supervision of its programmes to the Nepali government.

Like the Bhutanese government, the Nepali government has been unwilling to take effective international action aimed at resolving the plight of the refugees. Nepal, however, has stated that it will not accept local integration of the refugees. But as political will to find a solution wanes and humanitarian organizations cut their services, the conditions in the camps will become so poor that the refugees will be forced out.

There have been reports that newcomers applying for refugee status at the Nepali government screening center have had their identity documents confiscated. These documents are vital for refugees to prove their identity, if they are to return to Bhutan or for resettlement in a third country. It suggests that there may be a growing trade in illegally-obtained Bhutanese documents to establish asylum claims in various countries in Europe.

Tibetan refugees

In 1995, Nepal forcibly repatriated more than 300 Tibetan refugees fleeing Chinese persecution. The action has been condemned by governments and human rights organizations around the world. Nepal has denied it. The refugees were handed over to Chinese authorities across the border at Dram, known in Chinese as Zhangmu. Among the refugees were three former political prisoners who faced particularly harsh reprisal from the Chinese authorities.

The forced repatriations continued throughout the first half of 1995, despite strong protest from the USA, Australia and the UNHCR. However, Nepal's then Deputy Prime Minister, Madhav Kumar Nepal, insisted that there had been no change in the policy concerning refugees. But confronted with facts and figures, the then Home Secretary Rewati Raman Khanal admitted that some Tibetans had been handed back to China because they had asked to be repatriated.

Forced deportation is however only a part of the tragic story of Tibetans trying to escape Chinese persecution. Over the last several years, there have been persistent reports of Tibetans being fired upon by border guards and being beaten up by the Nepali police. As a result, many fleeing Tibetan refugees have been killed or injured. Escaping Tibetan refugees invariably report that soon after capture by the Nepali police, they are robbed of all their belongings. But the Nepali government persistently maintains that such abuses do not take place and that there is no policy of forced repatriation of Tibetan refugees escaping from Tibet.

Conclusion

Finally, I would only like to quote Professor James C Hathaway. "UNHCR's recent efforts to prove its relevance to governments have, regrettably, lent credibility to the politics of *non-entrée* and to the containment of refugees, UNHCR should instead focus on the development of dependable mechanisms to share-out equitably responsibility for the protection of refugees among states. By proposing the standards and mechanisms to implement common but differentiated responsibility toward refugees, UNHCR could prove that international law is still an effective framework within which to manage involuntary migration."[22]

Notes

1. Originally a backward-looking instrument, this Convention was adopted in order to address the unresolved refugee crisis that emerged from the Second World War. As such, it applied only to persons who became refugees as a result of events occurring prior to the Refugee Convention's adoption. This temporal limitation was removed by the Protocol Relating to the Status of Refugees of January 31, 1967, whose Preamble recognized that "new refugee situations have arisen since the convention was adapted." The pre-Convention definition did not take into account the reasons for the refugee's departure from his/her home nation.
2. *Human Rights : A Compilation of International Instruments,* United Nations, New York, 1988.
3. Under the Constitution of India, powers and functions are divided into Union List (federal government) and State List (provincial government or state government).
4. C.H. Alexanderowcz, "International Law in India", *International and Comparative Law Quarterly*, Vol. I (1952), p. 291.
5. The expression in this Article includes not only enactments of Indian legislature but also common law of the land as administered by courts in India before its independence. Gurdeep Singh, "Status of human rights convenants in India", *Indian Journal of International Law*, vol. 28 (1988), p.218.
6. Summary Records of the Third Committee meeting 259 (10 November 1949), GAOR, Sixth Session, p. 8143; and Mrs Kripalani, ibid., mtg 263 (15 November 1949), p.8144.
7. India, Lok Sabha Debates, vol. XVII, 7 May 1986, col. 32.
8. Writ Petitions Nos. 450/83; 605-607/84; 169/87; 732/87; 747/87; 243/88; 336/88/ and 274/88; SLP (Cr) Nos. 3261/1987; 274/1988 and 338/1988.
9. "Sri Lankan Tamil Refugees in Tamil Nadu Camps - Voluntary Repatriation or Subtle Refoulment", South

Asia Human Rights Documentation Centre, New Delhi, January 1996.

10. Ibid.
11. Ibid
12. "No Secure Refuge", South Asia Human Rights Documentation Centre, New Delhi, 14 February 1994.
13. *The Hindustan Times*, New Delhi, 28 November 1995.
14. "Returnee Refugees : Frustrated at not getting promised help" - A report of Bangladesh Manab Adhikar Sammanay Parishad, National Committee for the Protection of Fundamental Rights in CHTs, Jatiyo Mahila Ainjibi Samiti, Ain-O-Salish Kendra and Human Rights Journalist Forum, Dhaka, Bangladesh, 27 May 1994.
15. "Report on the visit of Jumma refugee team to the Chittagong Hill Tracts, Bangladesh on 14 & 15 March 1995", Takumbari, Tripura, India, 4 April 1995. See also Memorandum of Returnee Jumma Refugees 16 Points Implementation Committee, Khagrachari, Bangladesh, 15 October 1996. The Returnee Jumma Refugees 16 Points Implementation Committee states that out of the 1,027 families consisting of 5,186 individual refugees, 25 returnee Jummas refugees who had earlier been employed in various government jobs were not reinstated in their previous jobs, 134 returnee Jumma refugee families could not settle in their own lands due to the misappropriation of their lands by the security forces and Bengali illegal settlers and 79 families were not given back their lands as it was under forcible occupation of the illegal settlers from the plains. The Bangladesh government also registered false cases against 23 returnee refugees.
16. *Human Rights Newsletter,* National Human Rights Commission, New Delhi, July 1996.
17. Draft Report of the 47th Session of the Executive Committee of UNHCR Geneva, Dec. 7-11, 1996.
18. "The Status of Refugees under the Protection of UNHCR in New Delhi" SAHRDC/0131/1/95 of 1 May 1995, New Delhi.

19. This was stated by the Chief Secretary of Mizoram State Government in a hearing on the harassment of the Chakmas at the National Human Rights Commission on 8 November 1996.
20. Draft Report of the 47th Session of the Executive Committee of the UNHCR, Geneva 7-11 October 1996.
21. UNHCR's office in Nepal, however denied that there was any decision to reduce budgetary support for the camps in Jhapa in Nepal. However in absolute terms there could be a reduction in budgetary outlay compared to earlier years as investments had already been made to build up the infrastructure of the camps, leaving essentially maintenance and running costs.
22. James C. Hathaway, Can International Refugee Law be Made Relevant Again? *World Refugee Survey 1996*, US Committee for Refugees, Washington D.C. 1996 p. 19.

SECTION TWO

Bangladesh, A Land of Shifting Populations

Meghna Guhathakurta

History and geopolitics have combined to make Bangladesh a land of shifting frontiers and fluid population movements.[1] Together with West Bengal, Bangladesh sits on one of the largest deltas in the world, large parts of which even until the last century remained uninhabitable.[2] As the rivers shifted eastwards, dense forests gave way to agricultural land. Political and ideological configurations also changed with the growing rise of transforming religions, Buddhism, Islam and the Bhakti cults of the medieval period were all grafted onto an older civilization. But as modernity emerged in the crucible of colonialism and heralded the advent of the nation-state, this fluidity came to a standstill.

Violence was by no means a new phenomena in the history of the subcontinent, but the violence which accompanied the Partition of the subcontinent derived its legitimacy from the *raison d'etat* of the two new nations, India and Pakistan. The consequence of this violence was one of the largest population movements of South Asia in recent times. Two regions, Punjab and Bengal, were dissected into two and families who until then had shared a common language and a common culture with their neighbours became virtual strangers. Hindus and Sikhs migrated from West Pakistan and Bengali Hindus from East Pakistan to India while Muslims from all over India flocked to Pakistan. Technically speaking a 'refugee' situation was not allowed to develop since both states took emergency measures to accommodate new arrivals.[3] But the trauma of this experience, the sense of feeling uprooted, lasted well into the next generation.

Unlike West Pakistan, where the transfer of population was almost total, the exodus from East Bengal was comparatively not great at the time of Partition. It was the subsequent communal riots of the 50s and 60s that caused the Hindu population to flee their homes in then East Pakistan. The political economy of this exodus and the parallel influx from West Bengal needs to be studied in a systematic manner. However, focusing on the major population movements taking place to and from Bangladesh from the time of its independence in 1971, it is possible to categorize them as the following: i) movements as a result of deliberate politics of the nation-state, ii) movements due to economic and environmental pressures, iii) movements into Bangladesh and iv) internally displaced persons. Each head can be further divided:

i. Politics of the nation-state
 a. Bangladeshi refugees in 1971
 b. Biharis in Bangladesh
 c. Migration of Bangladeshi minority groups to India
 d. Refugees of the Chittagong Hill Tracts

ii. Economic and environmental pressure
 a. Bangladeshis abroad
 b. Trafficking in women and children

iii. Influx into Bangladesh
  a. Rohingyas
  b. others

iv. Internally displaced people
  a. Displacement due to environmental reasons
  b. Displacement due to demographic/economic reasons
  c. Displacement due to political reasons
  d. Displacement due to social reasons

i. Politics of the nation-state

a. Bangladeshi Refugees in 1971

It is said that "violence and subsequent forced movement of people constituted the Partition of India."[4] Similarly the forced movement of 10 million people across the border into India during 1971 and the countless millions of internally displaced people as a result of the ruthless and savage acts of genocide against unarmed civilians of East Bengal by the Pakistan authorities, constituted the making of an independent Bangladesh.[5] However unlike 1947 which saw the birth of two states based on majoritarian religions, the 1971 Bangladesh ideology was built on a linguistically based nationalism. The persecutory practices of the Pakistan state was therefore aimed against the forces of Bengali nationalism. In the Pakistani official discourse this meant the Awami League and Hindus, both of them, were regarded as Indian agents. As a consequence of this attempt by the Pakistani authorities to communalise the crisis, the percentage of Hindu refugees increased manifold than the Muslim refugees. In August 1971, for example, the communal composition of the refugees figured 671,000 Hindus and 541,000 Muslims.[6]

In 1971, the millions of people who fled across to India and some to Burma, were given refugee status and the international community and organizations as well as the Indian government undertook massive measures to 'look after' them as far as practicable. The refugees gave India the opportunity to draw international attention to the crisis, legitimized Indian involvement and enabled the camouflaging of political motives in humanitarian concern. After the independence of Bangladesh, most of these refugees were able to return to their home within a few short months, though their precise numbers are not available.

b. Biharis in Bangladesh

But the creation of a new independent state of Bangladesh created refugee-like situations for other communities. The story is that when Bangladesh achieved its independence in 1971, there were 1,000,000 non-Bengalis stranded in Bangladesh. Since most were Muslims originally from the Indian state of Bihar, they were called Biharis. Partition gave Bihar to India with its 4 million Muslims. Mass killing of the Muslim population prior to Partition precipitated the movement of Muslim Biharis into Pakistan. Of the 1.3 million Bihari Muslims who moved to Pakistan, about 700,000 chose to settle in East Pakistan.

But the Biharis remained a distinct community in Bangladesh. Their role in support of the Pakistani army during the Liberation War of 1971 precipitated retaliation against them, both during and after the war. Around a thousand Biharis were reported to have been killed during this time. Many Biharis left for West Pakistan during 1971 but among those who were left behind, a large proportion stood by their allegiance to Pakistan and demanded repatriation to Pakistan. About half of them chose Bangladesh as their homeland. Those seeking repatriation enlisted their names in a list prepared by the International Committee of the Red Cross (ICRC) during 1972-1973. In the first phase of repatriation about 170,000 non-Bengalis returned to Pakistan. This left about 250,000 to 300,000 in camps in Bangladesh.[7] The ICRC, after a few months of facilitating repatriation stopped, for reasons of financial constraints. Since then Pakistan has been evasive about taking back the Biharis.[8] Successive governments in Bangladesh have given them neither refugee status nor the right to citizenship.

As regime after successor regime came and went both in Bangladesh and Pakistan, the dispute failed to get resolved. At one point in 1980, the Pakistan Foreign Secretary stated, "Since we have no dispute there is no question of an agreement being reached."[9] The issue has become more controversial in the wake of the polarised atmosphere in Sindh. A prominent member of the National Assembly of Pakistan from Sindh, Maqdoom Khaliquzzaman, had reportedly announced his withdrawal from the Committee for Repatriation of Biharis, maintaining that the stranded Pakistanis did not belong to any of the four provinces of the country and as such the question of their repatriation to this part of the world did not arise.[10] Domestic politics has complicated the repatriation of the Biharis, as evident from the former Pakistani Prime Minister Benazir Bhutto's suggestion that the Muslim *ummah* should be the solution for these people.[11] Subsequently, a breakthrough seemed possible when Bangladeshi Prime Minister Khaleda Zia on a visit to Pakistan in December 1992, indicated that Pakistan had agreed to repatriate 3,000 families to Pakistan by December 1992. It failed to materialise when Sindhis in Pakistan demonstrated against any further repatriation of Bihari refugees.

c. Migration of Bangladeshi minority groups to India

The newly independent state of Bangladesh thought it could put an end to the legacy of communal strife of the pre-partition and Pakistan days by emphasizing the Bengali identity of all citizens, hence giving language predominance over religion and by incorporating secularism into the constitution. The first only managed to alienate non-Bengali speaking minorities such as the Biharis and the minorities of the Hill Tracts. As for the second, the principle of secularism in the beginning turned out to be ambiguous in state practice and after the change of regime in 1975, it was scrapped altogether from the constitution. In 1977, it was replaced by the phrase "absolute trust in Allah". Islam was made the state religion by the Eighth Amendment of 1988, thus giving legitimacy to religious majoritarianism. More than anyone else this hurt the religious minorities.

What most affected the everyday lives of the minorities and contributed to their departure, was not simply a matter of abstract state principles but specific discriminatory laws which had been enacted in Pakistan and continued under successive regimes in Bangladesh. The first of these laws, popularly known as the Enemy Property Act was enacted in 1965, during the 17-day India-Pakistan war to prevent the use of enemy properties against the war effort of Pakistan. The second was purportedly enacted to take care of the properties of those who left the newly independent Bangladesh for Pakistan.[12] Given Pakistan's traditional hostility towards India and with India being seen as a Hindu majority state, these laws affected the Hindu minority more than anyone else. In a study on these laws it was said that, "If there was no out-migration of Hindus from East Pakistan and Bangladesh during 1961-1991, there would have been

16.5 million Hindus in Bangladesh, instead of the official figure of 11.2 million recorded in the Bangladesh census of 1991. According to our calculation, from 1964 to 1991 a total of 5.3 million Hindus, that is, on average 200,000 per year, have gone 'missing'."[13] According to the census report the Hindu population has declined from 28.3 percent in 1941 to 12.6 percent in 1991.[14]

These laws were intended to be temporary, but came to be much abused. They were virtually used as strong arm tactics on vulnerable sections of the minority population to force them to sell off their land at dirt cheap prices or to stop them from acquiring new land. The procedure entailed declaring minority-owned lands or property as "enemy's" or abandoned or vested. More often this was done through fraudulent practices. It has been estimated that a million acres of land held by the minority community, out of total arable land of 21 million acres in the country, has been subjected to transfer from minority owners to the dominant sections of the society. About a third of all minority households have been adversely affected by these laws.[15]

Apart from these chronic problems, communal clouds have been brewing over South Asia ever since a surge in the fundamentalist parties or forces from the early nineties. Bangladesh has not been free from such influences. The attack by the Bharatiya Janata Party on the Babri Masjid had repercussions on all minorities in Bangladesh, not only the Hindus. It is a blow from which they are still reeling. Most minorities complain of discrimination in the workplace, especially in government jobs and business. In times of a communal flare up, security of life and property is threatened as during the post-Babri Masjid incidents. The minorities blame the administration for not giving them adequate protection.[16] All this makes them feel like second-class citizens. It is little wonder therefore that given the opportunity they want to migrate to India.

d. Refugees of the Chittagong Hill Tracts

The Chittagong Hill Tracts cover 10 percent of the total area of Bangladesh and lie to the south-east of the country bordering the Indian states of Tripura and Mizoram and the Arakan state of Myanmar. It is home to 13 different ethnic peoples of which the Chakmas, the Marmas and Tripuras make up 90 percent of the population. They are Buddhists, Hindus, Christians and animists, in a predominantly Muslim country. .

Most of the Chittagong people migrated to the south between the 16th and 19th centuries . When in the 17th century, Bengali settlers started inhabiting the coastal areas, the original settlers were driven to the hills. The British gave the CHT people the right of self-rule in internal matters.[16] The CHT Regulation of 1900 specifically excluded non-tribals from settling in tribal areas [17].

The Partition of the subcontinent in 1947 along religious lines, found the CHT with its majority population of non-Muslims, falling to the Pakistani side. The people of CHT at first defied this decision. They left the Indian flag hoisted in Rangamati, the district headquarters, until the Pakistani army came and brought it down. From then started the first outflow of refugees towards the bordering Indian states of Tripura and Mizoram. Many of the first batch of refugees left their homes with the intention of settling down in India, as did many Hindus from the plains. But whereas the Bengalis were allowed to intermingle with the Indian population, the Chakma ethnic refugees in Tripura were cordoned off from the rest of the populace and resettled in then North East Frontier Province (NEFA) or present day Arunachal Pradesh, on the tense Sino-Indian border. The purpose was to provide a buffer in the area against possible Chinese infiltration. It may be mentioned that until this day many of these people are still living in isolation from the general populace and have not been given Indian citizenship. [18] They live in clustered settlements under the supervision of district councils.

After the independence of Bangladesh, the flow of refugees to India increased, instigated by direct state violence. The Mujibur Rahman regime denied the autonomous status of the Hill Tracts, but it was General Zia ur Rahman's regime which aggravated the issue by re-settling Bengali landless peasants, from the coastal areas, on land occupied by the CHT hill tribes.[19] The CHT was looked upon by the government as empty land on which to resettle landless peasants and thereby relieve pressure on land and defuse political tensions. The people of the Hill Tracts resented this policy and as a consequence violence erupted. The Jana Samhati Samiti (JSS) with its military wing, the Shanti Bahini, was formed by the people of the Hill Tracts to resist the government forces and give shape to the movement for autonomy. The government instead of trying to solve the problem politically, chose military intervention. From then on the history or CHT has been a series of killings, violation of human rights and displacement of people from their homes and land. Counter insurgency operations in CHT have produced fresh waves of refugees into India, most notably in 1979, 1981 and 1986.[20] Not only have people fled to India, but military repression has forced them to retreat further into the hills. From the perspective of the indigenous people of the Hill Tracts, it is the settlers from the plains who are the refugees or *shoronarthis*.

The subsequent government of President H. M. Ershad, made the matter worse by initiating a plan of clustered settlements in which plains people were brought to live in CHT, and protected by an arc of military camps. Later such villages were also built for refugees returning from India. The inhabitants of these villages are virtually cut off from the rest of the population and do not have the freedom to move about freely. A dusk to dawn curfew is clamped on the whole area. Conditions within these villages are miserable since people cannot move about freely and earn their livelihood. They cannot cultivate their land or harvest the crops and the government rations, too, are meagre. The government does not allow monitoring by UNHCR and the operations of NGOs in the area are, banned. Although amnesty has been offered to Shanti Bahini on different occasions, it is only Shanti Bahini leaders who surrender who are given the benefit of some kind of rehabilitation programme. The rest are left to fend for themselves.

Talks were indicated between the Ershad government and the JSS to settle the issue but instead of responding to the demands of the JSS, President Ershad set up three district councils to administer what was once known as Parbotya Chattgram or the CHT. The dialogue between the JSS and the successor government of Khaleda Zia also failed. The JSS demanded the withdrawal of all Bangladesh military forces, disbanding of the district councils, dismantling of the clustered villages, prohibition of further settlement by people from the plains, retention of the CHT Regulation of 1900, economic development aimed at the ethnic peoples, release of JSS prisoners and the involvement of UNHCR or ICRC in the implementation of any agreement. But the responses from the Bengali side has been largely negative.[21]

Furthermore, there has been criticism from the *paharis,*

or hill peoples, about the nature of the peace process itself. The Hill people have claimed that the cease-fire and talks have been used for buying time and the sincerity of the government in resolving the conflict has been found wanting. They claim that the period of cease fire has actually been used to drive away a lot of paharis from populated areas and establish army camps in their place. The location of the talks too has been questioned. During the Ershad period the location of the talks was shifted in the middle of the process and this had a negative effect.

During the June 1996 elections, the Awami League, which eventually came to power, had made specific promises to solve the problem, politically. A cease-fire was negotiated and a national committee formed to look into the issue of the JSS. The withdrawal of the military presence remains a key issue for the near future, though some attempts at exploring the possibility of strengthening civilian administration has already been made.

One thing is certain. If the Parbottyo Chattogram issue is to be resolved, it needs to be brought into the mainstream political discourse. Some think that the talks need to be shifted to the capital Dhaka, where there will be a chance of getting more media attention and hence transparency. But in order to enhance the peace process a much more long-term strategy needs to be evolved by the Bengalis which involves a rethinking of the nationalist discourse which has alienated, even to the point of elimination, the minorities. They have been deprived of their homes, their livelihoods, their land and their heritage in the name of this majoritarian nationalist discourse.

Economic and environmental pressure

a. Bangladeshis abroad

Politics and economics can not really be separated. Through the ages, economic and environmental pressures have played an important and often primary role in causing population movements. Current day Bangladesh is a witness to such a phenomena. Poverty, population pressure on the land, unemployment and inadequate planning have generated a "push factor" which is driving Bangladeshis to more affluent lands. In recent times environmental factors have also been responsible for the movement of population. In particular, the western areas of Bangladesh are drying up partly because of the diminished flow of the Ganges due to the construction of the Farraka Barrage[22] and partly for reasons such as indiscriminate sinking of tubewells which deplete the water table and make for the eastward movement of rivers. This has resulted in a westward movement of people, usually landless labourers, to the Indian state of West Bengal. These labourers are Muslims as well as Hindus. Thus the main push factor in this case is economic and not religious or political persecution. In fact, it is also probable that the higher agricultural wage structure of West Bengal constitutes a "pull factor", for migration.

The government has generally tended to encourage migration as it has proved to be an important source of foreign exchange in the form of remittances sent back to the families. It also relieves pressure on the government to provide its citizens with land and employment. But it is not a path that is strewn with roses, especially, for those who migrate illegally.

According to the latest figures, more than a million Bangladeshis are currently living and working in the Middle

East and the Far East.[23] The total number of Bangladeshi migrants in the world is around three million. For many of these people temporary migration has proved to be profitable especially to those with professional skills. But for the large majority who are engaged in menial tasks, the hardships are many, including arrest, prolonged detention and deportation. In August 1996, Malaysian jails were reported to be holding 25,000 Bangladeshis. An earlier announcement by the Malaysian government in October 1995 had indicated that 38,000 illegal Bangladeshis were to be deported. In 1995, Saudi Arabia announced the planned deportation of 40,000 Bangladeshis. Thousands of Bangladeshis arrived in Chittagong port in November 1995. UAE is in the process of deporting 15,000 illegal Bangladeshis and Thailand claims to have more than 30,000. Within South Asia, the Indian government claims that there are eight million Bangladeshis living illegally in India. Pakistan maintains that 1.5 million Bangladeshis are in Pakistan, most of them in the port city of Karachi.

But despite the measures adopted by the government to facilitate economic migration, like setting up the Bureau of Manpower Employment and Training, it has proved totally powerless in the face of push back strategies of foreign governments. Initially the push back came from countries with contiguous territories like India and Pakistan, but more recently, it is West Asian countries like Saudi Arabia and UAE. Deportation apart, much worse is the inhuman treatment meted out to illegal immigrants. They languish in jails in miserable conditions, especially in Malaysia and Pakistan.

In an overview of "Refugees and Migratory Movements in Bangladesh", the writer S. Malik[24] observed that the current legal system does not take into account the requirements of this vast number of people working abroad nor are government agencies in a position to take effective measures to provide support to such people abroad. Consequently, the current legal and administrative system dealing with migration needs to be re-evaluated and overhauled. Possibilities of NGO intervention in this area also need to be considered.

b. Trafficking in women and children

Trafficking of women and children is one of the obvious indicators of growing poverty. It takes place in two ways: one, selling women for prostitution both within and outside the country and two, the trafficking of men, women and children for work outside the country. Here women and children form the most vulnerable group. In most cases, where such women or children get stranded in foreign lands, often ending up in prison, they are deprived of the minimal succour which a refugee is entitled to by international conventions, as neither home nor host country acknowledge their existence. Recent cases show that there is an ever increasing number of Bangladeshi women to be found in prisons or engaged in illegal activities in India, Pakistan and Malaysia.

It has been estimated, in a joint report of SAARC and UNICEF, that annually about 4,000 women are being trafficked into Pakistan.[25] The "flesh trade" is deeply embedded in the socio-political system of both countries and allegedly involves the law enforcement agencies especially in the border areas. Only a handful of these women have been caught. According to an article on the Bangladesh-Pakistan 'trade route' in the Karachi based weekly *The Herald*[26], the number of women caught at the time of smuggling numbered 75 in 1988, 941 in 1989 and until May in 1990, 308. Only about 35 *dalals* (agents) were apprehended at the time of smuggling. In a more recent report[27] the total number of men, women and children who were rescued from the hands of the racketeers from September 1995 to June 1996 numbered 124. About 65 *dalals* were arrested.

The number of women migrating legally in search of jobs from Bangladesh was estimated to be about 8,837 from August 1991 to August 1996[28]. But this figure included multiple exits by the same women. The largest number of women went to Malaysia and then came the West Asian countries. However, an official was quoted as saying that the actual number of women migrating could be at least 20 times the official figure.[29] The overwhelming majority of Bangladeshi women, nearly 90 percent, in West Asian countries work as domestic maids. In other countries, they work in the industrial sector, in electronics, plastics, garments and fish processing. South Korea officially categorizes migrants as "trainees".

It is therefore clear that although a certain section of women are being forced into the flesh trade, a sizeable number of Bangladeshi women want to go abroad and work honestly, for a living. That is their right under the constitution of Bangladesh. But the negative aspects of migration inherent in the flesh trade and the victimization of women workers in foreign countries has led the government to put a tight squeeze on immigration formalities, thereby often affecting this right. In addition, to the various application forms all migrants are required to submit, women must obtain a no objection affidavit from their guardian, a husband or a father. These, though are easy to doctor and sometimes women are allowed to go abroad without an affidavit. Those women planning to work as domestic maids must in addition seek permission from the Ministry of Labour and Manpower. There is a tendency in the government's migration policy (as in all policies relating to gender issues) to opt for patriarchal control as a remedial measure rather than rectify the ills of the system.

Influx into Bangladesh

a. Rohingyas

The Rohingyas are ethnic Arakanese from Myanmar and 40 percent are Muslims.[30] They inhabit the Arakan province, a long stretch of land along the coastline in the Bay of Bengal. The northern tip of the region adjoins Bangladesh and there is a 281 km long common border between the two countries. Both the Chittagong region of south eastern Bangladesh and the neighbouring Arakan region of Myanmar came into contact with Muslim Arab merchants in the first millenium. A large number of inhabitants of both the regions subsequently became Muslims. An Arakanese king occupied the Chittagong region in AD 951 and named it after him.[31]

In 1430, the Mughal governor of Bengal, Jala al-din Muhammad Shah helped re-install Narmikhila, the desposed king of Arakan, on the throne. Muslim influence in Arakanese affairs increased. But in 1785, the Burman king annexed Arakan into his kingdom and from then began the oppression of the Muslims of Arakan .The incorporation of Arakan into latter day Burma, brought the Burmans in direct contact with British India. The Arakanese refugees in the Chittagong area organized raids against Burmese rule. The Burman army in 'hot pursuit' led incursions into the British Indian territory. This led to the first Anglo-Burmese War of 1824-26, resulting in the annexation of Arakan and Tesessarim by the British.

The subsequent two Anglo-Burmese wars of 1853 and 1885 led to the establishment of British colonial control over the whole of Myanmar.

The advance of the Japanese army during the Second World War led to the exodus of tens of thousands of Indians who had earlier gone to Myanmar from India, as well as of Muslims from Arakan. Riots flared up between the communities and some 22,000 Rohingyas took refuge in the adjoining British territory of southern Chittagong. The Arakanese communities were divided in their loyalties, the Rohingyas were loyal to the British, rendering valuable services in work units, reconnaissance and espionage, while their Buddhist counterparts, the Rakhinese, sided with the Japanese. After the Buddhist dominated Burmese administration took control over Arakan, the sense of alienation of the Muslims grew and this was translated into armed resistance against the Burmese authorities. This further aggravated relations between the communities.

Gradually over the last few decades, the Arakanese Muslims came to be distrusted and prosecuted by the ruling powers of Burma. Sporadic demands for autonomy, armed clashes and discriminatory policies pursued by the government, led to the exodus of 1978. Thousands of Rohingyas from Myanmar came to Bangladesh in 1978 and again in 1991 as refugees. They were refugees because their condition coincided with the relevant criteria laid down in the 1951 Convention Relating to the Status of Refugees and the 1967 Protocol relating to the Status of Refugees. Although Bangladesh is not a signatory to the Convention and the Protocol, a memorandum of understanding was signed between UNHCR and the government of Bangladesh and with Myanmar. The MoU authorised the UNHCR to assume responsibility for the Rohingya refugees.

In 1978 some 200,000 Rohingyas had crossed the border into Bangladesh. At that time the Bangladeshi government claimed that there were as many as 252,000 Rohingya refugees while Myanmar acknowledged only 143,900, who according to the Burmese authorities, had absconded to Bangladesh in order to escape the Nigmin Project. Following negotiations between the two governments in June and July 1978, an agreement was reached on the repatriation of the refugees to Myanmar. The process commenced on August 1, 1978 and ended on December 29, 1978 and involved the repatriation of 187,250 refugees.

In March 1991, refugees started fleeing back into Bangladesh, persecuted by the junta troops and the Myanmar police. Systematic and massive human rights abuses like, forced labour, rape and confiscation of houses, land and farm animals by the troops of 23rd and 24th regiments of the Myanmar army, reportedly, triggered off this mass exodus. The destruction of mosques, the ban on religious activities, the harassment of religious priests and the denigration of Islam, reflected the intolerance of the authorities towards the religious rights of this minority community. Between 1991 and 1992, an estimated 250,000 refugees took shelter in Bangladesh. According to refugee sources, the reason for their persecution was that they had voted for the National League for Democracy led by Daw Aung San Suu Kyi during the 1991 elections and had supported the democratisation of Myanmar.

The Bangladesh government allowed the refugees to enter. Initially it tried to solve the issue on a Bangladesh-Myanmar bilateral basis and to manage relief efforts on its own. But the government of Myanmar disclaimed all responsibility, insisting that these so-called refugees were actually Bangladeshi citizens. This was despite the fact that many of these refugees possessed identity cards issued by the Myanmar government. After a visit by the Bangladesh Foreign Minister in November 1991, Myanmar agreed to take back the refugees. But nothing happened.

The situation was further complicated by the firing across the border by the Lunthan troops of Myanmar. They attacked the border area of Bangladesh near Rejupara, and this set alarm bells ringing in official circles. A potential crisis was defused at a flag meeting between the two sides where securing Myanmar's assurance of non-aggression was considered more important than the return of the refugees . However, what made the situation even more explosive was that as the Rohingyas were Muslims, the Jamaat-e-Islam in Bangladesh took a keen interest in housing and feeding the refugees. It was reported in the media that the organisation was also giving them armed training to fight a Rohingya Liberation War and funds were liberally pouring from Saudi Arabia and Pakistan. [32]

But the Bangladesh government reeling under the blow of a cyclonic disaster, realized rather belatedly, that it could not possibly undertake the burden of clothing, housing and feeding 100,000 extra mouths. Observing that international public opinion was lukewarm in condemning the Myanmar government, Prime Minister Khaleda Zia took the issue to the United States and to the Security Council. UN Under Secretary General John Eliassen, started talks with the Myanmar government and this paved the way for Bangladesh and Myanmar to enter into bilateral talks. In the meantime, the Myanmar government, faced with international pressure, agreed to take back the refugees on terms mutually agreed upon, provided that it was portrayed as a humanitarian gesture. Ultimately, the UNHCR was invited to provide assistance to the refugees in 1992.

Bangladesh viewed the refugees as a temporary problem. It is on this premise that the government signed a memorandum of understanding with Myanmar on April 28, 1992 under which Myanmar agreed to take back those refugees who could establish bona fide residency in Myanmar prior to their departure for Bangladesh.

After the initial hospitality and cordiality extended to the refugees, by 1992 the mood of the Bangladesh government had changed as evident in the joint statement signed with Myanmar. During 1992 and 1993, human rights groups and the UNHCR expressed concern at reports of coercion and forceful repatriation of refugees by the Bangladesh authorities. Following objections by UNHCR, the Bangladesh government blocked its access to the camps, disregarding the October 1992 agreement with UNHCR. As a result, the UNHCR withdrew from the repatriation programme on December 22, 1992. The 11,216 persons who were repatriated after the withdrawal of the UNHCR, were deemed to have been forcibly repatriated.[33] The repatriation process also came in for criticism from the US Department of State which viewed it as "coerced repatriation". Subsequently, the Bangladesh government suspended its unilateral repatriation on late January 1993 and announced plans to discuss the issue with the UNHCR. Negotiations for a fresh MoU began soon thereafter. Finally a MoU was signed on May 12, 1993.

The two most important concerns of the UNHCR were safeguarded in the MoU, namely, protection of refugees in the camps and voluntary repatriation, guaranteed by private interviewing of refugees by UNHCR. For the Bangladesh government, the linking of the MoU to the Bangladesh-Myanmar Agreement of April 1992, was an important achievement. One ambiguity however remained. It did not clearly spell out that repatriation would be promoted only when there was an appreciable improvement in the conditions and thereby the safety of the refugees could be ensured. This issue became a major bone of contention between the aid agencies, human/refugee rights groups and the UNHCR on the one hand and the Bangladesh government on the other, in the later phases of repatriation. According to official UNHCR estimates, the repatriation which started on April 30, 1994 resulted in the return of an additional 150,000 persons by the end of August 1996, reducing the present camp population in Bangladesh to less than 50,000.[34]

Internally displaced persons

There is a category of people in Bangladesh who have been rendered homeless, i.e. displaced from their original homes, by various factors — environmental, economic, political and social. But instead of crossing national or political boundaries, these internally displaced persons have remained within the borders of Bangladesh. Unlike migrants or refugees they are not recognized by most official agencies, although increasingly development agencies are becoming aware of the problem of IDPs.

a. Displacement due to environmental reasons

Bangladesh is a riverine country and subject to frequent flooding and river erosion. This has had its effect on the population and population movements. In the major floods which occurred between 1974 to 1988 about 20 to 50 million people were affected throughout the country.[35] But whereas flooding may cause temporary movement of population, river bank erosion may dislocate families permanently and that too might occur several times in the lifespan of a family. For example among the households of Kazipur in Serajganj, 46 percent of the population experienced displacement during 1980-86 and 42.9 percent of the displacees had experienced dislocation more than four times earlier.[36] The homeless often take shelter, many for several years, on roads, embankments and in some *khas* (government) land. Women specifically suffer because they are handicapped by the socio-economic structure.[37]

b. Displacement due to demographic/economic reasons

Rural-urban migration is a general feature to be seen in most developing countries. Bangladesh is no exception. For example in 1990, the rural-urban in-migration was calculated as 16.2 percent for women and 4.6 percent for men while urban in-migration has been calculated to be 30.1 percent for women and 34.5 percent for men.[38] Studies have been done to investigate the phenomena from the point of view of employment and demographic pressure.[39] But what is of concern to us is that inherent in such economic or demographic pressure is an element of displacement. Land poor farmers, for example, may be cheated out of their land and forced to leave their village, or lack of work for a poor labourer may force him to leave his village home. Until and unless these persons are settled and find security, they will remain dislocated in their behaviour and lifestyles. The millions of "floating population" inhabiting the streets of Dhaka, are the internally displaced.

c. Displacement due to political reasons

Not all politically persecuted people leave the country. For example, many Bengalis did not cross the border in 1971 but wandered from village to village to escape the onslaught of the occupying Pakistan army. But political reasons for displacement may also be inherent in the insensitive development policies initiated by the state. The building of the Kaptai hydro-electric project in the 60s for example inundated 40 percent of fertile arable land in the CHT and displaced about 40,000 hill people.[40] Other development or counter-insurgency measures like jungle clearing or logging displace indigenous people, destroy indigenous culture and destroy nature.[41] In the plains, the much talked of Flood Action Plan, could, it is feared, result in a major ecological and human disaster for the dwellers of the flood plains.

d. Displacement due to social reasons

Much of the violence against vulnerable sections of the population such as the poor, women and minorities is caused by the perpetuation of social structures which embody strict orthodox values such as segregation of men and women. In recent years some religious leaders with a rural support base have taken upon themselves to issue *fatwas* (religious decrees) which punish women for seeking employment, taking part in development activities or transgressing what they define as moral boundaries. Not only has this led to an increase in gender-based violence but it has also caused several families who have been targets of such *fatwas*, to leave their homes for security. The source of the violence is not only located in orthodox structures, but also in modern consumer-oriented values. There are many cases where women or young girls have become targets of sexual harassment, often at gun point, by *mastaans*, groups of rowdy youths, who live off their "friends" in political and administrative power. Attacks against minority girls are frequent and that is why many minority families who decide to stay back in Bangladesh still want to send their daughters away to "somewhere safe".

Conclusion

In the above review of the Bangladesh situation we can see clear cases of refugee situations like that of the Chakmas or Rohingyas, migrant situations if Bangladeshis working abroad, stateless persons like the Biharis who exist in a limbo between their allegiance to Pakistan and Bangladesh and internally displaced persons who live within the borders of Bangladesh but who have been rendered homeless. While each individual case has its defining political, economic social and demographic factor, the refugee/migrant situation needs to be looked at from a holistic viewpoint. Prime Minister, Sheikh Hasina in a speech at the UN in 1996 mentioned the issue of migration as a reality facing the world today. But apart from looking at the problem from an economic perspective, she gave no clue as to how she intends to deal with it politically or socially. No doubt a lot of work still needs to be done in terms of research and documentation and not only in well publicised areas like the Rohingyas or Hill Tracts, but in the areas which are not so well known and which may determine the futures of the people of Bangladesh, South Asia, and the world.

NOTES

1. S. Malik, *Refugees and Migratory Movements : An overview of and Situation Analysis on Bangladesh,* internal paper written for UNHCR, Dhaka, Bangladesh, 1996.
2. M. Mamoon, *Unnish Shotokey Purbo Bonger Shomuj,* (19th Century East Bengal Society), CSS, Dhaka, 1986.
3. S. Malik op. cit.
4. G. Pandey, The Prose of Otherness, in D. Arnold and D. Hardiman (ed) *Subaltern Studies VII,* Oxford University Press, Oxford, 1994.

5. M. Guhathakurta, The Bangladesh Liberation War : A Summon to Memory in Abul Kalam (ed) *Bangladesh: Internal Dynamics and External Linkages*, UPL. Dhaka. 1996.
6. I Ahmed, Refugees and Security: The Experience of Bangladesh in S. D. Muni and Lok Raj Baral (ed) *Refugees and Regional Security in SouthAsia*, Konark Publishers Pvt. Ltd., Colombo, 1996.
7. Minorities Right Groups, *Biharis in Bangladesh* cited in S. Malik, op. cit.
8. A. T. Salahuddin Ahmed, "Bangladesh-Pakistan relations: An Evaluation" paper presented at the National Seminar on Bangladesh and SAARC: Issues, Perspectives and Outlook, organized by Dept. of International Relations, Dhaka University and BIISS, Dhaka, 1992.
9. Syed Serajul Islam, "Bangladesh-Pakistan Relations: From Conflict to Cooperation in Emajuddin Ahamed (ed) *Foreign Policy of Bangladesh: A Small State's Imperative*, UPL, Dhaka, 1984.
10. M. H. Askari, "Eighteen years and still stranded" *Dawn* 11 Oct. cited in Salahuddin Ahmed, A. T. op. cit.
11. Mahfuz Anam, "Benazir for Muslim ummah Solution to stranded Pakistanis" in *The Daily Star*, 15 July 1992.
12. A. Barkat , et al. *Impact of Vested Property Act on rural Bangladesh: An Explanatory Study*, (mimeo) Association for Land Reform and Development, Dhaka, 1996.
13. *Ibid*
14. S. Nahar, *Shonkhaloghu Shomprodai* (A Comparative Study of Communalism in Bangladesh and India) Dhaka, Prokashon, 1994.
15. S. Malik, op. cit.
16. P. Tripura, The Colonial Foundation of Pahari Ethnicity" in the *Journal of Social Studies*, No. 58, Dhaka, CSS.
17. Father Timm, . *The Adivasis of Bangladesh*, A Minority Rights Group International Report, Vol. 92/1, 1992.
18. A. Mohsin, and B. Chakma. "The Myth of Nation Building and Security of Bangladesh: The Case of Chittagong Hill Tracts," The Case of Chittagong Hill

Tracts", Paper presented at the National Seminar on Bangladesh and SAARC : Issues, Perspectives and Outlook, op. cit.

Also see I Ahmed op. cit. for breakdown of Hill people and Bengali people population in the CHT pp. 131-132.

19. F. Timm, op. cit.
20. A. Mohsin, *The Politics of Nationalism : The case of the CHT*, Bangladesh, 1995, unpublished thesis.
21. Individual studies as yet unpublished have been done by Ashok Swain and Imtiaz Ahmed.
22. S. Malik, op.cit.
23. Ibid.
24. Cited in *Naribarta*, Newsletter of Women for Women, Dhaka. Sept. 1996.
25. *The Herald,* 10 November 1990 cited in B. Moudud, *Pakistaney Bangladesher Nari Pachar* (Trafficking of Bangladeshi Women to Pakistan), Bangladesh Mohila Parishad, Dhaka, 1991.
26. Ain O Salish Kendra (ASK) *Documents*, Dhaka, 1996.
27. ASK's interview with S. Bonik, Statistics Officer, Bureau of Manpower, Employment and Training, Bangladesh.
28. Ibid.
29. Cited in I. Ahmed, op. cit.
30. This section of the paper is based on research done by C.R. Abrar, Repatriation of Rohingya Refugees paper presented at Regional Consultation on Refugee and Migratory Movements, Colombo, 25-27 September 1995 and S. Malik, op. cit.
31. *The Daily Shongbad*, September 1992.
32. cited in C.R. Abrar, op. cit.
33. UNHCR, *Voluntary Repatriation and Reintegration : Bangladesh/ Myanmar: Situation Update*, Geneva, Sept. 1996.
34. K. M. Elahi, Riverbank Erosion, Flood Hazard and Population Displacement in Bangladesh: An Overview in Elahi, et. al. (ed) *Riverbank Erosion, Flood and Population Displacement in Bangladesh, Riverbank Erosion Impact Study*, Jahangirnagar University, Savar, 1991.

35. Ibid.
37. Bureau of Statistics, *Women and Men in Bangladesh: Facts and Figures 1970-1990*, Dhaka, 1994, p. 69.
38. See J. Pryer, Purdah, Fertility and Population Movements: Perspectives from Bangladesh, in S. Chant (ed) *Gender and Migration in Developing Countries*, Belhaven Press, London, L. Boer, Migration and Social Mobility in Bangladesh in the *Journal of Social Studies*, 13, Dhaka. Also see, A. Rahman, Migration and Food Security, BIDS, and M.A. Jabbar, Some Aspects of Unemployment: Migration and Income in the Bangladesh Rural Labour market in the *Bangladesh Journal of Agriculture Economics*, Dec. 1988.
39. M. K. Chakma, Counter Insurgency : A Multi-dimensional Process of Marginalization of the CHT Jummas, Paper presented in a Workshop on The CHT Jummas: Struggle for Identity, Calcutta, 28,29 April, 1996.
40. K. Chakma, Development, Ecology and Indigenous Women in the Chittagong Hill Tracts of Bangladesh, unpublished paper.
41. Meghna Guhathakurta, The Aid Discourse and the Politics of Gender in the *Journal of Social Studies*, no. 65, Dhaka, 1994.

Biharis in Bangladesh

Forgotten Pakistani citizens

Muhammad Nur Khan

Biharis who had migrated to East Pakistan from Bihar in India, languish in camps scattered across Bangladesh, waiting with a sense of despair and displacement to be repatriated to a land that refuses to give them recognition — Pakistan. These people have been living in subhuman conditions in 66 camps for the last 25 years.

Historical background

British era

At the Allahabad session of the Muslim League, held in 1930, Sir Mohammed Allama Iqbal declared that the "formation of a consolidated North-West India Muslim state appears to me to be the final destiny of Muslims at least of North-West India".[1] However, Sir Iqbal did not advocate a sovereign independent state for the Muslims. In 1933, Rahmat Ali described the Indian Muslims as a nation and prepared a plan for the establishment of Pakistan which was to include the Punjab, Kashmir, Sind, Baluchistan and the

North-Western Frontier Province. He also referred to the establishment of Osmanistan of Hyderabad and Bangi-Islam of Bengal and Assam. Till 1937, the Muslim League refused to approve the idea of Pakistan. It was in 1938 that Mohammad Ali Jinnah demanded the division of India. By January 1940, Jinnah referred to two nations, one of the Hindus and the other of the Muslims in India.

Presiding over the Muslim League session at Lahore, on March 22, 1940, Jinnah declared that the Muslims were not in a minority, they were a nation by any definition. Jinnah contended that "the Hindus and Muslims belonged to two different religions, philosophies, social customs and literature. They neither inter-married nor inter-dined. They belonged to two different civilizations which were based mainly on conflicting ideas and conceptions. Their aspects on life and of life were different. .... To yoke together two such nations under a single state, one as a numerical minority and the other as a majority, must lead to growing discontent and final destruction of any fabric that may be so built up for the Government of such a state".[2]

On March 23, 1940, the Pakistan Resolution was passed by the Muslim League at its Lahore session. The Resolution stated that no constitutional plan would be workable in India or acceptable to the Muslims unless geographically contiguous units were demarcated into regions, which should be so constituted that the areas in which the Muslims were numerically in a majority, as in the north-western and eastern zones of India, should be so grouped as to constitute independent states. The Lahore Resolution was the highest culmination of Muslim aspirations from the time of Sir Syed Ahmed Khan. It gave the League a new objective and a new programme. Renewed stress was laid on the two-nation theory and communal differences were exaggerated with redoubled energy. The Pakistan Resolution was a personal triumph for Jinnah and won him great popularity among the Muslims in India. It established his dictatorial leadership beyond all possibility of being overthrown.

On account of the Second World War, the British government began to rely more and more on the support of the Muslim League and Jinnah took full advantage of it. The conflict between Congress and the Muslim League, intensified over the question of the formation of the Interim Government of India in 1946. Communal riots took place in Bihar, Garhmukteswar, Lahore, Punjab, Rawalpindi, Calcutta, Barisal, Noakhali and in parts of East Bengal. The spread of communal disturbances, involving mass murder, arson and loot, obliged all parties including the British government to consider the whole communal and political situation afresh. The only way out of the difficulty appeared to be the partitioning of India.

It is a fact, that it was during British rule in India that Hindu-Muslim riots took place and in those areas where the nationalist movement was strong. Between 1889 and 1894, there were about 90 Hindu-Muslim riots, 44 riots in Bengal alone, nine in North-Western Provinces and Oudh, 17 in Madras and one in the Punjab.[3] The British government in pursuit of the policy of "Divide & Rule", encouraged riots wherever there was political activism to undermine the nationalist movement.

However, following communal riots in 1946, Lord Mountbatten proposed Partition plan of June 3, 1947 provided for the establishment of two separate dominions of India and Pakistan and British withdrawal from India on August 15, 1947. Pakistan and India were declared two sovereign states.

Pakistani era

As the movement for Pakistan and its creation was based on the two-nation theory founded on religious ideology, it was clear to all that only those areas where Muslims were in majority would form part of Pakistan. Millions of Muslims from other parts migrated to these Muslim majority areas. Among the peoples who migrated to what became East Pakistan, the 700,000 Muslims of Bihar comprised the vast majority. That is why this entire group was generally known as Bihari. For their socio-economic and cultural under-development, they blamed the Hindu zamindars and upper caste Hindus. They believed that Pakistan would guarantee them socio-economic, cultural and religious security. They expected to find positions of self-respect and self-reliance in Pakistan. The Biharis were, as such, mentally, ideologically, historically and legally tied to the umbilical cord of Pakistan.

History has this fact on record that Pakistan came into being as a result of the sacrifices made by the Muslims of the minority areas of India. The August 18, 1947 Id message of Jinnah, as the first Governor General of Pakistan, acknowledges this debt. "Let us not, on this occasion, forget those of our brethren and sisters who have sacrificed their all, so that Pakistan may be established and we may live. Those of our brethren who are minorities in Hindustan may rest assured that we shall never neglect or forget them.... I recognise that it is the Muslim minority provinces in this subcontinent who were the pioneers and carried the banner aloft for the achievement of our cherished goal of Pakistan. I shall never forget their support, nor I hope the majority Muslim provinces in Pakistan will fail to appreciate that they were the pioneers in the vanguard of our historic and heroic struggle for the achievement of Pakistan, which today is an accomplished fact."[4]

But the people who migrated from India to East Pakistan were different from those who migrated to West Pakistan. Moreover, the people living in East Pakistan were different in language, culture and historical origin from those in West Pakistan, though they had a common religion and the same national flag. It is a bitter irony that the Bihari people migrated to East Pakistan to settle in a Pakistan which for them meant a definite ideology, the full flourishing of their language, Urdu and the preservation of their culture.

Ever since Pakistan came into being in 1947, the Biharis consistently supported its policy on the sensitive national language issue. Controversy over the national language issue became the rallying point for Bengali nationalism which eventually led to the independence movement of Bangladesh. The Biharis were used to spearhead Pakistani policy in East Pakistan. Despite the danger to their life and property, they stood by Pakistan in 1971 during the armed and well organised struggle for its dismemberment. The Biharis came to East Pakistan to be Pakistanis but not to be "sons of the soil". As a result, at Pakistan's direction they opposed the creation of Bangladesh and lent the Pakistani army full support. The Biharis even took active part in colluding with armed groups in looting, arson, mass rape and the genocide of Bengalis.

Bangladeshi era

But in 1971, when Pakistan was defeated in the war for the liberation of Bangladesh, millions of Pakistanis branded as "Biharis", were left behind, insecure. Driven out from various parts of the new Bangladesh where they had been living when it was an integral part of Pakistan, they herded together in areas where the hoped to be safe and secure. Eventually, they took refuge in camps jointly organised by the Geneva based International Committee of the Red Cross and the government of Bangladesh, to await repatriation to Pakistan.

An estimated 462,000 Biharis fled to Pakistan but about 400,000 were left behind. They were given a straight choice between Pakistani or Bangladeshi citizenship. Some opted for Bangladeshi citizenship and have done well. But most of them opted to stay Pakistani in the misguided belief that Pakistan would accept and welcome them. They are still waiting to go "home" to a country they have never seen and which does not want them. They have one fixed idea : "I am a Pakistani and will die a Pakistani".

Bangladesh wants to repatriate those Biharis who want to be Pakistani. But Pakistan refuses to accept that the Biharis have any claim on it. Neither country wants them. They are now a lost people stranded by a war that created a Bengali-speaking country 25 years ago. They are non-Bengalis and speak Urdu. Theoretically, they should have Pakistani citizenship. They fought for the creation of Pakistan and left their land of origin, India, for Pakistan. They fought for the preservation of Pakistan's sovereignty and territorial integrity over East Pakistan. They fought alongside the West Pakistan army to maintain its domination over East Pakistan. But Pakistan has turned its back on them.

These stranded Pakistanis live in 66 camps scattered across Dhaka, Chittagong, Saidpur, Rangpur, Khulna and other districts. Lack of water and sanitation facilities has made these camps breeding grounds for epidemics. After 25 years in the camps there are those like Mohammad Ayub , 65 years old, who resignedly says, "If Pakistan does not accept us and if Bangladesh gives me citizenship, and can provide me with a job, I am ready to stay and live in Bangladesh. I don't want anybody to use us for their political game." Ayub, lives in New Colony Kailashpur Housing estate, Khulna where Bihari families live crammed in 8 ft by 8 ft rooms. There is one latrine for 25 families, little water and no electricity. "In 1995, a fire broke out in the camp. We lost everything but nobody came forward to help," he said.

In 1948 he had come from Bihar, when communal riots broke out in Calcutta, Bihar and other parts in India. Left behind were three acres of land and a small business. Once in East Pakistan, Ayub worked in the jute industry. He was working as a spinner in Crescent Jute Mills Ltd at Khulna when the backlash began against the Biharis for colluding with the Pakistan army. After December 16, 1971, Biharis stayed shut in the camps fearful of being killed if they ventured out. A few months later, the dead body of an old man, a Bengali, was found. The camp was attacked from all sides, many Biharis were stabbed and slashed to death. Dead bodies were moved away by the police and army.

Children in the camps have little access to education, especially as schooling is in Bengali. In some camps the community is running its own primary school. But most of the children in the camp live off their daily wages. For most it is difficult to find work even as a labourer even though the Biharis are willing to work for half wages. Ayub today works as a cook.

But whereas Ayub is resigned to staying on in Bangladesh, preferably as a citizen, there are others who are determined, even after 25 years, to go to a Pakistan that does not want them, even though their sisters or children may have got married and settled down in Bangladesh.

Citizenship and repatriation

The Biharis assert they are Pakistani citizens and are determined not to forget their identity as Pakistanis. They are still waiting to be repatriated to Pakistan, their imaginary homeland. Though Pakistan had signed agreements and made several statements in favour of the repatriation of all the Pakistani Biharis it is reluctant to accept them. About 163,000 Biharis have been repatriated to Pakistan within the last 25 years; and the last batch of 53 families were flown out to Pakistan in January 1993. But there still are 238,000 people of 41,000 families left in Bangladesh who live in the 66 "Geneva Camps". Stateless, they live in perpetual fear.

Children born in these camps, many of whom are in their late teens, are paying the price for the wrongs, if any, committed by their forefathers. Their plight needs to be resolved not within the narrow confines of refugee and citizenship laws but by invoking human rights and humanitarian principles.

General principles governing nationality in consequence of state succession lay down negotiations between the predecessor and successor states. Negotiations between Pakistan and Bangladesh did result in the transfer of 163,000 Biharis to Pakistan during the 25 years since the formation of Bangladesh. But the negotiations regarding the rest seem to have come to a halt. The situation has become further complicated by the linkage of the issue of the Biharis with that of the allegedly illegal movements of hundred of thousands of Bangladeshis to Pakistan.

However, irrespective of the bargaining and negotiating stances of Bangladesh and Pakistan and the claims and counter-claims of the two sides, the basic principle is that the states are obliged to prevent statelessness, particularly when such statelessness is consequent upon state succession.

Given the long-standing residence of the Biharis in Bangladesh and their legal entitlement under the citizenship laws of the country, there does not seem to be much justification in denying the Biharis their citizenship status, if they so desire.

According to the laws of citizenship of Bangladesh, the Biharis who are in the territory of Bangladesh are eligible to become citizens. Article 3(d) of the Bangladesh Citizenship Act, 1951 specifies the following criterion: "Who before the commencement of this Act, migrated to the territories now included in Bangladesh from any territory in the Indo-Pakistan subcontinent outside those territories with the intention of residing permanently in those territories".

Furthermore, Article 2 of the Bangladesh Citizenship (Temporary Provisions) Order, 1972 (President's Order 149 of 1972) provides :

i. who or whose father or grandfather was born in the territories now comprised in Bangladesh and who was a permanent resident of the territories now comprised in Bangladesh on the 25th March 1971, and continues to be so resident; or
ii. who was a permanent resident of the territories now comprised in Bangladesh on the 25th day of March 1971 and continues to be so resident and is not otherwise disqualified for being a citizen by or under any law, for the time being in force;

As most of the Biharis came to the territories comprising Bangladesh from the Indo-Pakistan subcontinent with the intention of residing there permanently and virtually all of them were permanent residents before March 25, 1971, a plain reading of these two sections would confirm their entitlement to the citizenship of Bangladesh.

However, article 2B of the Bangladesh Citizenship (Temporary Provisions) Amendment Ordinance 1978 (Ordinance No., VII of 1978) added that a person shall not qualify to be a citizen on Bangladesh if he "owes, affirms or acknowledges, expressly or by conduct, allegiance to a foreign state...."

But the pertinent issue concerning the legal status of the Biharis revolves around their stated desire to migrate to Pakistan, on the one hand and the reluctance of both Pakistan and Bangladesh to grant them citizenship, on the other. The problem of Biharis is thus not only a legal one. Apart from any other considerations, the problem is one of Pakistan's honour and moral integrity. The fundamental question is, should Pakistan betray a community that has consistently supported its policy even before its creation, sacrificed everything for its territorial integrity and sovereignty and fought against the liberation of the land where they now live? Is it honourable for Pakistan that the world should think that Pakistan is not ready to be responsible for its citizens, the Biharis, because it doesn't need them any more. This is despite the statements made and agreements concluded by Pakistan in support of the repatriation of the Biharis.

— On March 2, 1972, Pakistan Prime Minister, Z. A. Bhutto told *The Guardian* newspaper, "Of course in principal, I'd say they have every right to take up that position. I'd like to see what can be done to bring as many as possible here ... and some of them say two, three-four hundred thousand ... perhaps a little more then the ones who go from here then that would be better."

— On March 19, 1972 President Bhutto in a public meeting at Lahore said, "every Bihari (Muslim migrant from India) was a Pakistani and had the right to go to Pakistan."

— The Delhi Agreement, August 28, 1973, provided for the repatriation of "a substantial number of non-Bangladeshis who have opted for Pakistan with ICRC in 1972-1973 in exchange for the Bengalis in Pakistan and the return of Pakistan POWs (Prisoners or War) and civil internees in India."

— On June 28, 1974. Prime Minister Bhutto, speaking at an official dinner in Dhaka said, "The problems of these poor and unfortunate people (non-local Pakistanis) is a humanitarian one and we must not allow human considerations to be submerged by consideration of diplomatic advantage or political convenience."

— On September 26 1974, the Prime Minister of Bangladesh Sheikh Mujibur Rahman said at the UN General Assembly, "The plight of 63,888 Pakistani families who have reaffirmed their allegiance to Pakistan and have registered themselves with ICRC for repatriation to their country remains a pressing humanitarian problem. Bangladesh on its part was and remains ready to move forward towards reconciliation. We expect ... a successful conclusion."

— On July 9 1988 an agreement was signed between the government of Pakistan and Rabita Al-Alam Islami Makkah Al Mukrramah in Islamabad resulting in the setting up of a Trust. As seed money, Zia ul Haq, President of Pakistan, donated Rs 25 crores and Rabita Al-Alam Islami donated Rs 5 crores towards the Trust Fund. The Rs 30 crores is still lying unutilised by the government of Pakistan.

— On November 11, 1991, the first meeting of the Board of Trustees resolved, "that 2,000 families (10,000 persons) of stranded Pakistanis (Biharis) would be brought to Pakistan within the next few months."

After living in subhuman conditions in the camps, the Biharis started to organise themselves in their struggle for repatriation to Pakistan. The Stranded Pakistanis General Repatriation Committee (SPGRC) was formed in 1976. Through mass rallies, demonstrations and hunger strikes, it has been seeking to pressurize both the governments of Pakistan and Bangladesh to continue the process of repatriation. The SPGRC's programmes are aimed at attracting world attention to the sad plight of the stranded Pakistanis. Printed leaflets, brochures and posters provide information about the humanitarian issue. Several delegations of the SPGRC have met representatives of both governments to expedite the repatriation of the remaining 238,000 Pakistanis. Representations have also been made in various regional and international fora. But Pakistan's recalcitrance about taking back its citizens, remains.

Plight of being unwanted

For the stranded Pakistanis, in contravention of government orders, eviction from their homes and shops has become routine because of inter-departmental disputes on appropriation of land belonging to them. The Bangladesh government also does not have any clear policy in this regard. Sometimes, the requisite notice is not served in advance to enable the inhabitants to manage alternate shelters.

Relief supplies (wheat) to stranded Pakistanis in different camps, administrated by the district administration has been abruptly stopped on several occasions, since August 1992, without any reason being assigned.

The safety and security of the stranded Pakistanis living in different camps has been threatened in view of deteriorating law and order situation. In a few camps, people are contemplating fleeing to safety.

The SPGRC has urged Pakistan government to:

- immediately start repatriation of Pakistanis in

Bangladesh, as envisaged in Joint Declaration of August 12, 1992,

- release of assets by the Pakistan government,

- release of frozen *shaheed* and unclaimed funds lying with Habib Bank of Pakistan,

- release of Bihar relief and refugee relief funds,

- grant substantial funds from Baitul Maal of Pakistan for the reconstruction of damaged camps, education and medicare facilities.

They have also urged the Bangladesh government to undertake :

- immediate repair of 276 damaged latrines of Geneva Camp, Mohammadpur in Dhaka, as it is a health hazard.

- measures to stop eviction and demolition of camps and shops.

- provision and restoration of basic amenities in all camps and restoration of water supply in Chittagong and electricity in Rangpur, Khalishpur and Ishurdi.

- the safety and security of Stranded Pakistanis in Bangladesh be ensured.

- repair and renovation of all camps on a priority basis.

In view of the plight of the stranded Pakistanis, the international community should come forward to create effective pressure on both the governments, especially Pakistan, to take the necessary decision and initiate steps in favour of repatriation. And till the repatriation problem is solved, the Bangladesh government should recognise their refugee status and ensure respect for their rights in accordance with international refugee protection standards. Given the limitation of Bangladesh government, UNHCR and other regional and international organisations should cooperate with the Bangladesh government.

The problem of the Biharis should not be considered from the point of view of politics but from a humanitarian and human rights perspective.

NOTES

1. See V. D. Mahajan, *Advance History of India*, Part III, p. 318.
2. ibid, pp. 318-319.
3. p. 312.

SECTION THREE

Destination India

A political study of international migrations

Partha S. Ghosh

From time immemorial India has been an attractive destination for all kinds of people ranging from travellers to looters, from warriors to adventurers. Even the Aryans are known to have come from outside. No wonder then that the theme caught the imagination of the great Bengali poet Rabindranath Tagore who underlined this unbounded hospitality of India in his celebrated poem *Bharat-Tirtha*.

No one knows to whose clarion call
Peoples responded and came
In streams
And joined the ocean !
Hither came the Aryans, the non-Aryans,
The Dravidians, the Chinese, the Sakas,
The Huns, the Pathans, the Mughals—
And merged into one body and soul.
Today, doors to the West are open
New ideas are flowing
Incessant giving and taking
Meeting and mingling are on
They will not return
From this supreme ocean of Humanity
That is India. *(Free translation from Bengali)*

The phenomenon did not stop even after Partition although the Partition itself, was anathema to the phenomenon. The subsequent second partition which saw the creation of Bangladesh, encouraged the process further. The difference between the earlier experience and the post-independence one was that while during the earlier phase, the immigrants were from outside South Asia, in the later phases they were from within the region with some minor exceptions. Indeed, this was to some extent inevitable because the geographical limits of India themselves got truncated with the coming of independence.

This paper attempts to study the phenomenon of arrival of people from all over the region either as refugees, temporary workers, unauthorised migrants and permanent settlers and then relate it to the politics of the country. The essential thrust here would be to see the question from a human angle and argue that the elimination of regional disparities in the national context together with regional cooperation in the South Asian context can alone address it, holistically.

Some definitional problems

Any study of movements of people from one place to another confronts some definitional difficulties. These difficulties arise because in the modern world, both on account of technological advances as well as the growing awareness of people about their rights and well-being, international boundaries are no longer the dividers of people either culturally or emotionally, as it used to be in earlier times. Moreover, with the process of decolonisation which witnessed state formation prior to nation formation, the sub-problematique of cross-national ethnicity and sub-nationalism has arrived at the centrestage of intellectual inquiry. Its cumulative effect is to reveal the inadequency of finding a suitable and universally acceptable definition for social phenomenon.

Still, for the purposes of clarity and delineation of the scope of this paper, it is essential that an attempt be made in this regard, howsoever, limited its efficacy may be. Definitionally, "migrations" and "movements" are all distinguishable terminologies to a demographer. Migration has generally been defined as "a permanent change in place of residence by the crossing of specified administrative or political boundaries. The persons who fulfil these two criteria are regarded as migrants."[1] The word movement generally connotes "a change of residence within the same political or administrative boundary."[2] By the broader expression "population movement" one understands the migration of large groups of human beings from one part of the world to another, either for reasons of economics, security, food or for ecological considerations.

Insofar as the definition of a refugee is concerned, the UN Convention on the Status of Refugees 1951, defines a refugee as "any person who owing to well founded fear of being persecuted for reasons of race, religion, nationality, membership of a particular social group or political opinion, is outside the country of his nationality and is unable, or owing to such fear, is unwilling to avail himself of the protection of that country ..." Since then there has been considerable progress in the discourse to add human rights, military and environmental angles to the working definition to make it as broad-based as possible.[3]

For the purposes of this paper all these various expressions have been used interchangeably for the types of human migration we are discussing here fall in either one category or the other or in more than just one category. To put it simply, our concern is with almost all kinds of movement of people from parts of the South Asian region to India, both voluntary and involuntary and permanent or quasi-permanent. It may be noted that internal migrations, for example, of the rural poor to urban centres, or from one province to another for economic reasons or from one part to another within the same province for security reasons such as the migration of Kashmiri Hindus from the valley to Jammu town, is beyond the purview of this paper.

India, the final stop

If we accept the these broad definitions of migration, movements, population movement and refugee, it would be found that during the last half a century, India has, when compared to other countries in the region, hosted the highest number of people either permanently or quasi permanently from outside its borders, and most of them from South Asia itself. Estimatedly, about 25 million people have been pulled into this continuing flow of peoples to India, driven by the search from security against the threat to life, property or faith and culture or pushed by war, hunger and work or drawn by ethnic, racial, ideological or religious homogenisation.

From a strict methodological point of view based on theories of nation building all the different types of migration to India may be put in two or three typologies. For example, both the Hindu migrations after the Partition and the Bengali refugee influx in the wake of the Bangladesh liberation war, can be considered together in terms of the failure of nation building. But such strait-jacketing would not be useful for the purposes of this paper, the thrust of which is to view the problem from the point of India's political development. To further clarify the point, it may be argued that though both the above cases were nation building related, in the case of the Hindu migrants they became the direct vehicles through which the Hindu-chauvinistic politics of India was carried forward. But in the case of the Bangladeshi refugees both the Hindu nationalists and their enemies closed ranks. The fact that the majority of the refugees were Muslim mattered little to either of the groups.

Keeping in view the primary focus of this paper together with the various types of migrations to India both in terms of causality as well as their impact on domestic politics, seven categories of migrations may be considered although some overlapping is unavoidable. These categories are :

i. Hindu migrations caused by the Partition,

ii. Bangladeshi refugees as a result of the civil war in Pakistan,

iii. Sri Lankan Tamil, Burmese Indian and Bhutanese Nepali refugees due to inter-ethnic strife,

iv. Nepali, Bangladeshi and Pakistani settlers due to open or virtually open borders,

v. Developmental and environmental refugees from Bangladesh,

vi. Indian Tamil (Sri Lankan) repatriates as per contractual obligations,

vii. Tibetan and Afghan refugees as a result of military intervention by extra-regional powers.

The Partition fallout

The migration of Hindus that took place from Pakistan immediately before and after the Partition and which continued for several years thereafter, fall in this category. The nation formation related ideological conflict between the Congress and the Muslim League had created such distrust between sections of Hindus and Muslims that when the decision to divide the country was taken it resulted in unprecedented communal carnage at several places. In the wake of the Partition a large number of Hindus migrated to India. Estimatedly, about seven million Hindus were involved in the process. During the fifties, another four million Hindus migrated to India.[4] In the 60s, East Pakistan witnessed frequent communal strife causing a further exodus of Hindus, particularly to the neighbouring Indian states of Assam, Tripura and West Bengal. From Partition to 1964, the number of such refugees was estimatedly 5.5 million.[5]

Bangladeshi refugees

The denial of democratic rights to the East Pakistan based Awami League to form the government in Pakistan following the general election of 1970 in Pakistan sharpened the already existing political divide between the East and the West wings of Pakistan. The people of East Pakistan, claiming a distinctive linguistic and cultural identity of their own, around which developed the phenomenon of Bengali nationalism, came in conflict with Pakistani, or more precisely, Punjabi, nationalism. The Bangladesh liberation movement resulted in massive repression by the Pakistani military junta causing mass exodus of East Pakistanis to India. An estimated 10 million refugees arrived in India.

Ethnic strife

The arrival of a large number of Sri Lankan Tamils as refugees on account of the Sinhala Tamil ethnic conflict, the arrival of many Burmese Indians following the nationalisation of trade and industry there and the flight of thousands of ethnic Nepalis from Bhutan fall in this category. The anti-Tamil riots of July 1983 in Colombo forced many Sri Lanka Tamils to take refugee in the neighbouring state of Tamil Nadu in India. It was estimated that about 30,000 Tamils took refugee in India at that time. The flow continued with varying degree of intensity and by May 1985 it touched the figure of 100,000. Many of these refugees settled permanently in India. A 1990 estimate showed that approximately 120,000 Sri Lanka Tamils were living in refugee camps while about 80,000 were living outside the camps.[6] Following the assassination of Rajiv Gandhi in May 1991 the non-camp refugees were asked to register themselves with the police. By July 1991, more than 26,000 persons had registered. Soon afterwards, the police launched an operation to pick up those who had not registered. 1,800 arrests were made under the Foreigners' Act.[7]

According to recent reports there are 115 refugee camps in Tamil Nadu which shelter 56,746 refugees. The last phase of repatriation which took place between January 21, 1992 and March 20, 1995, had effected the repatriation of 54,188 people.[8] Lately, since the defeat of the LTTE in Jaffna and Killinochchi, once again there has been a surge of refugee movements towards India. Between July 31, 1996 and October 10, 1996, about 13,000 Sri Lankan Tamil refugees reportedly arrived on the Rameswaram coast of Tamil Nadu.[9]

In Myanmar, the policies of the government after independence in 1948, aimed at indigenising the society and polity, caused an exodus of Indians in the 40s through to the 60s. Before 1937 when Myanmar was part of the British Indian empire there were about 900,000 Indians in the country holding important commercial and professional positions. After Myanmar's independence when the new government embarked upon a policy of indigenisation which included making the Burmese the official language, a majority of Indians left the country and returned to India. During the 60s yet another exodus took place. This was caused by the policy of nationalisation of trade, industry, banking and commerce which made the role of Indians there redundant, as most of them had been engaged in these profit-making sectors. About 150,000 Indians were involved in this return migration.[10]

Again in the last decades, there has been a renewed flow of refugees from Myanmar to neighbouring countries which includes India, largely on account of the repressive policies of the ruling State Law and Order Restoration Council (SLORC). Most of these refugees belong to the Chin tribe and have come to Mizoram, some are also Nagas who have taken shelter in Arunachal Pradesh and Nagaland. Altogether there are about 40,000 Myanmarese refugees in India.

The ethnic strife in Bhutan between the majority Drukpas (Ngalongs and Sarchops combined) and the minority Lhotsampas (ethnic Nepalis) has forced a large number of the latter to leave the country and take refuge in India and Nepal. Although the majority of these 90,000 persons of Nepali origin who fled Bhutan in 1990 are in Nepal, estimatedly, about 20,000 are in India spread across the north-eastern states of Arunachal Pradesh, Assam and West Bengal. 7,000 of them who are in the Bomdila region of Arunachal Pradesh have been threatened with deportation because of the anti-foreigner campaign launched there by the All Arunachal Pradesh Students Union.[11]

Open border

The Indo-Nepal border is an open border which has resulted in substantial Nepali immigration into India. Nepali immigration has largely been to the north-eastern states of India and the northern districts of West Bengal and Uttar Pradesh. In the 70s it was estimated that nearly 5 million persons of Nepali origin had permanently settled in India for more than a generation.[12] According to more recent estimates, there are at least 6 million, perhaps even 10 million people of Nepali origin in India.[13]

While the border between India and Nepal was made an open border by the 1950 treaty, the border between India and Bangladesh is a de facto open border. It has resulted in large scale movement of Bangladeshis into India. As a consequence of the haste with which Cyril Radcliffe accomplished the task of partitioning India coupled with the inherent fallacy of the whole exercise in mixed Hindu-Muslim localities along the border between India and Bangladesh,[14] the border hardly gives the impression of an international border. A scholar who visited some of the border areas found the utter inefficacy of the system that was supposed to politically separate India from Bangladesh. He wrote: "We have drawn a line on paper, but where is that line on ground ? ... This situation was illegal but not unnatural. In this convoluted milieu I soon learnt how categories changed .... (Here) illegal meant routine; infiltration was migration; smuggling was trade, these were less Indian villages, but more border villages."[15] Economic and social interaction across the international boundary are as common now in many places as they were before the Partition. As a result, many people have come and settled on the Indian side of the border as a matter of routine.

The 1981 census revealed that in the eight border districts of West Bengal the population grew at over 30 percent between 1971 and 1981 whereas the remaining districts reported growth rates below 20 percent. In the extreme case of a town in northern West Bengal, the population jumped from 10,000 to 150,000. [16] According to estimates provided by the Indian census report, the number of people who have migrated illegally from Bangladesh to India totalled 1,729,310 from 1961-71 and 559,006 from

1971-81. These figures do not include the estimated 600,000 who entered Assam during 1971-81. It is possible that many of the Bangladeshi infiltrators were called Biharis.[17]

According to some estimates quoted by the media in the 1980s, on an average about 2,000 people were pushed back by Indian's Border Security Force (BSF) every month. However, the actual number of Bangladeshi nationals illegally entering India through the sparsely guarded 1,300 km long border is suspected to be at least ten times as high. According to the figures supplied by the government of India, in 1992, 1993 and 1994, 37,891, 23,559 and 16,991 infiltrators, respectively, were intercepted on the Indo-Bangladesh border.[18] To these numbers one should also add those Bangladeshis who enter India on forged travel documents or even valid ones but who do not return to their country of origin at the expiry of their visas. In the 1980s the West Bengal government claimed that at least 400,000 passport holders from Bangladesh who had entered West Bengal over the last ten years had disappeared into the Indian community. In reality, there is hardly any deportation of illegal immigrants back to Bangladesh, despite the hue and cry made in the country over the matter. From 1989 to 1994, only 3,189 illegal Bangladeshi immigrants were deported.[19] Presently, there are millions of unauthorised Bangladeshis living in various parts of India, generally doing menial jobs. Demographers agree that such out-migrations of people from poorer regions to neighbouring less poor ones are bound to take place, just like water seeks its own level. Earlier, these settlements were concentrated in neighbouring Assam and West Bengal but of late more remote areas like Bombay, Delhi, Haryana, Punjab and western UP have seen this trend.[20]

Another case that can be added to this category is that of clandestine Pakistani migration across the borders of

Gujarat and Rajasthan. This border is 512 km long in Gujarat and 1,335 km in Rajasthan. People living in the border areas often have kinship ties across the border. Smuggling is a way of life there and trafficking in drugs and arms, particularly after the Punjab crisis, is a growing problem for the Indian authorities.

In India, some of the border villages in the districts of Barmer, Bikaner, Ganganagar and Jaisalmer in Rajasthan have registered a much higher rate of growth than other villages. For example, between 1971 and 1981, the population of Bandha village went up from 172 to 5,888, of Muhar village from 9 to 247, of Kuldar from 32 to 240, of Modana from 422 to 1,198, of Mota Kilon-ki-Dhani from 48 to 540 and of Madasar from 445 to 1,171.[21] While part of this growth is attributed to the construction of the Rajasthan canal (Indira Gandhi Nahar) which attracted people from other districts, part of it is due to migration from Pakistan.[22] There has been a rise in the number of Muslim majority villages along the border. In this connection it may be noted that in the wake of the 1965 and 1971 Indo-Pak wars many Indian Muslims crossed over to Pakistan and settled there. They, however, managed to retain their Indian citizenship, thanks to local district politics. These people had a unique status of holding dual citizenship of both India and Pakistan and continued to cross the border with relative ease.[23]

Developmental and environmental refugees

In this category one may include the migration of the Chakma tribals of Bangladesh to some of the north-eastern states of India. The construction of Karnafuli (Kapatai) hydro-electric project in 1964 submerged 54,000 acres of settled and cultivable land affecting about 100,000 people, 90 percent of whom were Chakmas. In addition, state-sponsored resettlement schemes meant for plains people in the traditional "homelands" of the Chakmas, made them aliens in their own habitat. All this led to disaffection, civil strife, militancy, and eventually, state repression resulting in the flight of the tribals to neighbouring India for safety. By August 1987, there were about 33,000 such refugees spread over several camps in the North-East.[24] More recently, Bangladesh and India have agreed upon a process of repatriation. The pace though is slow. By April 1995, only 1,027 refugee families had been repatriated.[25]

There is also the case of Bangladeshis who enter India in large numbers in search of livelihood. Several studies have shown that the construction of the Farakka barrage in India on the Ganga near the India-Bangladesh border has contributed to the impoverishment of people of south-western Bangladesh, particularly of the Khulna and the Rajshahi divisions. Khulna was traditionally a high growth division but during the last two decades it has registered a drastic fall which is largely attributed to the impact of the Farakka dam on its agriculture. The exact number of out-migrants from these two divisions to India can never be known but it would not be too much of an exaggeration to put the figure at two million or so.[26]

Contractual obligation

Within this category falls the repatriation of a certain number of Indian Tamils from Sri Lanka to India. In 1953 it was estimated that there were 975,000 stateless persons of Indian origin in Sri Lanka. According to the Sri Lankan census of 1981, the Indian Tamils were 825,233 in number, constituting 5.6 per cent of the island's population. The Shastri-Sirimavo pact of October 30, 1964, provided that of the 975,000 stateless persons of Indian origin in Sri Lanka, registered in 1953, 300,000 persons and their descendants would be granted Sri Lankan citizenship while 525,000 their descendants would be granted Indian citizenship. The status and future of the remaining 150,000 people and their descendants would be decided later by a separate agreement. Subsequently in 1974, it was decided that both governments would grant citizenship to 150,000 persons left undecided by the 1964 pact in a 50:50 ratio.[27] The agreements could not be implemented properly because of the inherent problems associated with eviction from one's homestead. By January 31, 1989, 116,000 families had been repatriated to India but their rehabilitation was far from satisfactory.[28]

External intervention

So far, there are two cases of this variety. It includes the Tibetan refugees who crossed over into India following the Chinese annexation of Tibet and the small number of Afghan refugees, following the Soviet intervention in Afghanistan. Tibetan refugees started arriving in India first in 1950. It was during that year that the People's Republic of China started asserting its sovereignty over Tibet. However, it was only in 1959 that a large number of Tibetans fled to India and Nepal in the wake of the Chinese military action in the plateau. The reports of the International Commission of Jurists (ICJ), published in 1959 and 1966, documented several cases of religious persecution, torture, forced sterilizations and destruction of families, perpetrated by the Chinese authorities. It is difficult to ascertain the exact number of Tibetans who were forced to migrate. By 1966, it was estimated that about 80,000 to 90,000 Tibetans had taken refuge in India.[29]

The Soviet intervention in Afghanistan in December 1979 resulted in a huge inflow of Afghan refugees into

Pakistan. Some Afghans also moved to India and stayed on, mostly in Delhi. According to the UNHCR as of October 31, 1996, there were 18,500 Afghan refugees in India and most of them in Delhi.[30] Their presence attracted attention when following the hanging of former Afghan president Mohammed Najibullah by the Taliban in October 1996, Afghan refugees prevented his widow from entering a mosque in Delhi to pray for his departed soul.

The political connection

Of the seven categories mentioned above except for the first and probably the last, the movement of peoples coming across is a continuing phenomenon. In the absence of the kind of colonial and imperial system that operated in India prior to independence, there is little likelihood of a replay of the 1947 Partition. Similarly, after the end of the cold war and the growing change in the Chinese political strategy in South Asia, there is little possibility of China or Russia following an expansionist policy. But whether the phenomenon of cross-national movements of people is past or contemporary, it has a lingering effect on the politics of the country. It is, therefore, important to grapple with the issue from the perspective of the interface between the refugee problem and domestic politics.

Three points need to be borne in mind in this regard. In the first place, migrant populations affect the politics of the host country by their direct or indirect involvement in the local politics of their hosts. This has been evident in the examples of the Hindu refugees from Pakistan in Delhi and Punjab, the East Pakistani and Bangladeshi settlers in Assam and West Bengal, Nepali settlers in northern West Bengal, Sikkim and some north-eastern parts of India and the Sri Lankan Tamil refugees in Tamil Nadu.

Secondly, in all the cases of migration discussed above, there is a strong element of communal and ethnic underpinning which complicates the problem further. For example, since the majority of Bangladeshi infiltrators are Muslims, it gives a handle to the Hindu chauvinistic parties in India to communalise the issue. Similarly, Sri Lankan Tamil refugees in Tamil Nadu contribute to strengthening the Dravidian element in state politics.

Thirdly, some of the refugee groups bring with them a connection with insurgent groups active in their places of origin, thus spreading violent politics to the refugee receiving country. Sri Lankan Tamils in Tamil Nadu provide one of the best examples. As one Indian scholar noted, prior to the arrival of these refugees the political fights in the state even if they went to a physical level "rarely went beyond cycle-chains, sticks and stones. Never guns. The Jaffna 'boys' have introduced guns. That really worries the establishment, both in Tamil Nadu and in Delhi."[31]

Some conceptual issues

Population, society and politics : There is a dynamic and intricate interaction between the issues pertaining to population on the one hand and those pertaining to society and politics on the other. In India, however, population issues have largely been the forte of demographers who have not paid enough attention to this interaction.[32] It is only of late that it has been recognised by sociologists and as a result academic literature has started pouring in. In their reckoning, the basic premise is that ecological demography (a partnership between demography and human ecology) promises the most systematic and comprehensive treatment of the core of sociology, namely, the study of societies and social systems and vice versa.[33]

So far as the interaction between demographic issues and politics is concerned, it has been theoretically and empirically demonstrated that the demographic characteristics of a society invariably influence the politics of that society. The argument being that "many problems which are viewed as strictly political have, in fact, demographic roots. Conversely, policy interventions that are proposed with demographic intentions often result in distinctly political consequences. It is this dual interaction between population and politics that has contributed to the increasing politicisation of demographic issues in the world today."[34]

Demographic variations as a factor influencing politics, however, can be of various types. It can result from internal migration, increased birth rate, reduced mortality rate, cross-border migration or the dismemberment of a country. For example, the Partition of India, overnight turned the Hindus into a minority in Pakistan. Later, the secession of Bangladesh, overnight turned the Punjabis into a majority in what had been a linguistically and ethnically pluralistic Pakistan. Even such issues as abortion or sterilisation can become highly sensitive political issues. The massive defeat of the Congress party in India in 1977 was to some extent attributed to the government's forced sterilization drive.[35] Similarly, the question of abortion became a major political issue in several Muslim countries on the eve of the International Conference on Population and Development held at Cairo in September 1994. In Bangladesh mass rallies were organised to force the government to withdraw from the Conference.

Population growth and migration

Against the backdrop of Thomas Malthus's doomsday warning against England's uncontrolled population growth in the nineteenth century, the close connection between population growth and migration has been recognised. During the 1970s when the North-South dialogue was high on the intellectual agenda of the world, many tended to underemphasise the danger of population growth in the Third World on the ground that after all, the world resources, if pooled equitably, were good enough to feed many more millions. It was argued that the real problem lay with the skewed distribution system.[36] But as the years rolled by, it was evident that there was hardly any progress towards a global approach to societal problems and nation-states remained parochial in their thinking. As it has been noted, "we can speculate about how the world might get organized, but individual nation-states, as Karl Deutsch was fond of pointing out, face a condition, not a theory. This condition dictates action. To be sure, an appropriate policy for one country, given its resources, social values, and ability to organize and carry out policies, may or may not be appropriate for another country."[37] Through the ages, hardly any country has had a population policy. Instead, the easiest escape from an impending population explosion has been migration to "greener pastures".

Malthus in his celebrated "Essay on Population" (1798), had dwelt extensively upon the growth of population in England and virtually predicted its doom. Three developments seemed to have saved England, namely, the industrial revolution, the growth of the British empire and the migration of Britons in large numbers. In the 1820s more than 200,000 Britons emigrated. The figure trebled in the following decade and reached almost 2.5 million in the 1850s.

Between 1815 and 1914, around 20 million Britons left the country. In 1900, Britain's population was 41 million. Had a massive population movement not taken place, this population would have been to the tune of 70 million.[38]

The disequilibrium syndrome

Migration as a field of demographic study has been viewed differently by economists and political scientists, although both subscribe to the disequilibrium theory. In explaining cross-border migrations, economists argue that there is a disequilibrium between the sending and the receiving countries. Compared to the receiving country, in the sending country wages are low, employment opportunities are fewer and agricultural land use is low. All these result in out-migration from the sending country. The so-called "push" factor is in operation. In contrast to this, political scientists stress the disequilibrium within the sending country itself and not between the sending and the receiving country. Since there are regional and other disparities within the sending countries, the disadvantaged people migrate to other countries to escape misery. In the process, they eventually contribute to the disequilibrium in the receiving countries as well. Thus, "while economic explanations of migration induce one to think about ways to reduce economic differences between sending and receiving countries in order to reduce unwanted international population movements, political explanations for migration induce one to think about ways to resolve political differences among ethnic groups within the sending country or between a people and their government."[39] On account of this hiatus in perception "a politically driven model of international migration is a highly conflictual one, both for sending and receiving countries."[40]

Better wage-cheap labour logic

While migrants leave their country in search of better wages, prospective employers in the receiving country welcome them for the cheaper labour they provide compared to the native workers. What should logically follow from this is that there should be opposition to their entry from the labour unions. However, in the case of India as regards the Bangladeshi migrants, we see nothing like that. The Bangladeshis pose no threat to the organised labour for they are mostly unskilled and are engaged in the unorganised sector as menial workers. But even in the United States of America where illegal immigrants, particularly from Mexico, pose some sort of an economic challenge to the poor African Americans, there does not seem to be any serious opposition to these illegal Mexicans from the African Americans.[41] This suggests that immigration may not provoke any nativist reaction unless it is projected as a racial, communal or ethnic threat. Correspondingly, as the empirical evidence from South Asia suggests, where migrations are politically determined they "often diminish the ethnic heterogeneity of the country of origin whereas economic migrations have made the countries of destination more heterogeneous."[42]

Politics of inter-state migrations

The phenomenon of cross-border population movement, together with the inter-state conflicts they generate, is becoming a major concern for elites all over the world. Since the phenomenon is closely linked to the principles of self-determination, national integration and the politics of nation building, its nature and dimensions often get extremely complicated. Symptomatic of this complexity is the dissimilar stand taken by states with regard to such questions as ethnic loyalties or secessionist movements, when it is within as opposed to when it is outside their respective national boundaries. It is more a norm than an exception for a state to take a particular position with regard to these issues when it comes to dealing with it internally and quite a different one when dealing with it in respect of other nations. What should follow from this is that the external posture of a state on these questions is generally uniform. But even that is not so. It varies, depending upon the nature of the relationship that exists, at a given point of time, between and among nations.

Within the scope of cross-national migration, two broad categories of international conflicts may be considered. In the first place conflicts can be caused by population pressure upon resources leading to expansionist tendencies.[43] Secondly, clandestine population movements affect the demographic balance of the host region to the detriment of the political future of the local elites, forcing the latter to enter into a conflictual relationship with the country of origin of the migrants. In the 70s, Jacques Chirac, the former French Premier lashed out against immigrants, when he said that "a country with 900,000 unemployed but with two million immigrant workers is not a country with an insoluble labour problem". In 1973, there were brutal attacks on Algerians in Marseilles, prompting Algeria to temporarily cut off emigration to France.[44]

Of the demographic factors impinging upon politics, the most complex are those which have religious and ethno-nationalistic roots. Since both religious nationalism and ethno-nationalism draw their sustenance from human emotions which are often irrational, inter-state conflicts rooted in ethnic and religious discords are the most intractable and the most violent. Comparatively discord over resources, being much more concrete, is more amenable to a compromise, if not a solution.[45] Nazli Choukri summarizes the various political consequences of the problem of migration in the following words:

> "Population size many function as a political parameter when, for example, it generates population pressure upon resources that lead to expansionist tendencies. Population composition may be a parameter of a conflict when it sets the cleavages in a society, generating tensions that result in ethnic or religious conflict. So, too, the population distribution may be a political parameter when, for instance, tribal allegiance crosses national boundaries and generates overt conflict, or when the migration of population changes the ethnic composition of the receiving community and results in nativist reaction."[46]

Impact on domestic politics

India presents a good case study for the theory that international migrations influence the politics of the host country. From the time of the Hindu refugee influx in the wake of the Partition to date, when the country is experiencing a virtually constant flow of refugees of all kinds from neighbouring countries, though in smaller numbers, the politics of several parts of India has been influenced by the phenomenon. The ethno-religious dimension of it often makes the problem more complex.

Large-scale migration of Hindus from Pakistan after the Partition substantially influenced Hindu nationalist politics of India. The birth of the Hindu chauvinistic Bharatiya Jana Sangh in 1951 can be directly attributed to the post-independence communal strife. The linkage of the Jana Sangh with the Hindu nationalist Hindu Mahasabha and the Rashtriya Swayamsevak Sangh (RSS) is too well known to be recapitulated here. The founder of the Jana Sangh, Shyama Prasad Mukherji, constantly emphasised the refugee factor as one of the most important compulsions behind the launching of the new party. The refugee settlements, particularly in Delhi, constituted the initial base of the Jana Sangh..

Together with the Hindus, a large number of Sikhs had also arrived as refugees from Pakistan. While the Sikh ethnic identity remained as before, the Punjabi Hindu ethnic identity under went a change. The Punjabi Hindus began to identify themselves more closely with Hindi as opposed to the Sikhs who continued to emphasise what had been the common mother tongue of both, Punjabi. The origin of militant Sikh separatism that rocked Indian politics in the 70s and 80s can to some extent be traced to the communalisation of the Sikh mind after Partition. The Hindu-Sikh differences which surfaced over the question of language during the 1951 census, were largely created by the conflicting approaches of the two communities on this issue. The subsequent bifurcation of Punjab and the creation of Haryana, in the 60s, was the inevitable consequence of this controversy.[47]

Bangladeshi refugees

During the Bangladesh liberation war, millions of Bangladeshi refugees had taken refuge in India, particularly in Assam. Not all of them returned to Bangladesh after its creation. On the contrary, there was a constant flow throughout the seventies, largely on account of the deteriorating economic situation in Bangladesh. The magnitude of the flow came into sharp focus when the Indian Election Commission released the electoral lists for the state of Assam in 1979 on the eve of the 1980 parliamentary election.[48] The All Assam Students Union (AASU) which had launched an agitation in 1978 against unauthorised Bangladeshi settlers, now intensified its stir. Eventually, in August 1985, the Assam Accord was signed between the agitationists and the government of India, and a formula worked out to evict unauthorised foreigners. Considering the impracticality of the AASU demand that all be deemed "foreigners" who had arrived in India after 1951, it was eventually conceded that March 25, 1971 would be the cut-off date. All those who had arrived after that date would be repatriated. With regard to those who came between January 1, 1966 and March 24, 1971, the accord stipulated that they would continue to stay in India but would become full citizens with voting rights only after ten years.[49] Because of the almost impossible task of identifying illegal migrants, it was evident from the beginning that the accord was doomed to failure. Even after a decade, there is little evidence of illegal foreigners being actually identified and repatriated from Assam.

In 1981, there was no census in Assam due to the disturbed situation there. In 1991 when the census data suggested that the foreigners problem had been exaggerated, the then Chief Minister of Assam, Hiteshwar Saikia took full political advantage of it. He had a strong following among the Muslims and he found the census convenient to consolidate his base. Drawing attention to the fact that Assam had registered the lowest population growth of 53 percent during the last twenty years (which was a percentage point lower than the national average) and particularly much lower when compared to the other north-eastern states,[50] Saikia refuted the statement of the Union Home Minister S. B. Chavan that illegal immigration continued unabated in the state. He said emphatically that "if anybody can identify a single foreigner in Assam, I am willing to quit politics forever."[51]

But soon after Saikia's death in 1996 and with the return of the Assom Gana Parishad (AGP) to power, the foreigners issue surfaced again. Although the AGP and the AASU did not subscribe to the Bharatiya Janata Party's communal politics of treating Hindu foreigners as refugees who should be given shelter and their Muslim counterparts as "foreigners" who should be deported, their opposition to granting voting rights to 670,000 foreigners was indication enough that the pot was still boiling.[52] The Bodo threat to the Muslim settlers added an element of violence to this otherwise political problems.[53] The present demand of the Prafulla Kumar Mahanta-led AGP government of Assam is that the Illegal Migrants' (Determination by Tribunals) Act (IMDT Act) of 1985, a part of the Assam Accord, be replaced by the Foreigners Act of 1946. According to the 1946 Act the onus of proving that one was not a foreigner was on the accused, unlike in the IMDT Act where the onus was on the accuser. The United Front government at the Centre, has been sympathetic to the demand.

The demand, however, got diluted under political compulsions. The AGP has itself become ambivalent on the question. Since the replacement of the IMDT Act by the Foreigners Act was opposed by Assamese Muslims, behind whom was Congress party, it has not been an easy political decision for Mahanta to remain steadfast. Besides, the controversy had its reverberations on national politics. The Congress, the CPI, the CPI(M), the Indian Union Muslim League (IUML), all supporters of the United Front government, were opposed to any change in the situation. Home Minister Indrajit Gupta who belongs to the CPI was only prepared to accept that the "mechanisms for detection and deportation of illegal immigrants need to be strengthened."[54] Against this background Mahanta found discretion the better part of valour and his favourite phrase became "IMDT or no IMDT, we would like to make it clear that the minorities of Assam will not be harassed." Since the AGP itself had developed cold feet and there was no demand as such from any other political quarter, except sections of the AGP led by Bhrigu Kumar Phukon and Brindaban Goswami, there was hardly any justification for Prime Minister H. D. Deve Gowda's government to alter the legal position with regard to the detection of illegal foreigners.[55]

The question of infiltration of Bangladeshi nationals into India has caused considerable consternation to many Indians, most notably the supporters of the BJP. By mixing this issue with the rising population of the Muslims which the 1991 census revealed, these political forces argued that while this growth can be attributed to the disregard of the Muslims of family planning measures,[56] it is also due to unchecked Bangladeshi infiltration.[57] In Maharashtra where the Hindu chauvinistic Shiv Sena and BJP are in power the controversy is most pronounced. The Shiv Sena-backed BJP government has made a big noise against Bangladeshi slum dwellers in several parts of Bombay, where they are supposed to be concentrated.[58] In the 1996 general election, the BJP made it one of their major polls issues and campaigned vigorously in the border towns of West Bengal.[59]

The Nepali question

The growing visibility of Nepalis in India, and the fact that hard data on their numbers is almost impossible to get, has made the subject politically sensitive. The policies followed from time to time by India to restrict the flow of Nepali immigration, have served as an irritant not only to Indo-Nepal relations but also to Nepalis settled in India. Both questions are intricately linked. In October 1976, the Indian government, in response to a series of demonstrations in Nepal against India's "annexation" of Sikkim in August 1975, imposed a Restricted Area Permit on all foreigners, including Nepalis. Thus restrictions were put on the travel on Nepalis to certain areas including parts of Arunachal Pradesh, Assam, Manipur, Meghalaya, Nagaland, Sikkim, Tripura, Uttar Pradesh and West Bengal. Considering the fact that India and Nepal are tradition and treaty bound by India-Nepal Treaty of Peace and Friendship of 1950 to keep their borders open, Nepal resented the decision.

Various state governments of India have imposed this requirement of a restricted area permit to restrict the immigration of Nepalis to their states to the detriment of local Nepali political interests. Indeed, the restrictions caused difficulties not only to prospective Nepali emigrants but also to about five million Indian nationals of Nepali ethnic origin who have close relatives living in Nepal. The government of India, however, has not eased upon this requirement. Even the Janata government (1977-80) which was committed to improving relations with neighbouring countries did not alter the decision. In 1980, the government introduced a system of identity cards in the state of Sikkim to control Nepali emigration into the state and thereby prevent distortions in the electoral rolls.

The Nepali question in Indian politics is a curious mixture of the politics of Nepali nationals on Indian soil and that of ethnic Nepalis of Indian nationality. The question found its most articulated political expression in the politics of Nar Bahadur Bhandari of Sikkim and that of Subash Ghising, the leader of the Gorkha National Liberation Front (GNLF) of Darjeeling in West Bengal. The GNLF movement assumed international dimensions when on December 23, 1986, Ghising wrote a letter to the King of Nepal. Copies of the letter, 16 in all, were endorsed to various governments and international agencies. It pleaded for justice for "the unpardonable historical crimes against humanity on the still unresolved question of the very political existence or future status of ... Gorkha in the Indian Union." It sought "fresh new treaties for a permanent political settlement of the ... victimised Gorkhas as per ... the provisions of the Charter of the United Nations" taking into account "the future status of their ceded land and territories."[60]

In Assam, too, the Nepalis were unhappy at Rajiv Gandhi's statement in December 1986 in Darjeeling that there was no question of granting citizenship rights to Nepalis who had immigrated after 1950. Protesting against this, the Assam Gorkha Sammelan and the All Assam Gorkha Students Union argued that it was unethical to brand one section of immigrants as citizens, the Bangladeshis, and the others as not.[61]

India and Sri Lanka

The Sri Lankan Tamil refugees in India presented a problem for Indian politics which was somewhat unique compared to other situations, namely, the Bangladeshi or Nepali nationals in India or Hindu refugees in the aftermath of the Partition. The number of Sri Lankan Tamil refugees has never been large yet they disproportionately influenced the politics of Tamil Nadu where the majority of them had taken shelter. On account of the very nature of Tamil Nadu politics and the emotive response that the refugees evoked locally, the problem assumed relevance for Indian politics, particularly so as Tamil Nadu had a record of nurturing a secessionist movement during an earlier phase. Both the contenders for power in Tamil Nadu — the Dravida Munnetra Kazhagam (DMK) and the All India Anna Dravida Munnetra Kazhagam (AIADMK) — relied heavily on their capacity to project themselves as the champions of the Tamil cause.

The Congress party ruling at the centre kept shifting its alliance, from one to the other, depending upon the prevailing political exigency. As it happens in this kind of a competitive situation, the party in the opposition had the added compulsion to assume an ultra-chauvinistic stance to which the ruling party was forced to respond in almost equal terms.

The intermeshing of Sri Lanka Tamil politics with that of Tamil Nadu and then with that of India at the national level, found its most dramatic expression in the assassination of Rajiv Gandhi in the run up to the parliamentary elections of 1991. The assassination which was masterminded by a suicide squad of LTTE took place on Tamil Nadu soil itself. As a result the ruling DMK government came under severe political pressure from its rival, the AIADMK, which routed the former in the assembly elections that took place in January 1992. At present, although the DMK is back in power with the support for the Tamil Maanila Congress, a splinter group of the Congress Party, the Sri Lanka Tamil factor is for the time being dormant. However, it has the potential to assume centrestage.

In perspective

One of the paradoxes of the problem associated with refugees in India — "teflon citizenship meets symbolic xenophobia" [62] — has been the way in which the political rhetoric of expulsion of unauthorised immigrants has increased in direct proportion to the inability of politicians and the state to control their movement. The problem, indeed, is both massive and complex. Almost all the types of immigration that we have discussed, are a continuing phenomenon and given the regional disparities and security-related asymmetries among the nations of South Asia, they are likely to accentuate. But what would really keep the pot boiling is the massive poverty of the region and the regional strategic asymmetries.

South Asia is one of the poorest regions of the world. Within the region, according to the World Development Report, India is poorer than most of the other states. Still, the on-going migrations are mostly towards India and not vice-versa. Regional development is lopsided in each of the South Asian nations. But for countries like Bangladesh and Nepal, being small in size, their capacity to absorb internal economic migrations is extremely limited. India provides a vast area where somewhere or the other, these migrants can earn a better livelihood.

The relevant literature on how to control illegal immigration is generally West-centric. As such, the problem has been viewed primarily from a North-South perspective. Some of the strategies being considered in the developed countries in relation to illegal migration, include more trade relations with the immigrant countries, more foreign direct investment and official development assistance.[63] Yet another strategy that has been worked out, particularly in France, is not to focus on totally eliminating the possibility of illegal immigration but to prevent illegal employment which would automatically discourage illegal immigration.[64]

None of these strategies seem to be effective in the Indian situation. Barring Bangladeshi and Nepali immigrants, all the other kinds have arrived in India for reasons other than economic. Even for Bangladeshi and the Nepali immigrants, the above-mentioned strategies have little relevance. With Nepal, apart from a treaty agreement which allows free entry of Nepalis to India, there exists wide ranging trade and aid relations. The same is true with Bangladesh. With regard to the solution about preventing illegal work, it may be said that most of the illegal immigrants are employed in the unorganised sector as domestic servants or daily wage earners, which no law can check, particularly when law enforcement itself is weak. There are other related problems as well. For example, given the rise in the crime graph, the police department of Delhi now insists on the registration of domestic servants with them. As a result, whenever a Nepali servant is caught for some crime, a whole lot of Nepali servants are rounded up causing consternation amongst the local Nepali community.

An Assamese author has suggested a solution which is worth considering, although it has several problematic economic and social implications. According to this : "India can consider issuing a residential and work permit along with traveling and re-entry permits for the same period to all foreigners, irrespective of their country of origin, after detecting and registering them. These people must be divested of voting rights in the elections to state assembly and parliament but may be allowed civic rights at the local level. They may be provided reasonable civic amenities, their rights may be protected by suitable legislations and part of their income may be allowed to be repatriated to their families back home. Such a humane, practical and profitable policy will ensure that the poor of our neighbouring countries are not uprooted from their hearths and homes and keep their roots intact. In most cases the families will stay back. This will also greatly diminish social tensions in Assam and the north-east."[65] But what would happen to those who get lost in the Indian crowd after the expiry of the permits. Let alone India, even the United States has not been able to prevent this from happening. In 1990, there were 90,000 illegal over-stayers in America.[66]

What is the solution then ? Barricades, fences and forcible evictions ? None of them has worked so far, nor is there any possibility of their working in the future, given the history, geography and society of the region. Probably there is no enduring solution. At best what can be expected is a reasonable management of the situation, from which there is no escape, through regional cooperation among the concerned states under the aegis of the SAARC.

NOTES

1. A.K.M. Nurun Nabi and P. Krishnan, "Some Approaches to the Study of Human Migration," in Kuttan Mahadevan and Parameswara Krishnan, (eds), *Methodologies for Population Studies and Development,* New Delhi, Sage, 1993, p. 83.
2. Ibid., p. 85.
3. S. D. Muni and Lok Raj Baral, (eds), *Refugees and Regional Security in South Asia,* New Delhi, Konark, 1996, pp. 2-5.
4. There cannot be any exact estimation of these refugee flows. But the figures given here are generally accepted to be accurate. See O.H.K. Spate, *India and Pakistan : A General and Regional Geography,* London, Methuen, 1957, p. 119. Also see Kingsley Davis, "India and Pakistan : The Demography of Partition", *Pacific Affairs, 22,* Vancouver, 1949, pp. 254-64.
5. Indian Commission of Jurists, *Recurrent Exodus of Minorities from East Pakistan and Disturbances in India : A Report to the Indian Commission of Jurists by its Committee of Enquiry,* New Delhi, 1965, pp. 309-12. For detailed figures of Bangladeshi immigration into Tripura, see Gayatri Bhattacharya, "Refugee Rehabilitation and its Impact on Tripura's Economy," Ph.D. dissertation, University of Calcutta, 1978, pp. 19-20.
6. Bertram Bastiampillai, "Sri Lanka Tamil Refugees in Tamil Nadu : Trouble to the Host," in Muni and Baral, (eds), *Refugees and Regional Security in South Asia,* p. 195.

7. V. Suryanarayan, "Sri Lanka Tamil Refugees in Tamil Nadu", in ibid., pp. 221-22.
8. V. Suryanarayan, "New Challenges in Sri Lanka," *The Hindu*, 10 July 1996.
9. *The Hindu*, 6 October 1996.
10. Myron Weiner, "Rejected Peoples and Unwanted Migrants in South Asia", *Economic and Political Weekly,* Bombay, 21 August 1993, p. 1738.
11. Ibid., 12 February 1996.
12. K.N. Sud, "Nepalese in India", *Hindustan Times,* New Delhi, 9 September 1975; A.C. Sinha, "Immigrants from Nepal," *The Statesman* New Delhi, 17 April 1982; Rudraman Thapa, "Nepali Migration into Assam: In Retrospect", *Journal of Politics,* Dibrugarh, 2, March 1995, pp. 86, 88.
13. N. N. Jha, "Minorities, Immigrants and Refugee Issues Both in the Context of India and India-Nepal Relations", Paper presented at the India-Nepal Colloquium, New Delhi, 26-28 September 1994, p. 7.
14. At the time of Partition, it was the border between India and East Pakistan.
15. Ranabir Samaddar, "A Twilight Zone that Divides a Road, a Village and a People," *The Asian Age,* 21 November 1995. The question of about 50,000 Indians in enclaves in Bangladesh also remains unresolved. While the transfer of Tin Bigha corridor to Bangladesh has given the latter access to its enclaves on Indian soil there has been no reciprocal arrangement to give India access to these enclaves. For details, see ibid., 21 October 1996. Migration of East Bengalis to the neighbouring Assam and Tripura also has a long tradition. The process continued even after the partition of India. See Lalit K. Pathak, "East Bengal Immigrants in Assam Valley - An Analysis of Census Data", Srinath Baruah, "Immigration Problem and Population Trend in Assam," and other articles in B. Datta Ray, (ed), *The Pattern and Problems of Population in North-East,* New Delhi, Uppal, 1986.
16. Ashish K. Biswas, "The Unchecked Influx," *The Hindu,* Madras, 17 February 1982.

17. Imtiaz Ahmed, "Refugee and Security," in Muni and Baral, *Refugees and Regional Security*, pp. 143, 150.
18. *Times of India*, 31 March 1995.
19. *India Today*, 30 April 1995, p. 79. The corresponding figure for Pakistan was 590.
20. As per some estimates, there were about 1.3 million illegal immigrants in the north-eastern states and West Bengal. See, S. Mukerji, "Migration in Easter India : How much of it is illegal", *The Journal of Family Welfare,* 37(3), September 1991, p. 71.
21. *India Today,* New Delhi, 15 September 1985, p. 53
22. The facelift that the canal has given to the local economy has been discussed in B.G. Verghese, *Winning the Future: From Bhakra to Narmada, Tehri, Rajasthan Canal,* New Delhi, Konark, 1994, pp. 67-73.
23. *Sunday,* Calcutta, 10-16 November 1985, pp. 15-22. See also *The Hindu*, 4 July 1995, for a recent report on the phenomenon.
24. *The Hindu*, 3 August 1987.
25. *Asian Age*, 5 April 1995; *Times of India*, 7 April 1995
26. For a detailed analysis, see Ashok Swain, *The Environmental Trap: The Ganges River Division, Bangladeshi Migration and Conflicts in India*, Report No. 41, Department of Peace and Conflict Research, Uppsala University, Sweden, 1996. See also Thomas Homer-Dixon and Valerie Percival, *Environmental Security and Violent Conflict : Briefing Book,* American Association for the Advancement of Science and the University of Toronto, 1996, pp. 10-16.
27. For details, See Partha S. Ghosh, *Cooperation and Conflict in South Asia,* New Delhi, Manohar, 1989, pp. 155-61.
28. L. Vedavalli, *Socio-Economic Profile of Sri Lankan Repatriates in Kotagiri,* New Delhi, Konark, 1994, pp. 38-39, 46-49, 154-55. See also Partha S. Ghosh, "The Other Tamils," *The Statesman,* 8 September 1990.
29. Dawa Norbu, "Refugees from Tibet : Structural Causes of Successful Settlement," paper presented to the Fourth International Research and Advisory Panel Conference on Forced Migration, Oxford University, 5-9 January 1994, pp. 1-3.

30. *Asian Age,* 1 May 1995.
31. Quoted by Mervyn de Silva, "Will the Ceasefire Hold?, *Lanka Guardian*, Colombo, 8(7), 1 August 1985. The scholar was not identified.
32. R. Jayasree, K.B. Kurup, Dominic E. Azuh and N. Audinarayana, "Population Research in India : 1970-1990," in P. Krishnan, Chi-Hsien Tuan and Kuttan Mahadevan, *Readings in Population Research : Policy, Methodology, Perspectives,* Delhi, B. R. Publishing, 1992, pp. 485-557.
33. For more on the point and relevant literature, see N. Krishnan Namboodiri, "Ecological Demography : Its Place in Sociology," in ibid., pp. 321-49.
34. Nazli Choucri, "The Pervasiveness of Politics",*Populi,* New York, 5(3), 1978, p. 30. See also W. Howard Wriggings and James F. Guyot, "Demographic Change and Politics : An Introduction," in W. Howard Wriggins and James F. Guyot, (eds), *Population, Politics, and the Future of Southern Asia*, New York, Columbia University Press, 1973, pp. 1-29.
35. V. A. Pai Panandiker and P.K. Umashankar, "Fertility Control-Induced Politics of India", monograph, Centre for Policy Research, New Delhi, June 1994.
36. This author was one of them. See Partha S. Ghosh, "On Drawing a Red Herring",*Alternatives* New Delhi/ New York, 8(1), 1982, pp. 131-138.
37. Richard L. Merritt, "Population Imbalance and Political Destabilization," *International Political Science Review*, 16(4), October 1995, pp. 412-13.
38. Paul Kennedy, *Preparing for the Twenty-First Century* New York, Random House, 1993, pp. 4-5.
39. Weiner, *Rejected Peoples*, pp. 1745-46.
40. Ibid., p. 1745
41. Lawrence H. Fuchs, "An Agenda for Tomorrow : Immigration Policy and Ethnic Policies," *Annals* Philadelphia, No. 530, November 1993, pp. 174-77.
42. Weiner, *Rejected Peoples*, p.1745.
43. S. Chandrasekhar, *Hungry People and Empty Lands : An Essay on Population Problems and International Tensions* London, George Allen and Unwin, 1954, pp. 102-6

44. Kathleen Newland, *International Migration : The Search for Work* Worldwatch Paper 33 Washington, D.C., November 1979, p. 23.
45. Robert Mandel, "Roots of the Modern Inter-State Border Dispute," *Journal of Conflict Resolution,* London, 24(3), September 1980, p. 435.
46. Choucri, "The Pervasiveness of Politics." For details, see her *Population Dynamics and Violence : Propositions, Insights and Evidence* Lexington, D. C. Health, Lexington Books, 1974; Nazli Choucri and Robert C. North, *Nations in Conflict : National Growth and International Violence* San Francisco, W. H. Freeman, 1975; Robert C. North, *The World that Could Be* Stanford, Stanford University Alumni Association, 1976. See also the chapter on "The Causes and Consequences of Migration," in J. Beaujeu-Garnier, *Geography of Population* London : Longman, 1978.
47. Satya M. Rai, *Partition of the Punjab : A Study of its Effects on the Politics and Administration of the Punjab (1) 1947-56* Bombay, Asia Publishers, 1965, pp. 198-205.
48. Myron Weiner, "Immigration : Prespectives from Receiving Countries," *Third World Quarterly* London, 12 (1), January 1990, pp. 157-58. Assam's Muslim population indeed has grown disproportionately during the present century largely on account of migrations from the neighbouring Bengal province during the British period and after independence from East Pakistan/Bangladesh. See Pathak, pp. 106-24; Biman Kar, pp. 285-96; all in Datta Ray, *The Pattern and Problems.* Also see Mukherji, *Migration in Eastern India,* pp. 69-73.
49. *India Today*, 15 September 1985, p. 27.
50. For details of the census date, see Raghubir Chand and Mahavir Chand Thakur, "Changing Population Profile," *Seminar* New Delhi, No. 378, February 1991, pp. 19-23.
51. *Times of India*, 22 August 1994.
52. *The Hindu*, 7 January 1996.

53. In 1994, Bodo attacks on Muslim villages turned 50,000 villagers into refugees, *India Today* 31 August 1994, pp. 68-71.
54. *Times of India*, 10 June 1996 and 13 September 1996.
55. *The Hindu*, 27 November 1996. Also see, Barun Das Gupta, "Gunning for Mahanta," ibid., December 8, 1996.
56. Some relevant literature are as follows : R.B.N. Sinha, "Attitudes of Hindus and Muslims to Family Planning," *The Journal of Family Welfare* Bombay, 37,(2), June 1991, pp. 47-49; Malika B. Mistry, "Hindu-Muslim Fertility Differentials in India," *New Quest* Pune, No. 94, July August 1992, p. 236; Pravin Visaria and Leela Visaria, "Demographic Transition : Accelerating Fertility Decline in 1980s," *Economic and Political Weekly*, 17-24 December 1994 p. 3286.
57. See the resolutions adopted by the BJP at its national executive meetings held on 27 February 1993 at New Delhi and on 10, 11 and 12 April 1993 at Calcutta. *BJP Pamphlet*, New Delhi, n.d. See also the interview of noted demographer Ashish Bose in the *Times of India,* 2 December 1995. According to him : "The Muslim growth rate is substantially higher. If we assume that the Muslims are growing at the same rate as Hindus and growth rate is two percent every year, then migration is about 33 percent . But the truth lies somewhere in between. Migration could account for 15 to 33 per cent of the increase."
58. For details, see *India Today.* 30 April 1995, pp. 78-79.
59. *Asian Age,* 25 April 1996.
60. Text of the letter in *The Hindu*, 24 December 1986.
61. Lok Raj Baral, *Regional Migrations, Ethnicity and Security: The South Asian Case,* New Delhi, Sterling, 1990, p. 55.
62. The phrase has been borrowed from the report prepared by John Stone for a workshop organised by the Woodrow Wilson Center, Washington, D.C., on "Ethnic Conflict in the Post-Cold War Era: Problems in Advanced Industrial Societies," January 1995, p. 5.

63. W.R. Bohning, "Helping Migrants to Stay at Home," and Gary P. Freeman, "Can Liberal States Control Unwanted Migration?," *The Annals* Philadelphia, No.l 534, July 1994, pp. 165-77 and 25-27 respectively. See also, Doris Meissner, "Managing Migrations," *Foreign Policy* No. 86, Spring 1992, pp. 66-83.
64. Claude-Valentin Marie, "From the Campaign against Illegal Migration to the Campaign against IllegalWork," *The Annals* Philadelphia, No. 534, July 1994, pp. 118-32.
65. Dhruba Jyoti Borah, "Social Alienation and Tension in the North-East," paper presented to the symposium on "Focus on North-East" on the occasion ofThe Shillong Times Golden Jubilee.
66. Freeman, "Can Liberal States Control Unwanted Migration?," p. 23.

Sri Lankan Tamil Refugees in India
Accords, people and UNHCR

Fr. C. Amal Raj

A nation cannot be built by employment of force. It can be built by getting the diverse people in a plural society involved and committed to unity. This could happen if the diverse groups are trusted by the numerically dominant and entrusted with the responsibility for engaging in nation building as equals; then the clamour for separation is rendered meaningless. In finalising the devolution proposals it should be recognized that only the strong can afford to compromise, the weak could negotiate.

Betram Bastiampillai
Ombudsman
Human Rights in Sri Lanka

Sri Lanka, a tiny island of 25,000 sq km in the Indian Ocean, just thirty km from India, is inhabited by two fiercely competitive races, the Sinhalese and the Tamils, both migrants from India. Ethnic harmony was short circuited when the ruling class started using linguistic differences for parochial political ends. The Tamils felt aggrieved by the aggressive ethnic postures of the Sinhalese politicians. The Sinhala Only policy,[1] the reservation policy coupled with the government aided colonisation policy and the gradual disappearance of the Tamil language from official usage, eroded the confidence of Tamils. From 1954 they struggled through non-violent means.

As the US Committee for Refugees, describes it, "for two decades younger generations of Tamil watched a succession of Sinhalese dominated governments conspire to undermine cultural heritage, linguistic rights, traditional homelands and educational and employment opportunities. They watched their own leadership suffer defeat upon humiliating defeat in Parliament in a futile effort to secure at least equal rights or limited autonomy."

After occasional ethnic riots and some sterile interludes of dialogue, communal carnage erupted with fury in June 1983. An estimated 5,000 Tamils were burnt during one night in a pogrom of violence. "In three days of rioting some 200,000 people were driven from their homes. Between 27,000 to 30,000 sought refuge in India".[3]

India's role in the Sri Lankan crisis springs from more than having to play host to thousands of Tamil refugees. Culture and economics makes Sri Lanka very important to India. Moreover, Sri Lanka has the potential to complicate India's security. The location of the strategic natural harbor of Trincomallee had drawn in the big powers into the region during the cold war era. Sri Lankan politicians also tend to use the enmity of India and Pakistan to their own advantage. When there used to be two wings of Pakistan, in times of war, it was Sri Lanka which provided refueling facilities for planes from West Pakistan.

Sri Lanka has squeezed out concessions from the Indian government by threatening to provide facilities to the big powers. One such concession was the Srimavao-Shastri pact considered by many as paving the way for the first refugee flow from Sri Lanka. 500,000 Tamils of Indian origin were made stateless and sent back to India.

When India was actively involved in the "liberation" of Bangladesh, refueling facilities were made available to Pakistani aircraft by Sri Lanka. Prime Minister Indira Gandhi, was not pleased. An opportunity to get back at the Sri Lankan government soon offered itself in the form of support for disgruntled Sri Lankan Tamil students in Madras. India's successful adventure in East Pakistan by organizing local guerrilla groups, encouraged Indian rulers to try an "encore" in Sri Lanka. Tamil militant groups were born. As Rajesh Kadian in *India's Sri Lanka Fiasco*[4] documents, at first, there were 27 militant groups, but slowly five groups became dominant— LTTE, PLOTE, TELO, EPRLF and EROS. Indian officials both in the formal and covert foreign policy establishments saw it in their interest to keep the groups divided, while Indian politicians entangled them in competitive local politics.

Sympathy for the Tamil cause ran very high in India till the mid-80s. Both the central and state government of Tamil Nadu encouraged a frenzy of emotional support with the media becoming a willing ally by highlighting the atrocities committed against the Tamil peoples. Emboldened by the sympathy of India and backed by sophisticated training in arms and strategy, the militant groups launched some daring attacks against the Sri Lankan government. The Sinhala politicians exploited the opportunity to set the majority Sinhalese community against the Tamils. The violence that erupted in July 1983 shocked the world.

Prime Minister Rajiv Gandhi brokered a peace accord on July 29, 1987 between the Sri Lankan government and the Tamil militant groups. The refugees went back hoping to live in peace. But the fragile peace accord put together over the heads of the Tamil militant groups, especially the LTTE, fell through. The LTTE fought a ferocious war against the Indian Peace Keeping Force (IPKF) killing 1,155 Indian soldiers, the highest in any war fought by India.

Under pressure from both the Sri Lankan government and the LTTE, India withdrew in March 1990. Two months later, on June 11, LTTE guerrillas attacked 17 police stations in the eastern province and captured an estimated 600 policemen. Eelam war II started and by July 880,000 people were displaced all over the island in 640 welfare centers. By 1991, 210,000 refugees had fled to India again.

Fear of human rights violations, fear of random violence and fear of persecution has seen an increased flow of refugees. According to statistics released by the Rehabilitation Ministry of the Sri Lankan government, in July 1996, there were 810,000 internally displaced people. Operation *Satjaya* (True Victory) launched in July 1996 in Killinochchi displaced nearly 200,000 more. In October, Operation Riversea, displaced thousands more from Jaffna. Some 20,000 moved towards Vauniya. *1*

Army commanders in the border town of Vavuniya control the flow of food into LTTE held areas where l,600,000 people still live. Delaying tactics and limiting food supplies, effectively draws the starving multitude towards the army controlled zones. Refugees reaching India, speak of continuous starvation. This is in total contravention to the Geneva Conventions of 1949 and the Second Additional Protocol of 1977. Sri Lanka has ratified this Convention. Article 17 (1) of Protocol II, specifically forbids starvation of civilians as a method of combat including attacking or removing for that purpose "objects indispensable to the survival of the civilian population such as foodstuffs."

As the International Committee of the Red Cross (ICRC) commentary makes clear, Protocol II does not allow the argument of military necessity to be used to justify starving the civilian population. As soon as there is a lack of "indispensable objects", international relief action provided for in the Article 18 should be authorised to fulfil the obligation following from Article 14. ICRC further elaborates: "The fact that consent is required for a relief action to be undertaken does not mean that the decision is left to the discretion of the parties. If the survival of the population is threatened and a humanitarian organization fulfilling the required conditions of impartiality and non-discrimination is able to remedy this situation, relief actions must take place."[5]

The food embargo was relaxed in August 1991 but by the end of the year there was still a lengthy list of prohibited items, including medicines, soya based food, sanitary napkins, surgical equipment, bandages, batteries, gasoline and matches. All goods transported to the north-east are subject to military approval and anything which is potentially useful to the militants is banned, no matter how essential to the general public. The embargo was relaxed again during the peace interlude in 1995, but was reimposed the next day, after the LTTE broke off the peace talks. A desperate people are forced to fall back on a flourishing back market where things are sold at ten times the market price .

The whole of Mannar Island has been reclassified as a "conflict zone" by the army after the recent attacks by the LTTE from the Mannar mainland. In October 1996, the UNHCR representative in India, Irene Khan confirmed[6] that the Sri Lankan army entered the UNHCR camp in Pesalai in Mannar Island. This set off another exodus of refugees back to India. 750 refugees fled in August 1996 and another 1,000 in September. The refugees alleged that the security forces were rounding up young boys and girls and taking them to the barracks, causing panic among those who had sought refuge in the Pesalai camp.

The majority of the people who fled to India had been repatriated from India just four years before. The UNHCR has been obliged to play a role which is more in consonance with the interests of the two governments rather than humanitarian considerations. This is evident from the reports of Asia Watch on the repatriation process. Its August 11, 1993 report stated that, UNHCR and Sri Lankan government officials had both assured that the refugees received adequate information from "informal channels of communication" about conditions in Sri Lanka. Given the repeated complaints of refugees in both countries about curtailed mail delivery such reassurances are not convincing. Letters from home are the best source of information about security.

Many repatriates in camps in Sri Lanka told Asia Watch that they had little idea about the conditions to which they were returning. Many were given the false impression that they would be able to go back to their villages. Most indicated that they left India because conditions in the camps had become intolerable, because officials pressure them to leave and because they expected to be able to return to the homes they had left. In spite of the plea of many to not to be sent back to a war zone, the Indian government had thrown them back into an area of high density conflict.

This is in contravention of the right of *non-refoulement* which is the basis of refugee protection. Article 33 of the 1951 Convention on the Status of Refugees and the 1967 Protocol, prohibits the repatriation of refugees to countries where life or fundamental freedoms would be endangered. *Non-refoulement* provisions are also included in Article 3 of the Declaration on Territorial Asylum and in other UN Documents. Although the Indian government has not acceded to the 1951 Conventions the right of *non-refoulement* is accepted as customary international law, regardless of a country's accession to specific UN instruments.

India's displeasure at the latest influx of refugees has forced the Sri Lankan security forces to fortify the transit camps in Pesalai. But more people from the Vanni region are also moving towards Vidathathivu in an effort to come to India. According to the refugees who reached India in 1996, 30,000 were waiting to cross over.

Both the Sri Lankan army and the LTTE continue to hold on to and draw in people into the zones held by them. The 24 hour pass system and the age limit system, namely, no passes for people below 26 years, hamper the movement of people from LTTE-held zone. Neutral agencies are kept out of the process of registering new arrivals in the Veppankulam camps in Vavuniya. The army continues to pick up youngsters coming out of LTTE zones. The use of non-LTTE militant groups to screen newcomers is a matter of deep concern.

The government determines the movement of NGOs. Inside the LTTE-held zones, its frontline organization the Tamil Rehabilitation Organization (TRO) controls NGO activities. A section of the Buddhist clergy continues to term any NGO activity as "pro-LTTE activity" In the east, complaints are heard that Muslims continue to get favoured treatment in rehabilitation. In villages surrounding Kalmunai this discriminatory treatment is evident.

India and Sri Lankan refugees

After every outbreak of violence, civilians have been forced to flee to India. The decision to flee is not taken lightly.

Those who flee do so because they are in danger of being killed, tortured forcibly recruited , raped, abducted or starved. Once a family decides to leave it usually treks along jungle trails avoiding minefields, sometimes walking for 21 days at a stretch before reaching a boat that can take the family to India. Women and children have to survive a night's ordeal in the rough sea. When they reach the northern-most point of the island, boats can ferry them to the Indian side. Middlemen charge as much as Rs. 1,000 per head for a journey that would ordinarily cost Rs. 150. Boats meant for ten, load forty. Rejected by the country of their birth, tossed on the waves, the refugees survive the journey only if they can get away from the ever vigilant Sri Lankan navy patrols. If they are caught, the young among them are taken south never to be heard of afterward. Occasionally the restless sea demands its pound of flesh, gulping in an overcrowded boat. Boatmen often become greedy and in the middle of the sea they ask for more gold. Death of children is a regular occurrence in the boat.

Life in the refugee camps

Initially, faced with an emergency situation, the Tamil Nadu government accommodated the refugees in ad hoc shelters. The Indian government was loath to send the refugees to other Indian states because of the language barrier. Camp sites were a yard, a marketplace, rice godowns or even open air toilets. Hutments put up for just a month in 1990, continue to shelter some 58,000 Sri Lankan Tamils in 100 camps in Tamil Nadu. Physical conditions in the camps are deplorable. The extensive damage to physical surroundings has reduced the camps to a culture of slums. Housed in temporary hutments made of tar sheets, the scorching heat makes life in the camp intolerable. Each refugee is given a *per diem* of Rs 5 (20 cents), obviously inadequate, considering the fact that most of the Sri Lankan Tamils use coconut in their food.

A welcome feature has been the lifting of the ban on educational facilities. But the ban on NGOs continues and the UNHCR is still not allowed direct access. As India refuses to accede to international protection regimes for refugees, international aid agencies do not have access to the camps.

Social scientists find refugees disoriented beings. The refugee mind is in constant confusion. His life is determined by officials of an alien land. His "house" is restricted, his movement monitored and his food rationed. He is an object under the gaze of officials and charity groups, denied even a modicum of privacy. Life is oppressively monotonous. This disintegration of his sense of self is an aspect rarely considered. On top of this he lives in the midst of a hostile environment where local politicians have made the Sri Lankan Tamils a scapegoat for all ills.

After the assassination of Rajiv Gandhi, allegedly by an LTTE suicide bomber, the refugees have got sucked into a whirlpool of fear and insecurity. The common man in Tamil Nadu is convinced that any Sri Lankan Tamil is a militant. In 1983 the refugee was welcomed as a wounded brother but since 1991 he is seen as somebody who wounds you.

The refugees have been subjected to arbitrary arrests, detention, coercion and violations of the principle of *non-refoulement*. In 1990 January, the Tamil Nadu government picked up 1,700 camp refugees, including 72 children below 12, and incarcerated them in Vellore till 1995. They were kept in maximum security prison in Vellore and the government indulged in a gymnastics of nomenclature calling them "special camps" to protect "vulnerable" refugees.

Appeals to UNHCR to uphold its protection mandate in India, failed to yield any response.

Among the new arrivals, the Tamil Nadu police have arrested 18 boys and moved them to a "special jail". In addition 87 refugees still continue to be in the special camps of Chenglepet and Vellore. Except for a few hard-core militants, most others are ordinary refugees picked up from the various camps under the Foreigners Act by the previous state government.

Government policies towards refugees are ad hoc and on occasion refugees have been used for political leverage. India tends to politically manipulate its humanitarian response. Its relationship with UNHCR has been an uneasy one. Like all other SAARC countries in the region, India, continues to be firm against any direct involvement. After the Bangladesh relief operation where UNHCR played a major role. UNHCR closed its offices in Delhi in the early 80s. The Afghan and Sri Lankan crisis brought thousands of refugees again to India and a fresh role for UNHCR in India.

UNHCR compromising its protection mandate

In India the UNHCR is allowed a limited protection role but NGOs concerned with refugee relief work feel that UNHCR, instead of maximising the mandate allowed by local governments, has colluded with the Indian government in hastily repatriating the refugees back to Sri Lanka. In rushing through the 1992 repatriation of refugees, without taking into adequate consideration the situation on the ground, UNHCR gave legitimacy to what was an act of deportation by the Indian government. As part of its protection mandate, the UNHCR is expected to share information with the Tamil refugees about the conflict situation in the country of origin. It informed the refugees that "certain liberated zones" were safe for them to go back to. Repatriated back to Sri Lanka, the refugees found that they could not go back to their native place. Many sought refuge again, in the Pesalai camp and other UNHCR-run transit camps. With the outbreak of fresh conflicts, the refugees are returning to India.

In Sri Lanka, the UNHCR has tried out the novel concept of open relief camps, namely, camps where people can come from the villages and stay in case of an emergency and go back. How fragile the sanctity of these sanctuaries are, was tragically exposed when the Sri Lankan army stormed into the Pesalai sanctuary in July 1996 and picked up refugees for questioning. This was in violation of the understanding that no group will enter any UNHCR camp. Army harassment resulted in the flight to India by some 74 families from the camps. Protest from the government of India against the fresh influx of refugees, has pushed the Sri Lankan authorities to lay a virtual siege on the UNHCR camp in Pesalai. The recent arrivals from the UNHCR-run camps to India indicate that all the refugees want to flee back to India.

In the wake of the historic Jaffna exodus in October 1995, UNHCR's efforts to strengthen its office in Killinochchi with communications equipment was thwarted by the army. The army in an effort to draw to civilians towards its zone prevented the UNHCR food conveys from crossing into the conflict zones. After Operation *Satjaya* in July and August 1996, three weeks of starvation forced the people to come to the army zone. UNHCR's protests were feeble.

UNHCR in South Asia exists at the will and sufferance of local governments, none of whom have acceded to the international protection regime. UNHCR in its 1996 report to the Excom indicated that its overall programme objective in India was "to solicit greater participation of Indian Government and organizations and institutions dealing with refugee affairs in order to create greater public awareness of refugee situations and issues in India and promote a legal framework for the protection of refugees".[7]

But UNHCR in the process of not alienating local governments, has politically colluded with the Indian government in acknowledging who is a refugee and who is not. The 58,000 Sri Lankan Tamil refugees in India are not listed in the UNHCR World Survey of Refugees. The Indian government has denied UNHCR access to them.[8]

The death of more than 40,000 civilians in Sri Lanka and the massive displacement of people, calls for an urgent regional effort. As a starting point both groups, the Sri Lankan government and the militant groups, should start by respecting the basic rights of movement, food and shelter for civilians in the conflict zone. In civilian areas the use of aerial bombing and mortal shelling must be stopped. A safe zone for fleeing refugees can be created in Vavuniya and Mannar Island and these can be monitored by an international body. Free Access to NGOs, both in Sri Lanka and India must be encouraged. International monitoring of the refugee movement inside Sri Lanka is very vital.

Notes

1. The Sinhala Only Act of 1956 makes Sinhala the sole official language. Mr S W R D Bandaranaike, the father of the present President was then Prime Minister Also in July 1957 after widespread language riots, Prime

Minister Mr. Bandarnaike concluded a pact with Mr. S J V Chelvanayakam, the Tamil leader, called The Bandaranike- Chelvanayakam Pact 1957. Parity of languages and certain devolution of powers through regional councils for north and eastern provinces was provided for. Mr. J R Jayawardene led the opposition to the Pact resulting in the ignominious abrogation of the pact by Mr. Bandaranike.

2. *World Refugee Survey 1996*, US Committee for Refugees, Washington D.C., 1996. p 5.
3. ibid.
4. See Rajesh Kadian *India's Sri Lanka Fiasco*, Vision Books, New Delhi, 1990.
5. *Asia Watch* April 23, 1993.
6. *The Hindu,* October 17, 1996.
7. What is disturbing is that in the list of partners named by UNHCR in India, namely, National Law School in Bangalore, Indian Center for Humanitarian Laws and Research, Delhi, Aware, Andhra Pradesh and Voluntary Health Association of India, there are no field-based or human rights organisations. Owing to the ban on NGO involvement in refugee welfare work in India and the continued attacks on NGOs in Sri Lanka, a forum for Protection of South Asian NGOs had been mooted.
8. *World Refugee Survey 1996,* US Committee for Refugees, Washington D.C., 1996.

Nowhere Peoples

Burmese refugees in India

Rita Manchanda

Humanitarian considerations rather than law, have shaped India's policies towards the waves of people from the neighbouring countries, who have sought refuge. Asylum has been given and space made for thousands of "de-facto refugees"[1] to stay on in India on humanitarian grounds. This despite the fact that India continues to resist acceding to the international legal protection regime for refugees. It has denied the UNHCR and agencies like the ICRC access to refugees except on a restrictive basis. But its expansive tradition of accommodation of cross-border population movements has come under strain in the face of competing political and security concerns. Humanitarian considerations are no match for political considerations and India's adherence to the international principle of *non-refoulement* has come under pressure with local authorities pushing back refugees termed illegal migrants.[2]

Like other South Asian states, for India too, the category - *refugee*- is less a matter of law and policy and more a matter of political judgement and attitude. Still, India provides shelter to some 368,500 refugees from neighbouring countries.[3] But its policy or rather the absence of a policy, makes for erratic and ad hoc responses. As India's political interests shift, what was once an expansive policy of hospitality towards refugees becomes a ruthless "push back" policy, as the Burmese refugees in India are discovering.

India which had welcomed the fleeing Burmese pro-democracy student activists and even financially supported their passage in 1988, is pushing them back. Apparently, the pull of democratic and humanitarian sympathies for the Burmese refugees has lost out to the competing political imperative of "engagement " with Myanmar's military junta—the State Law and Order Restoration Council (SLORC).

The refugees have become pawns in India's geo-political competition for influence with China in Myanmar. Moreover, in the pursuit of quelling border insurgency in the North-East, the Indian authorities are cooperating with the Myanmar security forces to manage the porous border. And if it means sacrificing rather than shielding de facto refugees fleeing persecution or generalised violence, so be it.

Victims of insecurity at home, the Burmese refugees in India have become victims of the Indian state's internal security complex. Cross-border flows have got mired in national security concerns. As a consequence, the Union government will no longer stand in the way of the Mizoram state police terrorising, the dominant Burmese refugee group—40,000 ethnic Chin-Burmese refugees—and threatening them with deportation.

Despite assurances given by the Ministry of External Affairs to the UNHCR, the Mizoram state government is pushing back the refugees to Mynamar where they face "forced labour", "forced porterage" or a firing squad. The thousands of Chin-Burmese refugees are a stateless people in the making. In India they are "illegal migrants" and in Mynamar they are not accepted as citizens as they have not had the identity cards issued by SLORC since 1994.

The situation of the ethnic Chin-Burmese "de facto refugees" shows the difficulty in making any useful distinction between refugees and economic migrants. The "pull factor" is complicated by the reality of the ethnic oppression of the Chins and official developmental policies which have left underdeveloped and poor the Chin border state.

Inside Burma

Five decades of civil war which pitted Burma's ethnic minorities against the majoritarian *Burman* ruling elites and now the military junta, has resulted in a million Burmese peoples crossing over to neighbouring countries to flee economic hardship and mass violation of human rights. Myanmar's "majoritarian" nation-state building project has locked it in armed confrontation with its distinct ethnic minorities. The dominant *Bhama* or *Burman* community makes up 69 percent of the population living in the Irrawady river valley. In the coastal and hill border areas are to be found the Shans comprising 8 percent of the population, Karens 6.2 percent and the Arakanese 4.5 percent and the remaining 11.8 percent is spread across the Mons and Chins.

The ethnic minorities had controlled the border and coastal areas. The military crackdown in 1988 on pro-democracy activists in central Myanmar, saw thousands of pro-democracy activists flee to the border areas and join local movements which had been struggling against the centralising power of the *Burman* state. SLORC turned its guns on the border areas pushing thousands of refugees to flee generalised violence and mass violation of human rights in the form of forced porterage and forced labour.[4]

In 1991, SLORC's largely adolescent army acquired $ 1.2 billion in arms from China to give it a lethal punch as it ravaged the rural areas. It resulted in a fresh exodus as tens of thousands of Burmese fled to neighbouring countries. The Christian Chins and the Muslim Rohingyas were specially targeted. Myanmar's Chins were one of the last ethnic groups to take up arms against the Burmese junta. Only in 1988 was the armed resistance group, the Chin National Front formed.

Burmese refugees in India

India does not recognise the influx of people from Myanmar as refugees.

There are four categories of people from Myanmar who have sought refuge in India.

i) Ethnic Chin-Burmese are the dominant group of Burmese peoples in India estimated to be about 40,000. Many have been in India for decades and may have come across as much for economic as political reasons. Historically, the trijunction of India, Burma and Bangladesh has been an integrated economic corridor, characterised by cross border population flows. Overlaying this is the reality of the Chins' fear of persecution as a Christian ethnic minority in the majoritarian Buddhist *Burman* state. After the military crackdown on the pro-democracy movement, thousands of Chin student activists fled to India. But whatever may be the "refugee like situation" of the Chins, the Indian government regards them as economic migrants.

ii) Ethnic Nagas fled Burma in 1992 following the army's crackdown on insurgents in the upper Sagaing division. An estimated 1,500 ethnic Nagas from Myanmar have crossed over into Arunachal Pradesh, Mizoram and Manipur. They are not recognised as refugees.

iii) Arakanese refugees have been crossing over from Myanmar's Arakan state since 1993. According to the South Asia Human Rights Documentation Centre (SAHRDC) their number is estimated to be 738. Arakan state along the Bay of Bengal borders Mizoram and the Chittagong Hill Tracts of Bangladesh. Earlier, in 1978 and 1991 there was a major exodus of Muslim Rohingya refugees from Arakan state into Bangladesh. The Arakanese refugees crossing over to India, are largely Buddhists fleeing the military occupation of their state. 30 battalions of Myanmar's western command are based in Arakan state to fight the rebel forces.

The 45 families who first crossed into India in 1993 fled because of the practice of forced labour for the construction of Kyauktaw-Paletwa road and the heavy levy of rice which had to be supplied to troops there.[5] Since then several hundred Arakanese refugees have fled torture and forced porterage in the Arakan. The refugees have built makeshift camps in the remote areas of Mizoram. The Indian government does not recognise them as refugees.

iv) Burmese refugees in India recognised by UNHCR are 267 in number.

Refugees or illegal migrants

Chin-Burmese

The ethnic Chins, the majority of whom are Christians, had been special targets of the Burmanisation programme of General Ne Win who toppled the civilian government of U Nu in 1962. Political and cultural resistance provoked severe repression. As the Chin language was banned in local schools, educated Chins crossed over to Mizoram and became teachers in schools there.

The trijunction of India, Burma and Bangladesh has historically been an economic corridor for cross border flows. Chins on both sides of the Indo-Burma border have been crossing over for decades. In Mizoram state 80 percent of the handloom workers are said to be from Myanmar.

The military crackdown on pro-democracy activists in 1988 saw a fresh exodus of refugees from Chin state. According to The Other Media, a Delhi based NGO working with refugees from Myanmar, about 500 had crossed over to Manipur state, while several hundred, largely Chins, went to Mizoram state. At the time the government of India announced that it would not turn back student refugees. The Indian embassy even offered student leaders financial support to come to India.

The failure of the democracy movement in Myanmar and the success of the military in keeping itself in power made the ethnic minorities even more vulnerable. Moreover, the military, to remain in power, sought to consolidate its position among the majority Bhama community, by pursuing a policy of "race and religion". It was used to divide the democracy movement and to woo the Buddhist monks alienated from the military because of the killing of Buddhist monks in the 1990 anti-government demonstrations.

The Indian government responded to the influx of student activists from Myanmar by opening up camps in Manipur and Mizoram. But in Manipur, the 300 Burmese students activists there got little sympathy from the local authorities. Clashes occurred and 160 Burmese students were repatriated and others were put in Imphal jail without trail. Intervention by Indian activists, eventually, secured their release. In the case of the Burmese refugees, the Indian courts have provided protection against expulsion orders of the government by staying deportation orders. For example in

Bogyi vs Union of India case, the Guwahati High Court ordered the temporary release of a Burmese man from detention for two months so that he could apply for refugee status with the UNHCR.[6]

Many Burmese student activists who had sought refuge in the North-East states made their way to Delhi to get recognised by UNHCR. 267 Burmese refugees are recognised by the UNHCR. However, some 80 to 100 Burmese refugees are still believed to be in Manipur.

Sanctuary violated

In Mizoram, the Chin student activists were initially welcomed by the locals. The Mizo and Chin tribals belong to the same ethnic family. In Mizoram two camps were opened. UNHCR was denied access to these camps. The government provided for the refugees. Some students chose to live in a rented house in Aizwal, the capital, working as daily wage earners on construction sites and as weavers. In an effort to assist these Aizwal students, Mizoram Chief Minister Lathanwala in 1990 sanctioned ration cards to be issued to them. These cards served them as identity cards protecting them from police action.

But by 1994, the welcome had run out. Rations in the camp had been slashed and the Chin-Burmese were forced to fend for themselves. As they started competing for local jobs, it fed the groundswell of hostility against "foreigners" and in the process, the 40,000 Chins , many of whom had been living in Mizoram for decades, became the special focus of the "quit Mizoram" campaign.

In September 1994, Lian UK, member-elect of the Burmese Parliament, alerted UNHCR[7] and concerned NGOs about the forcible repatriation of Burmese refugees to Myanmar. There is no authoritative information about how many Burmese were deported. Figures vary from 1,000 to 10,000 people who were pushed back into the hands of the Myanmar military. In Myanmar, the deportees were jailed for six months while awaiting trial by the military tribunal.

The Other Media has documented the case of Rothla Peng (30) a Chin-Burmese who fled Burma in 1989. He had been working as an evangelical teacher in a local school. Rothla Peng was among the 320 Burmese who were picked up by the Mizoram police, arrested and then deported in September 1994. The police had picked up 500 "aliens"—Chakmas and Burmese. The Chakmas had "permits". The Burmese did not. 320 Burmese were deported and arrested on the other side of the border. Those who were not jailed were either sent to do forced labour on the roads being built by SLORC or forced porterage for the army. Rothla Peng managed to slip back into India. But he dare not return to Mizoram for fear of being picked up by the police and again deported.

An international alert sounded by concerned NGOs moved the Indian government to make the state government halt the deportations. But India's Ministry of External Affairs, too, had begun to shift away from its earlier policy of opposition to the SLORC. India was keen to revive diplomatic relations with SLORC. The initial enthusiasm for the pro-democracy movement which saw Aung San Suu Kyi awarded the Jawaharlal Nehru Award for International Understanding in 1993, had by 1994 turned into an embarrassment.

India was worried at the galloping spread of Chinese influence in Myanmar while it was pursuing a hands off policy towards the junta. India's strategic imperative demanded it do business with SLORC.

By 1995, the push back policy was resumed. This time

the xenophobic fervour whipped up by the local politicians in Mizoram found active backing from the Union Home Ministry. Driven by the internal security logic of quelling insurgency in the area, the Home Ministry saw the SLORC forces as allies in joint counter-insurgency operation.

Joint counter insurgency operations

India's North-East has been a bubbling cauldron of sub-national assertion by competing ethnic minorities and regional movements struggling to establish their identity against the Indian state's "majoritarian" nation-state building project. Armed opposition groups have been battling the army and the para-military forces in the area. At the trijunction of India, Myanamar and Bangladesh with its cross-border ethnic linkages, rebel groups from all three states have been crossing borders. Sanctuary and even military camps have been based across the border with varying degrees of cooperation from host governments depending on the shifting vagaries of national interest.

India has moved to shed its democratic sympathies for the pro-democracy alliance of ethnic groups fighting against SLORC to join hands with SLORC in stamping out insurgency in the area. What has fuelled the joint strategy, is the suspicion that the Chin National Front (CNF) and its armed wing the Chin National Army (CNA) were in league with the Nationalist Socialist Council of Nagaland (NSCN), People's Liberation Army (PLA) and the United Liberation Front of Assam (ULFA), armed insurgent groups at war with the Indian state in the North-East.

In April 1995, the Vice Chairman of the CNF, Sang Hlun crossed over to Parva border village in Mizoram for a scheduled meeting with the Border Security Force (BSF). According to Van Hmung,[8] a Chin-Burmese refugee who was the headmaster of the Parva High School, CNF leaders had come to clarify misunderstandings with the BSF over allegations of collusion with Indian armed insurgents. But before the meeting could take place, the BSF arrested them. Van Hmung who had been asked to be an interpreter, was also arrested and tortured. The BSF wanted to know about NSCN crossings in the area. After a week, he was released and told it was all a mistake. Sang Hlun, meanwhile was taken by helicopter to Aizwal and died in custody in an Assam Rifles army camp.

Soon after India and Myanmar launched a joint counter insurgency operation code named Operation Golden Bird. It was the start of "institutional mechanism" set up by the two governments to facilitate ground level cooperation for control of insurgent groups. The 1995-96 annual report of the Indian Home Ministry lauds the success achieved through intelligence sharing in intercepting insurgents on both sides of the border. "Five sectoral meetings and three national-level meetings have been held so far with the Myanmar authorities and the cooperation extended by them in curbing and containing insurgent activity has been very satisfactory."[9]

But the cooperation came at a price. Earlier at the Indo-Myanmar trade talks in February 1995 in Rikhwader in Burma, an understanding was reached that India would close down the refugee camps and aliens would be deported. Myanmar suspected that CNF activists were operating from the Champhai camp. According to a news report in *Sankeibaknei* newsmagazine, 30 Chin-Burmese refugees were to be deported every week.[10] In May a task force was set up under the Deputy Commssioner, Aizwal, to work out a process for identifying and deporting "aliens".

The Champhai camp was closed down on June 1,1995. Concerned NGOs appealed to the Union Home Ministry to intervene. But the Home Ministry justified the closure as there were only four inmates left in the camp and they were suspected to have "dubious links".[11] What was not acknowledged was that the state government had over the last couple of years squeezed to starvation levels the rations in the camps forcing the refugees to move out.

But even in the case of the "civilian" refugees, the Home Ministry readily turned its back. The Home Ministry claimed that Mizoram state authorities had informed them that "the Chins in Mizoram are not refugees who had taken shelter to avoid persecution by the Myanmar authorities. They have migrated illegally in search of gainful employment".[12] Taking refuge in the legally accepted definition of "refugees", the Home Ministry asserted "a distinction needs to be maintained between political refugees and migrants".

UNHCR too, appears to have accepted that the Chin-Burmese peoples in Mizoram were economic migrants and not a case of mass migration requiring their protection as they were in a refugee like situation. UNHCR has not been allowed access to the refugees, and thus has not been able to determine for itself the status of these refugees.

Fearing police action and deportation in Mizoram, several ethnic Chin and Burmese refugees came to Delhi in June 1995 to UNHCR for protection. UNHCR in Delhi, assured by the Ministry of External Affairs that there would be no push back of the Chin-Burmese, chose to give the refugees a take it or leave it offer. That is, stay on in Delhi without any assistance or accept a one timers Rs. 3,000 grant and travel allowance, if they returned to Mizoram.

Irene Khan, Head of Mission, Delhi UNHCR, was persuaded that in India, the Chins with their ethnic and linguistic ties with the Mizos, could find work and be assimilated in Mizoram as had happened over the last few decades. Even those Chin-Burmese who were among the few Burmese refugees to get UNHCR certification, were told the subsistence allowance available to Afghan, Iranian and other Burmese refugees, would not be extended to them. The Chins could fend for themselves.[13]

Already, branded as illegal immigrants in Mizoram, the Chins were virtually being asked by UNHCR to do something illegal and lay themselves further open to police and political action in Mizoram. Leng Mang, one of the Chin refugees recognised by UNHCR as a person of concern, was one of the refugees who left Delhi, urged by UNHCR to return to Mizoram. Within a month he was picked up by the CID agency of Mizoram, arrested and tortured to make him identify CNF activists. His UNHCR certificate afforded him no protection.

In July and August 1996, scores of Chin-Burmese in Aizwal were picked up by the state police. In Mizoram rallies were taken out demanding the immediate deportation of the Chins. The state Home Minister announced at one of the rallies—"Quit Mizoram". The provocation was the killing of an activist of the Young Mizo Association, in a border village on July 12, 1996. Local newspapers claimed that three members of the CNF had killed him. Police terror was let loose against the Chin-Burmese in Aizwal. Quit notices were served to 100 Chin-Burmese families in Aizwal. A state government circular warned refugees to leave by August 13, 1996.

The arrests were aimed at pressurising the CNF. For SLORC was putting pressure on its Indian allies as the CNF stepped up its military campaign in Myanmar. Moreover, CNF's blockade of goods across the Indo-Myanmar border in this sector had hit the thriving illegal and legal trade in this region. Mizoran Chief Minister Lalthanwala had hoped to garner Rs 5 billion for the state by opening up border trade. Mizo traders were loud in their outcry against the CNF. Mizo armed police went in hot pursuit of the CNF into Myanmar. Mizoram Chief Minister urged the Centre to send in the paramilitary Assam Rifles against the CNF.

SLORC was also insistent that India hand over deserters from the Myanmar army who had fled to India. In 1996 there was a dramatic increase in the number of soldiers from the Myanmar army crossing over to India. Many of these ex-soldiers had made their way to CNF camps in Bangladesh. In January and June 1996, former soldiers-deserters from the Burmese LIG 268 and 269 reportedly traded their arms with CNF activists for safe passage to India. The Indian government had refused to grant them asylum but it was understood, they would not be pushed back. SLORC wanted India to hand over ten deserters who had sought asylum in India.

On August 5, 1996 ten ex-soldiers of the Myanmar army were deported by the Indian authorities. A few of the refugees from Myanmar's Arakan state who were deported along with the deserters, managed to escape back to India in October and informed the Burma Students League that they saw the ex-soldiers held in jail by SLORC soldiers. Six were sentenced to death, others to life imprisonment.[14]

In August, 33 Burmese refugees were pushed back following the July 4, 1996 order of the Deputy Commissioner Chhimtuipui District, Saiha in Mizoram.[15] Among the deportees was Van Hmung a Chin-Burmese national. He had been headmaster of the High School in Parva village in Mizoram before being picked up by the army's "Black Cats" in April 1996. Despite the protestations of the village council, he was taken away to Saiha jail and locked up with other would be deportees. For Van Hmung, this was his second bout at the hands of India's security forces. A year before in 1995, the BSF had picked him when the CNF leader Sang Hlun had called him to be their interpreter at a meeting with the BSF. Instead they were all arrested by the BSF.

Van Hmung had been living in Parva village since he fled Burma in 1989 because as a teacher activist in the Chin state of Burma, he was wanted by SLORC. In Parva village, inhabited by the Bawn tribals a branch of the Chin tribes, Van Hmung built up the first local school, teaching in the Chin language. It was officially recognised in 1994. Van Hmung was appointed headmaster of the government high school.

In April 1996, Van Hmung was arrested, again, tied up and beaten but not interrogated. This time the security forces wanted nothing from him. All he knew was that he would be deported along with members of the Arakanese Liberation Party and other Burmese refugees. Once across the border Van Hmung managed to slip back to India, preferring to be hunted by the Mizoram police than SLORC. As an "illegal" and as an activist of the pro-democracy, capture by SLORC forces would mean death.

The Chin-Burmese are an "unwanted people" . They have nowhere to go. Back home in Myanmar, is persecution as an ethnic minority by a government bent on stamping out their religious and cultural identity. There is the prospect of forced labour, forced porterage, starvation, arrest and torture. In Mizoram, is hounding by the state police, arrest and deportation. On April 7, 1997 the Deputy Commissioner of Aizwal again served notice on illegal migrants. Within three months they would be deported.[16]

India may have its democratic sympathies as the then Indian Foreign Minister I K Gujral said. But they have lost out to the overall gameplan of war against sub-national assertion. SLORC has been able to convince the Indian authorities that its iron hand alone can contain the seething cauldron of Myanmar's ethnic communities. And what government in India wants the volatile north-eastern border to explode?

Caught in the middle are thousands of Chin-Burmese in a refugee-like situation. But the cross border population movement of the Chin-Burmese in India has got mired in the national security complex of India and Myanmar. The Chin-Burmese refugees are being sacrificed to the politics of expediency.

Notes

1. *Refugees : Human Rights Have No Borders.* Amnesty International, London, 1997.
2. For a comprehensive overview of India's legal position on the refugee issue see Smrithi Talwar, "Building a Regional Consensus on Asylum" in Regional Consultation on Refugee and Migratory Movements in South Asia, UNHCR, New Delhi November 1996, pp 44-54.
3. *Refugees in South Asia: A Report,* South Asia Forum for Human Rights, September 1997.
4. For details see Alan Clements and Leslie Kean *Burma's Revolution of the Spirit,* White Orchid Press, Bangkok, 1995 and *World Refugee Survey* 1996. US Committee for Refugees, Washington DC, 1996.
5. Country Report on Refugee Situation. South Asia Human Rights Documentation Centre (SAHRDC), Delhi, October 1995.
6. Civil rule no 1847/89 Guwahati High Court. S.Talwar. p.51
7. Lian UK, former elected Member of Parliament, National Assembly 7 Myanmar, Chin State, now refugee in the USA, wrote to the UNHCR, September 29, 1997.

8. Testimony of Van Hmung to The Other Media, September 1996.
9. Annual Report, Ministry of Home Affairs, 12995-96 p.16.
10. *Sakeibaknei*, bi-weekly magazine, February 10, 1995.
11. Union Home Ministry's response to The Other Media on alleged expulsions of Myanmar nationals, July 24, 1995, Delhi.
12. Ibid.
13. Based on correspondence between The Other Media and UNHCR Geneva, Aug. 12, 1996 and personal interview with UNHCR, Head of Mission Delhi, July 1996.
14. See Shar Aung "Burmese Refugees in India" in *Health for the Millions* special issue on Refugees vol 22, no 2 March-April 1996 and *Refugees in South Asia: A report,* SAFHR, Kathmandu, September 1997.
15. Order no D/225 JUDL-SHA/96 dated July 1996 Office of the Deputy Commissioner Chhimtuipui, District Saiha, Mizoram.
16. Van Hmung Testimony to The Other Media.

Development and Discontent
Displacement and rehabilitation in India

Malika Basu

Situations engendering refugees, as well as planned displacements caused by development, raise important issues of human rights. This paper discusses at length the state of development-induced displaced people in India, people who sacrifice their today for the nation's uncertain tomorrow. Like becoming a refugee, being involuntarily displaced from one's land and habitat is not only disruptive and painful, but also fraught with long-term risks of becoming poorer than before and again displaced.

Population displacement by development programmes is now a worldwide problem. Millions of people have been uprooted by planned development projects and by natural environmental disasters to become internally displaced peoples. The process of industrialisation, electrification and urbanisation in all countries — industrial as well as developing — can only increase, the number of development programmes causing *involuntary* population displacement over the next decade.

The term "involuntary displacement" is frequently associated with a wide range of related expressions such as forced removals, dislocation, expropriation, relocation, resettlement, and re-development. The United Nations uses the term "forced evictions" to describe the practice of the involuntary removal of people from their homes and the subsequent human rights violations stemming therefrom.

Involuntary displacement consists of two closely related yet distinct processes, displacing people and rebuilding their livelihood or rehabilitation, though more often it has come to mean, pure and simple, displacement of people.

Displacement concerns how land and other major assets are expropriated and people removed to establish a project intended for the overall "social good". Rehabilitation concerns the fate of the displaced people. In theory, the two processes — displacing and reconstructing/rehabilitating — are segments of a single continuum. In practice, the first is not always followed by the second.

Development-related displacement and refugees

The definition of refugees in 1951 Convention applies only to persons who are outside their country, "owing to well founded fear of being persecuted for reasons of race, religion, nationality, membership of a particular social group or opinion." The definition does not provide protection to those who have been internally displaced because of ethnic strife, civil disturbance, breakdown of law and order, denial of human rights and insecurity of food, land and water caused by forces beyond their control.

The 1969 OAU Convention covers persons displaced by ethnic strife, civil disorder, religious riots and persecution. However, it does not apply to persons who have been displaced by natural and man-made natural disasters or by the denial of food, land and water security.

The definitions currently accepted internationally for the term refugees tend to be fairly restrictive. They do not cover either the voluntary migrant or people forcibly displaced by planned development. Since many countries and international organisations provide for special entitlements to refugees, every attempt to define the term is underlined by the concern to avoid any confusion between a "genuine" refugee and a so-called "voluntary" economic migrant.

Involuntary displacement is distinct from voluntary population movements. Voluntary mobility, including rural-urban migration, stimulates economic growth and reflects people's willingness to pursue new opportunities. In contrast, involuntary displacement does not include the choice to remain, and those displaced, often face more risks than opportunities.

Refugees and peoples displaced by development programmes, however, resemble each other in that they are victimised by events, natural or man-made, for which they, as individuals, can not be held responsible.

Both categories are "displaced" populations undergoing a major disruption in their pattern of social organisation and culture. They are facing the same task of physically and culturally surviving this disruption by reorganising their economy and their way of life. Both relocate in previously unknown places, among host populations often suspicious or directly hostile. Both situations raise important issues of human rights.

But there is a sharp difference in terms of their legal status and entitlement to assistance. The responsibility of the state vis-à-vis development displaced people is of a different nature than its responsibility towards refugees. The first is assumed deliberately through the state's decision to enforce the legal principle of "eminent domain".[1] The state resorts to the exercise of "eminent domain" law when it constructs a new infrastructure essential for national development, satisfies the need of many beneficiaries, and generates gains otherwise unobtainable. Because such constructions entail the forced displacement of those in the 'way', the state voids the right of private individuals to hold on to their land and residence, compelling them to move elsewhere.

When people are displaced by a public development project, it is incumbent upon the government to ensure that the oustees are fully compensated and enabled to reconstruct their productive livelihood. If such assistance is not provided, development-displaced people are likely to become destitute and their situation, in essence, becomes similar to the refugees.

A sliding process whereby established inhabitants become oustees and soon refugees, happened for instance, to many people displaced by the Srisaliam Dam, in Andhra Pradesh or to the oustees from the Hirakud Multipurpose Dam Project in Orissa. The same process is being replicated in the Singruali region in Uttar Pradesh, where after the initial displacement in the 60s from the Rihand reservoir, some of the same families who have still to recover from the first displacement, are facing eviction once again, this time because of the construction of ash dykes of thermal plants in the area.

It is useful to point out both the similarities and differences between the status of refugees and the status of persons displaced from planned programs. For this will highlight the circumstances in which bad planning or abdication of government responsibility converts displacees into refugees. The purpose of resettlement policies must be to prevent the development-displaced people from sliding into a "refugee-like" condition.

Planned development in India

After independence, the Indian state accepted planned development as the strategy for improving the economic, social and political life of its citizens. In the quest for development, however, what was overlooked was what Nehru had thought to be the crux of India's planning, namely, "planning is not merely a question of drawing up a list of projects and finding resources to execute them... The financial aspect is important but is far less important than the human aspect".

This human aspect which Nehru so often emphasised, has been ignored. The consequences of this grave neglect has been the displacement of millions of people for development purposes. As a result, the displaced and the dispossessed, question the legitimacy of the developmental process, protesting that guiding principles like, "planning for the people", "people's participation", "people's needs" and "humanisation of development", are but mere rhetoric.

Development projects are consciously planned interventions to steer economic growth. No doubt, growth in India has occurred. However, instead of diminishing the problems it was meant to alleviate, it has widened the domestic inequalities of income, wealth and economic power. Only 16 out of every 100 households in India today, a mere four in the villages, have what is called first generation infrastructure facilities. That is, safe drinking water, electricity and toilets.

Economic growth is an important component of development, but it cannot be a goal by itself, nor can it go on indefinitely. At the start of the first development decade, the UN defined economic development as economic growth plus social change.

It is necessary to emphasize that a project however technically perfect, will not bear the desired results if we keep the *substance* out of it. *Substance* here refers to the people who constitute the nation. In this case, the people are those on whom a new status has been imposed, that of the displaced.

Magnitude and modalities of displacement

Development induced displacement takes diverse forms and is associated with different types of developmental activities. Though no reliable statistics are available, the fallout from all these activities would put the displacement figures into millions. The magnitude of forced displacement is likely to be much larger than the number of refugees. According to the UNHCR's *The State of the World's Refugees* 1997-98, while there are 13 million conventional refugees nearly 5 million IDPs, some 50 million can legitimately be described as victims of displacement.

In developing countries, the World Bank estimates that for the 300 large dams that, on average, enter into construction every year, the displacement toll is above four million people. Projects for urban development and transportation infrastructure entail the displacement of an additional six million people. The overall figure is greater because it should include displacees from projects such as thermal plants, mining, parks and forest reserves.

In India, the few estimates available, are conservative. A 1989 study by Fernandes, Das and Rao estimated that during the last four decades some 15.5 million people had been displaced by dams, mines, industries, wildlife reserves and other development projects.[2] Five years later Walter

Fernandes revised upward that initial assessment to about 21 million people.[3] If one includes urban displacement due to various deliberate or planned activities, then the number would rise even further.

Amongst all developmental projects, dams and reservoir construction, is the single largest cause of displacement. An estimate puts the number of persons affected directly or indirectly by irrigation projects over the past forty years in India, at 20 million, of whom only 25 percent have been rehabilitated.

The Sardar Sarovar Dam project on the Narmada river will lead to the forced displacement of at least 200,000 people in 237 villages in the states of Gujarat, Maharashtra and Madhya Pradesh. Another large, multi-dam project in the Uttar Kannada district of Karnataka will displace 200,000 people. According to official figures 55,000 will be displaced by the Koel-Karo dam while another study puts the number at 66,000.

A close look at the composition of the displaced population reveals that the majority of the displacees belong to the poorer and backward sections of society. Most displaced persons (DPs) are tribals, dalits and from other weaker sections of society, like landless, small and marginal farmers. Government estimates show that the tribals, who constitute a little over 7.8 percent of the country's population account for more than 40 percent of the displaced of dams, mines and industries and almost all of wildlife sanctuaries. A fairly large proportion of the displaced also appear to belong to the most oppressed group in the Hindu caste system, the scheduled castes. Even among these groups, women are the worst victims. But they are rarely taken into consideration while planning for the project and resettlement.

These estimates of displaced persons exclude a very large section of the affected population. That is, apart from DPs, there are the project-affected persons (PAPs), who are not physically displaced but have nevertheless been deprived of their livelihood due to the loss of their land and common property resources (CPR) or because the community to which they had till then rendered services, has been broken up. These people are often forced to leave the area as they have lost their source of livelihood or their access to the bio-mass resources on which they depended.

The point is, the modalities of displacement differ widely between regions, states, cities, communities and households. The form that it takes and the justification varies widely from one situation only to another. In some areas, mass forced evictions are not uncommon, whereas in others, individual households are affected.

Whatever may be the form, the voices of the displaced are a chorus, echoed in virtually every displacement situation, be it the Narmada, Singrauli, Koel-Karo, Netarhat and Korba in India or the Arun valley in Nepal. They reveal what it means to be a "displaced lot", namely a loss of social networks, severance from an ecosystem that sustained them and above all, a feeling of powerlessness and insecurity about the future.

Displacement is made all the worse by the fact that fewer than 25 percent of the displaced persons of planned development have been rehabilitated.

The re-establishment process

Initial resistance, even hostility, is natural in any displacement situation. What they lose is lost and gone forever and can not be replicated in a new set-up. The trauma of displacement begins well before the process, itself, actually takes place. It needs to be understood that neither displacement nor rehabilitation is a one-time event. They are two important parts in a long process that begins much before physical displacement and ends many years after resettlement.

Despite the magnitude of displacement caused by developmental interventions in the five decades since independence, there has been a total apathy on the part of successive governments, in both, framing a national policy and in enacting national and state legislations to protect those who have to be forcibly displaced in the so-called national or public interest.

There is no national policy or law for rehabilitation. The resettlement of the displaced is governed by policies and rules of the concerned state governments or those specifically formulated for the project. At present, only the states of Maharashtra, Madhya Pradesh and Karnataka have rehabilitation laws. The Karnataka Act passed by the legislature in 1987 received the President's assent only in 1994. Gujarat and Orissa have "land for land" policies for DPs of irrigation projects.

Since resettlement/rehabilitation is undertaken project-wise by independent authorities who have little or no coordination between them, the same people find themselves displaced more than once, each time as the result of a different project.

Korba, in Bilaspur district of Madhya Pradesh, reflects this problem of multiple displacement. The first lot of people were displaced by the Hasdeo Bango Dam. Subsequently, land was acquired for coal mining, thermal power plants, explosive manufacture and aluminium and fertiliser industries. Korba has the pride of place in the industrial map of our country for it is an exemplary instance of the enormous diversity of projects situated in a particular geographical area.

This "industrial belt", within an area of approximately 284 sq. km, however, has seen no uniformity in the programmes to rehabilitate the large number of people displaced or affected by the projects. There are different "resettlement and rehabilitation" (R&R) programmes for the same area and for people of similar socio-economic and cultural background. Sometimes members of the same family get different rehabilitation packages because they fall under different projects.

If a project covers more than one state as in the case of Pong Dam, involving the states of Rajasthan and Himachal Pradesh, the plight of the oustee is even worse. While each state wants the maximum benefits of the project, neither wants to share the responsibility for rehabilitation. While many Pong Dam oustees were not rehabilitated, others who were resettled found themselves not much better off. Having lived most of their life in the hills of Himachal, they found themselves unable to cope with the deserts of Rajasthan where they were offered resettlement. They found the conditions so inhospitable and alien that many returned to Himachal Pradesh.

When we scrutinise even some of the development projects where the planners and project authorities have applied their minds to preparing resettlement packages, we find that they have failed to understand the dimensions of the problem of rehabilitation in a holistic way. Under policies for resettlement the government and project authorities have changed, knowingly or unknowingly, people's rights into mere concessions. Rehabilitation can not be a welfare scheme planned by the government or project authorities but a right of the displaced persons and project affected persons.

Against the backdrop of the complexities of the displacement problem and the mounting pressure from activists for proper rehabilitation and resettlement, the government recently initiated the preparation of a National Rehabilitation Policy for displaced persons. But it has been argued by some activists that the policy has no teeth. It is an expression of good intentions. "It creates no rights. A law or an Act, on the other hand, gives actionable rights and the person whose rights are violated can invoke the courts to secure those rights".[4]

In India then, a citizen does not have a legal right to rehabilitation if he is displaced from his traditional habitat. The only legal enactment concerning displacement and compensation applicable to the entire country (except Jammu and Kashmir) is the Land Acquisition Act 1894, amended in 1984. The Act does not provide for resettlement. The rate of compensation, as also its nature, are decided project-wise. As a result, the displaced are often disposed of with a minimum cash compensation.

Where adequate financial compensation has been provided, as for persons displaced by Hirakud Dam in Orissa, out of Rs. 96 million earmarked only Rs. 34 million was paid out. Resettlement schemes also ignore the psychological costs such as alienation from one's culture and community and induction into the new industrial work culture. Forced migration, bondage, absenteeism and alcoholism are often the outcome of such neglect. Moreover, aspects like exposure to new diseases caused by environmental changes, are all but ignored while planning the project, compensation and rehabilitation.

A substantial number of the displaced persons or project affected persons are tribals dependent on common property resources for their livelihood. Communities with a high dependence on common resources or on the village as a community to which they render services for a living, suffer the most. Moreover, the Land Acquisition Act has *patta* as the basis of compensation. Only the landowner is compensated. Only individual land documents are considered valid.

As displacement has become a process of impoverishing those dependent on common resources and other landless persons, it is being argued in India that instead of financial compensation, these persons should be turned into shareholders in the project. The project will thus be jointly owned by capital investors and them.

A step in economic rehabilitation was initiated through the T.N. Singh formula of 1967, namely, one job per family displaced by mining and industrial projects. The formula had its shortcomings for no effort was made to train the local population for skilled jobs in the project. Most therefore got short-term unskilled contract jobs. The formula was abandoned in 1986 because of the trend towards mechanisation and the consequent shortage of unskilled jobs.

Amongst all categories, women are the worst victims of the present model of development. There is a need for gender perspective in issues related to displacement and rehabilitation. Since women seldom have ownership rights they are automatically left out. They are often kept in the dark by their own men. The men who complained of lack of dissemination of information regarding a project and its consequences, in turn treat their womenfolk no differently. During the course of our meetings in Korba, women facing displacement said, "We do not know when we will have to leave this place. One day they (our men) will suddenly ask us to pack up everything.... There is always this tension...."[5]

The basic needs approach

Among the many anthropological, sociological and geographical studies, which seek to explain what happens when people are forcibly displaced, one of the most influential models is that developed by Michael Cernea, Senior Advisor, Sociology and Social Policy in The World Bank.[6] He has outlined a pattern of eight typical interconnected trends which in varying intensities will be present in any displacement situation. Together they constitute a model of the overall impoverishment process. Very concisely, these are landlessness, joblessness, homelessness, marginalisation, increased morbidity, food insecurity, loss of access to common property and social disarticulation. Cernea's "Impoverishment Risks" analysis model is accepted by the World Bank for India in a number of Bank-assisted projects, as a methodological model which analyses, anticipates and articulates the risks of displacement. It has become a management and has participatory tool for resettlement planning to attain the Bank's Resettlement and Rehabilitation policy objectives of restoring, and over a period, improving livelihoods.

A close look at Cernea's model reinforces the reality that displacement dismantles what people have built over decades. A closer look reveals that in most cases of displacement "basic human needs" are infringed. The United Nations has identified the following list of basic needs: i) nutrition, ii) shelter, iii) health, iv) education, v) leisure, vi) security (both physical and economic), and vii) environment. Development is real only if it makes our lives better in terms of these needs.

The experience has been that people whose land is acquired for a development project benefit in no special way. For instance, in Singrauli the settlements of the displaced in the neighbourhood of the National Thermal Power Corporation plant, remain in darkness. "Look at their colonies ....", as an oustee stated, "they have light, proper drinking water, all basic amenities .... Development is (only) for them...."

Good resettlement can prevent impoverishment, even reduce poverty by rebuilding sustainable livelihoods. If resettlement is not adequate, the resettled end up worse off than before. It provokes local resistance, increased political tensions, entails extensive project delays, and postpones project benefits for all concerned. The benefits lost because of avoidable project delays sometimes far exceed the marginal cost of good resettlement packages. Ensuring that involuntary displacement is minimized, and when unavoidable, is carried out without impoverishing people, is necessitated on both economic and ethical grounds.

Conclusion

As development has been wrongly understood as a matter of technological development and economic inputs only, most of our projects have not benefitted the "people". The whole accent has been on increasing production and not achieving a just distribution of what is produced. Moreover, most development efforts have come from above. There has been little participation by the local people, especially the economically and politically disadvantaged people, in formulating policies and plans affecting them.

By successfully pushing the affected people out of the decision making process, in project after project, we have ensured in almost every case a failure of resettlement and rehabilitation. What is demanded is not alternative projects but an alternative approach to development. It also calls for decision making, through which people are given choices to develop alternatives for themselves.

If a particular development project destroys and disorients the lifestyles of the people, though it might appear to be in the "national interest", the people affected have a right to oppose it and the government, a duty to take the objections into consideration. Development means development for the people.

Notes

1. Michael Cernea, *Bridging the Research Divide: Studying Refugees and Development Oustees*, The World Bank Reprint Series, No. 481, Washington D. C., 1996.
2. See *Development, Displacement and Rehabilitation* edited by Walter Frenandes and Enakshi Ganguly Thukral, Indian Social Institute, New Delhi, 1989.
3. Walter Fernandes *Development, Displacement and Rehabilitation in the Tribal Areas of Eastern India*, Indian Social Institute, New Delhi, 1994.
4. Vasudha Dhagamwar "Comments on the two drafts of the Rehabilitation Policy", Paper prepared for the National Workshop. February 17-19, 1995, Indian Social Institute, New Delhi.
5. This is based on my personal experience as a member of the Multiple Action Research Group (MARG) team which is working in the area.
6. Michael Cernea, "Involuntary Resettlement in Development Policy Guidelines in World Bank Financial Projects", The World Bank, Washington D.C., 1988.

SECTION FOUR

Nepal's Refugee Burden

Hari Phuyal

The landlocked Himalayan Kingdom of Nepal, since ancient times has seen peoples both individually and in communities, crisscross frontiers, into Nepal and out of Nepal. The limited carrying capacity of the country's mid-hills has made thousands of people migrate to India's North-East and southern Bhutan. Nepali migration to northeast India and from there to Bhutan, began with the unification and expansion of Nepal under King Prithivi Narayan Shah. The treaty of Sugauli, 1815, saw the shrinking of Nepal's empire but left behind communities of Nepalis all across the Himalayan region.

The British policy of recruitment of young Nepalis in the Gurkha regiment in the British Indian army led to their settlement in North-East India. The British also imported Nepali labour to work in the newly established tea plantations.

Thousands of others migrated to escape repressive government policies, an exploitative labor system and famines and epidemics. The spread of peoples of Nepali origin all across the Himalayan region has raised the bogey of a "Greater Nepal" ethnic assertion. Nepali settlers in the North-East have become targets of "sons of the soil" movement and hundreds have migrated back to settle in the fertile Terai plains of Nepal.

Nepal, in turn, has a long history of playing host to streams of people who have sought refuge.[1] Political upheavals in the contiguous regions of Tibet-China and the Indian subcontinent have seen waves of refugees cross into Nepal — Tibetans, Bangladeshis, Burmese, Kashmiris, Nepali settlers and hill tribesmen from the North East and even Tamil refugees. The open border between India and Nepal in the south has become a corridor for inflow of not only refugees and migrants but also criminals and sex workers.

Nepal is host to some 20,000 Tibetan refugees settled in camps across 19 districts. They streamed across the border in 1959 when the Dalai Lama left Lhasa for India. In the case of the Tibetan refugees, Nepal has had to do a delicate balancing act between the competing interests of western donor countries and its neighbour China. Its earlier policy of hospitality, resettlement and even naturalisation of Tibetan refugees has given way to a more restrictive policy of asylum and reports of hundreds of new arrivals being pushed back.

More recent are the Bhutanese refugees who have been streaming into Nepal since 1990. In southern Bhutan some, 130,000 people of Nepali origin, have been pushed out and become refugees in India and Nepal. Nepalis had for centuries been crossing into Bhutan and settling in the malarial infested jungles in the south. But in he name of the policy of "One Nation One People", thousands have been disenfranchised. Peoples of Nepali ethnicity have been forcibly driven out. In 1992, 90,000 refugees fled to Nepal and have been living in seven camps in Jhapa and Morang districts.

In the immediate aftermath of the independence of Bangladesh in 1971-72, Bihari Muslims fleeing reprisals from the new government for their collusion with the Pakistani forces, crossed over into India and then into Nepal. With the assistance of the UNHCR and the International Committee of the Red Cross, all persons for whom Pakistan had taken responsibility were sent to Pakistan. A few hundred who did not know the proper procedure of registering as refugees are still in Nepal but by now assimilated as Nepali nationals or Indian migrants.

Nepal is not a signatory to the 1951 UN Convention on Protection of Refugees or the Protocol, and therefore policies towards refugees vary with different groups. Nepal, itself a poor country, has involved UNHCR and the international community to support the successive waves of people who have sought refuge in Nepal.

The social, economic and environmental burden of caring for 90,000 Bhutanese refugees for more than five years, has put an intolerable strain on the state's resources, even with the assistance of UNHCR and international NGO groups. Moreover with an estimated 10 million people of Nepali origin spread across the Himalayan region, there are enormous political costs of assimilating these "rejected peoples" of Nepali origin from Bhutan. It is UNHCR assistance which has kept alive the separate identity of these Bhutanese refugees of Nepali origin in the camps. The danger is that a squeeze on budgetary support and a resulting deterioration in camp conditions will push the refugees to leave the camps and melt into the South Asian night.

Tibetan refugees

Tibetans are the oldest refugee population in Nepal. In 1959, the establishment of direct Chinese control in Tibet and the flight of the Dalai Lama to India saw 20,000 to 30,000 Tibetans seek asylum in Nepal. Initially they entered via the Kodari Highway. According to the government of Nepal, there are 20,000 Tibetan refugees but the Tibetan Welfare Centre claims there are over 30,000. More than half of them live independently outside the 16 refugee settlements.[2] From 1989, with revival of political unrest in Tibet, fresh waves of Tibetans began to cross over to Nepal essentially using it as a transit point to India or for resettlement in a third country. By 1995 it was estimated that about 50 Tibetans a week were coming into Nepal. But as against its earlier policy of unrestricted asylum on arrival, Nepal now "unofficially" permits the Tibetan refugees to enter but without recognising them as refugees and without permitting them to remain in Nepal.

The earlier Tibetan refugees to enter Nepal have become naturalised Nepali citizens. Many second and third generation refugees are still residing in Nepal, though quite a few have moved on to India and the West. All camps, except the transit camp for new arrivals, are managed by the refugees themselves. Freedom of movement is not restricted and they are at liberty to pursue any profession they wish in Nepal. The Tibetan refugee community has been culturally and economically integrated in Kathmandu Valley. Approximately 80 percent of the refugees are involved in the carpet industry. Others also work in the hotel and garment industries.

Nepal claims that she has given asylum to Tibetan refugees on humanitarian grounds and has nothing to do with Tibeto-Chinese politics. However, the presence of Tibetans in Nepal has created an awkward situation for the Kingdom of Nepal. Often reports that some Tibetan refugees are involved in anti-Chinese activities hit the headlines in local and foreign newspapers. Public demonstrations by refugees demanding "Free Tibet" fuel fears of Nepal becoming a centre for anti-Chinese activities, complicating Nepal's relations with its huge neighbour to the north.

In cases of arrest of asylum seekers or any dispute in the process of status determination of Tibetan refugees, Department of Immigration works closely with UNHCR. A representative of the Tibetan Welfare Centre in Kathmandu will also be called in to assist in the process. The screening process isolates two options for the refugees, i) in case of insufficient grounds for seeking asylum they are to go back to Tibet, ii) if they are persons of concern, they will be permitted to stay for some time in Nepal and then sent on to third country.

In response to the first arrivals of Tibetan refugees in the 60s, the ICRC, Swiss Red Cross and UNHCR came forward to assist them. The government of Nepal also extended assistance. In the early years Tibetan refugees were given identity cards but their distribution was not very systematic. During the last thirty years Tibetan refugees have been registered and issued identity cards only once. Recently, the government of Nepal constituted a high-powered Citizenship Commission entrusted with the responsibility of screening Tibetan refugees to provide them with identity cards.

The contribution of the Tibetan refugees to the Nepali economy is significant, and if they are repatriated, the country may face serious economic problems, but if the refugees remain, especially if more settle here, it will create political problems for Nepal with its giant neighbour China.

Bhutanese refugees

By ethnic identity, most of the Bhutanese refugees in Nepal are of Nepali origin and they migrated to Bhutan several centuries ago. There is no historical evidence available about their migration from Nepal to Bhutan. According to a popular belief, a Tibetan King had taken some Nepali/Newari families to Tibet in order to construct some monasteries. The same people are believed to have constructed Paro Kyichu in Bhutan and it is strongly believed that they settled in the fertile villages of western and central Bhutan. This belief seems to be supported by the statement of the Bhutanese Foreign Minister, Dawa Tsering: "The Nepali have been settling down in our southern plains from the seventh century. We welcomed them because they were a hard working people. But they can't be permitted to swamp us".[3] Another historical line traces Nepali migration into Bhutan back to 1624 when the first batch of skilled Nepali artists went to the country. A formal document was signed between the Gorkha King Ram Shah and the first monk ruler of Bhutan Shabdurng Nawang Namgyel in this regard. British records indicate that the settlement of Nepali southern Bhutan was encouraged by them until the Duar war introduced a pattern of population movement which continued till the promulgation of the Citizenship Act of 1958.

The 1958 Citizenship Act and other restrictive measures have been introduced because the ruling Drukpas elite fear being outnumbered by the Lhotsampas of Nepali origin. The Drukpas are said to comprise 16 percent of the population, the Sarchops 31 percent, the rest are estimated to be southern Bhutanese of Nepali origin. The Bhutanese power elites fear that the Lhotsampas will follow the example of the Nepali political parties and push for democratisation of absolute monarchy in Bhutan.

The Bhutanese government adopted a number of legislations and policies to push the southern Bhutanese out of their country: i) the Marriage Act of 1980; ii) Bhutanization policy; iii) citizenship laws; iv) compulsory national work; v) green belt policy; vi) language policy, vii) religious policy; viii) no-objection certificate; ix) voluntary leaving certificate (VLC) and x) census of 1988.

India being the first country of asylum, many refugees first camped in India and then many moved on to Nepal. In India, the state governments of Assam, Meghalaya and West Bengal are against the presence of the Bhutanese refugees. The Union government of India also does not support them. While India still hosts 40,000 Bhutanese refugees, the local elites in the North-East are hostile to the re-entry of the same refugees who had crossed over to Nepal from India.

In Nepal, the Lhotsampas, first, spread to many parts of eastern Nepal but later on with the support of local people and the UNHCR, they were housed in refugees camps in the eastern districts. The Home Ministry has been entrusted with the management of refugees. At the central level it has created the National Unit for Coordination of Refugee Affairs with field level Refugee Co-ordination Unit (RCU) to take care of the refugees. In addition the maintenance to law and order, the RCU, in coordination with the UNHCR, undertakes the task of refugee verification and documentation.

Bhutanese asylum seekers are registered in the camps as refugees only after screening to determine whether they have genuine reasons for fleeing their country of origin. Refugees were initially interviewed and registered in the camps themselves but since May 1993 formal screening has been taking place at the Indo-Nepal border in Kakarvitta.

The support to refugees is being channelised through agencies of His Majesty's Government (HMG) of Nepal,

UNHCR, World Food Program (WFP), the Lutheran World Service (LWS), Save the Children Fund (SCF) UK, Oxford Committee for Famine Relief (OXFAM), Nepal Red Cross Society (NRCS), CARITAS- Nepal and Centre for Victims of Torture (CVICT).

The living conditions of the refugees in the camps[4] are not bad and have even created problems of resentment among the relatively deprived local population. Moreover, the pressure of 90,000 additional people on the limited environmental resources of Nepal makes the burden of shouldering the responsibility for the refugees, every year more difficult.[5]

Refugee leaders in the camps insist that until democratic institutions are put in place in Bhutan, there can be no protection of their human rights and no possibility of voluntary repatriation of refugees. At the least, the Bhutanese government must clarify its attitude towards the ethnic autonomy of the southern Bhutanese.

The Nepal government, on its part, has initiated seven rounds of bilateral talks with the Bhutanese government to resolve the refugee crisis. In addition, there were talks between the Prime Minister of Nepal and the King of Bhutan during the sixth SAARC summit in Colombo in 1991 and again in Vienna, Austria. A Bhutan-Nepal joint ministerial committee was constituted in July 1993. The second round of talks saw some serious discussion on the issue of categorising the refugees into four groups — i) bonafide Bhutanese evicted forcibly, ii) Bhutanese who emigrated, iii) non-Bhutanese peoples and iv) Bhutanese who have committed criminal acts. This categorization, however, was completely against the basic philosophy of constitutional refugee law.

There have been seven rounds of talks but they have failed to resolve the problem of 90,000 Bhutanese refugees in Nepal. The government of Nepal has also appealed to the international community. In 1991, as Nepal faced the first influx of refugees its prime minister called a meeting of the resident diplomats. Recently, the foreign minister of Nepal made an impassioned plea to the international community on resolving the Bhutanese refugee issue while addressing the meeting of the Executive Committee of the UNHCR. Internationalization of the Bhutanese refugee problem is also taking place by virtue of the activities of the Bhutanese refugees' human rights organisations.

Other refugee groups

The open border between India and Nepal, formalised by the 1950 treaty has facilitated the movement of refugees and migrants both from Nepal and into Nepal, for example, Tibetans transiting to India or Bhutanese arriving first in India and then moving to Nepal. It has also drawn to Nepal smaller groups of refugees fleeing conditions of violence and violations of human rights from all over South Asia. Under the 1950 treaty Indian and Nepali nationals are accorded equal treatment as nationals in each other's countries.[6] No visa is required.

Kashmiri migrants

Political insurgency in Kashmir has seen many thousands of Kashmiris leave their homeland. Some have made their way to Nepal. They are not officially recognised as refugees in Nepal and have not applied for refugee status either with the UNHCR or the government of Nepal. Their main place of residence is in Kathmandu's tourist areas like Thamel. Over the last few years there has been a mushrooming growth in the number of handicraft shops opened by these traders from Kashmir in Kathmandu and Pokhara. Estimates put the figure of these recent Kashmiris migrants at about 4,000 in Kathmandu and Pokhara. They are distinct from the Kathmandu Kashmiris of the valley whose ancestors are believed to have come to Kathmandu in the 16th century and have culturally assimilated. The recent arrivals have little or no interaction with the older residents of Kashmiri Muslim stock. They are watched, warily for possible linkages with militants from the Kashmir valley.

Sikh and Tamil refugees

Militant movement in India's Punjab to establish an independent state of Khalistan in the 80s led to some Sikhs crossing over to Nepal. Many of them have since migrated back to India, though some Sikhs can still be seen residing in Kathmandu, Birganj, Nepalganj and Dhangadi. Neither HMG nor UNHCR is aware of them.

A few Tamil refugees from Sri Lanka, escaping ethnic violence and displacement have made their way through India to Nepal. Press reports[7] claim that nearly 50 Tamils were residing in the vicinity of Pashupatinath temple and other areas of the Kathmandu Valley. The government of Nepal and UNHCR have not recognised any Sri Lankans as refugees.

Burmese refugees

Successive groups of Burmese citizens of Nepali origin have entered Nepal from Burma over the years because of continuing internal turmoil in that country. Most have been naturalised and rehabilitated by the government of Nepal. Many of the Burmese refugees have received Nepali citizenship.

Refugees from North-East India

Ethnic tension in the North-Eastern states of India like Assam, Meghalaya, and Arunachal Pradesh has pushed many ethnic Nepalis to return. Xenophobic "sons of the soil" campaign have on several occasions targetted the people of Nepali origin there. Many who have been made homeless have sought refugee in Nepal. Many were repatriated, while others stayed on in Nepal. There is no official estimate of their numbers. However, the situation is fraught with unsettling implications for Nepal as there are estimated to be seven million potential refugees of Nepali origin in the North-East. In the event of a spurt in ethnic tension targetted at the Nepalis as in Meghalaya in 1986,[8] there could be a mass influx of people of Nepali origin being published back into Nepal.

Indian migrants

The unique open border between India and Nepal has encouraged two way migration. Estimates of Indians seasonally migrating to Nepal and those settled in Nepal have become highly politicised since the 80s with a growing phobia about India's huge population swamping Nepal.[9] Some estimates put the figure at three to four million but it is likely to be as grossly exaggerated as is the reverse figure of three million migrants of Nepali origin in India. The 1991 Nepal census puts the figure of people of Indian origin in Nepal to be 418,982 and of Indian citizens in Nepal to be 68,489 persons.

Indian migrant workers have entered Nepal from northern India, a process facilitated by their ethnic similarities to Nepalis residing on the border in the Terai region. Thus, it is very difficult to identify who is an Indian and who a Nepali. In the 80s the government of Nepal sought to impose various legal and administrative restrictions to curtail their flow into Nepal.

UNHCR's other refugees

The UNHCR in Nepal has accorded refugee status to some Chinese (non-Tibetans), Iraqi, Afghan, and Somali refugees, but their numbers are few. Upon the breakup of the USSR, many Russians who had been staying in Nepal for some time, were helped to return.

Legal protection for refugees

Legally, refugees are treated under the laws applicable to aliens in Nepal.[10] The Citizenship Act 1975, section 3, permits the naturalization of refugees. The Immigration Act 1991 retains the power of expulsion of aliens on the grounds of national interests. The Extradition Act 1991, section 12 (1) supports the principle that political offenders are not to be extradited. This clause supports the philosophy of international refugee law. Similarly, the laws relating to marriage and passport are netural in this regard and thus in no way are hostile to the basic philosophy of refugee law.

The Foreigners Act empowers the government to regulate the entry of aliens into Nepal and their stay. The Passport Act deals with the power of the government to impose conditions of possession of a passport for entry into Nepal and the issuance of passports, travel documents and trekking permission.

As Nepal does not have any particular legislation to regulate the inflow of refugee into the country, it is being tackled by administrative measures. Government policy as regard to entry and stay of refugees and aliens has been quite liberal.

Environmental and developmental displacement

The causes of internal displacement can be classified as i) natural calamities; ii) socio-economic processes and iii) development. The main cause of displacement in Nepal are floods, landslides earthquakes and droughts. In addition, some development projects like wildlife and forestry conservation projects have displaced people. It is estimated that annually floods and landslides affect nearly 8,000 homes, displaced 40,000 people and destroy 12-15,000 hectares of paddy land.[11]

As regards socio-economic processes, internal migration is the most influential aspects of displacement. This occurs mainly from hilly areas to the plains and from rural to urban areas. The causes of internal migration are over-population, deforestation, an unsystematic system of agriculture and soil erosion. People migrate basically to secure employment. This kind of migration involves two aspects of displacement: landlessness and displacement of indigenous people.

Development projects like road and bridge construction and irrigation works have displaced many people. Hydro-electricity projects, dam construction, expansion of electric lines and establishment of wildlife conservation parks have also displaced many people. Systematic wildlife conservation started in Nepal in 1971. The first wildlife conservation project in Chitwan National Park displaced 22,000 people. Similarly, in Bardia National Park, and other wildlife parks have displaced 1,500 families.

Compensation offered to them is not sufficient for their rehabilitation. Many of them became landless and work as industrial labour. The problem of internal displacement has been brought about due to the non-accountability of the government and the lack of a responsive policy framework to meet the basic needs of the majority of the population.

Emigration from Nepal

Many people from the western and eastern hill regions have gone to India for employment and have stayed on as economic migrants. Migratory politics on both side of the Indo-Nepal border have made estimates of numbers, at best broad. Estimates of Nepali migrant workers in India range from 1.8 million to 3 million and that of Indians in Nepal 800,000 to 3.2 million.[12]

Many young people of Nepal are recruited in the Gurkha regiment of the British army and in the Indian army. Young Nepalis also go to the Gulf and East Asian countries for employment. A recent phenomenon is the massive expansion in trafficking of sex workers across the open border to India. More than 100,000 girls from Nepal are employed as sex workers in the different cities of India.

That there is a major problem of migration and survival in the hills is now coming to be recognised. But the government is yet to seriously develop the hinterland and in such a way that it does not cause more displacement. And yet Nepal with its limited carrying capacity with of 21 million people is carrying the burden of more than 110,000 refugees.

Notes

1. See Dhurba Bar Singh Thapa, paper presented at the round- table Asian Experts on current problems in the International Protection of Refugees and Displaced Persons, Manila, 14-18 August, 1980.
2. The Tibetan refugees camps are as follows; Chyaka of Solukhumbu, Syabrubesi of Rasuwa, Sawayambhu, Boudha and Jorpathi of Kathmandu, Jawalakhel of Lalitpur, Chandipokhari of Nuwakot, Hiletar ofTanahu, Hyanja and Chhorepatan of Kaski, Dorpatan of Baglung,

Chhoira of Mustang district. A new camp for the new arrivals has also been established in Kathmandu. These camps are basically used for the transit purposes.

3. *The Statement,* February 12, 1991.
4. The latest data of UNHCR shows that the registered number refugees is in the various five camps like Timai, Sanichare, Goldhap, Beldangi-1, Beldangi-2, Beldangi-2 (Extn)., Khudunabari (N), Khudunabari (S).
5. The estimated number of Bhutanese refugees outside the camps is 20,000. They are scattered in different parts of the country. Because of their ethnic identity they have been also trying to settle down in Nepal. For details see Hari Phuyal, Nepal's Response to Refugee Problem: A Case Study of Bhutanese Refugees in Eastern Nepal, *Nyayadoot,* Vol. 88, English Special Issue, 1996, pp. 80-94.
6. Article 7 of the 1950 Treaty of Peace and Friendship between India and Nepal states that the two governments "agree to grant on a reciprocal basis to the nationals of one country in the territory of each other the same privileges in matter of residence, ownership of property, participation in trade and commerce, movement and privileges of a similar nature."
7. More than four dozen Tamil refugees are reported in the news paper; see: *Shree Sagarmatha,* September 23, 1996 and October 12, 1996, Kathmandu.
8. North-East of India (Refer to Hari Phuyal, *Refugee Law*, Pairavi Books, Kathmandu, 1996, pp 76-83).
9. For further details, see the report on internal and international migration in Nepal, 1983, Kathmandu pp. 236-249 See also "Lies, Damn Lies and Numbers" by Dilli R. Dahal, *Himal South Asia*, Kathmandu, Jan-Feb 1997 p. 26
10. Articles 11, 12, 14, 15, 23 and 88 of the Constitution of the Kingdom of Nepal, 1990.
11. *Human Rights Year Book*, INSEC, Kathmandu, 1993.
12. "Lowly Labour in the Lowlands" by Kanak Mani Dixit, *Himal South Asia*, Kathmandu, Jan-Feb 1997 pp. 10-18.

Bhutanese Lhotsampas

Victims of ethnic cleansing

Rakesh Chhetri

Located in the eastern Himalaya, Bhutan is a tiny kingdom sandwiched between two Asian giants, India and China, with a geographical area of 46,500 sq km. and a population of little over 600,000. Bhutan is the last bastion of hereditary feudal monarchy. But Bhutan's tranquil image of Shangrila has received a battering over the last seven years as 20 percent of its population has been turned into stateless refugees. More than 100,000 Lhotsampas or Nepali speaking southern Bhutanese have been pushed out of Bhutan.

In the name of preserving the Bhutanese identity, the state policy of Bhutanisation or *Drukpaisation* has triggered off a series of politically erratic, racist and discriminatory policies against the Lhotsampas. The Lhotsampas and other ethnic groups are under pressure to assimilate their social and cultural identity with that of the politically and socially-dominant Drukpa ethnic group. The Bhutanese government's policies of assimilation and integration met with stubborn resistance, first from the Lhotsampas and then from the Sarchops, the second largest ethnic group after the Lhotsampas.

Bhutan has three major ethnic groups, Drukpas, Sarchops and Lhotsampas, living in culturally separate regions, in the north, east and southern foothills. All three groups are immigrants. The Drukpas, the ruling group migrated from Tibet around ninth century. They speak *Dzonkha* and inhabit the north-western parts of Bhutan. Drukpa refers to the followers of the Drukpa Kargyupa school of Tibetan Tantric Buddhism.

The Sarchops of Tibeto-Burman stock who supposedly migrated from North-East India speak *Changla* language and live in eastern and central Bhutan. The Lhotsampas speak Nepali language and inhabit the southern foothills from east to west. Historical evidence of the migration of these ethnic groups does not exist. But there is no history of communal or ethnic clashes in Bhutan.

In Bhutan, politics is practised along ethnic lines and has become the monopoly of a single ethnic group, the Drukpas. *Tshogdu*, the National Assembly of Bhutan has 150 members, of which a 100 members represent the people and 40 members are nominated by the king from among the bureaucracy and 10 members are nominated by the clergy, called Monk Body which has a strength of 5,000 monks and is dependent on government subsidy. It often interferes in the administration and legislative process.

The over representation of the Drukpa community in the government is evident. Out of thirteen ministerial posts twelve are held by them and out of nine Royal Advisory Councillors, five are from the Drupka community. At the officials level, eight of the nine secretaries to government, are Drukpas. High posts in the army, police and the bureaucracy are all dominated by Drukpas.

Nation building: Assimilate or quit

Bhutan was originally a religious colony of Tibetan Lamas who migrated from Tibet. State policy, was essentially directed at preserving Bhutan from Tibetan invasion. However after 1950, the Bhutanese state, concentrated on nation-state building, seeking to evolve a Bhutanese identity, culturally and ethnically, distinct from the Tibetans. Bhutan had watched the annexation of Tibet and cultural cleansing with gloom and foreboding.

Unlike most of the South Asian nations, nation building in Bhutan is not inspired by the nationalistic zeal against a foreign rule. Bhutan's geopolitical features, such as high mountains, rugged terrain, a difficult river system, inhospitable climate and poor communications have discouraged conquest. Moreover, British India's desire to keep the Himalayan kingdom as a buffer state between India and China explains why Bhutan maintained its independence from the colonial power. Geography and the absence of external threat from its southern neighbour had encouraged a sense of security in Bhutan.

Instead, internecine strife among regional chieftains resulted in group loyalties overriding nationalistic aspirations towards a strong national government. The existence of multi-ethnic and multi-linguistic groups with parochial regional attitudes and loyalties was also responsible for shaping the Bhutanese peoples' allegiance to group loyalties.

In the absence of a strong tradition of nation building, nationalism was by and large state sponsored. The state made it mandatory for all citizens to take an oath of allegiance to *Tsa- Wa-Sum* or the king, the kingdom and the people. This law has exerted profound influence in shaping and consolidating nationalism in Bhutan. *Tsa-Wa-Sum* demands complete allegiance of the citizens to the three elements. In fact, any "offence" to the three elements is punishable with a death sentence. Tek Nath Rizal, former royal advisory councillor was arrested for writing critically about the king and the government. Recognised by Amnesty International as a "Prisoner of Conscience", Rizal has been languishing in jail since November 16, 1989, serving a life sentence.

For the ruling Drukpa elites, "Bhutanese national identity" has meant "One Nation One People". Forced assimilation and integration, through eviction, by depriving the Lhotsampas of their nationality and through brutal intimidation and the use of force has been the hallmark of state policy. The state authority believes, "Pluralism is practical for a large country but not for a small country like Bhutan." Religion, that is, Buddhism, has been used as a political tool by the leadership. Buddhism and the feudal institutions of power are so intertwined that they have almost become synonymous.

Apprehensive about the democratic winds of change blowing across the subcontinent, threatening the feudatory monarchy in Bhutan, the king and his coterie have pursued an assimilationist strategy centred around One Nation One People, particularly targeted at the Lhotsampas, estimated to be from 30 to 52 percent of Bhutan's total population. The ruling elites viewed the Lhotsampas as a serious threat to the monarchy and the dominance of the Drukpas. The Lhotsampas are politically more conscious, better educated and more exposed to modernising and democratic influences of India and Nepal. Difficulties in integrating the Lhotsampas into the national mainstream defined in the image of Drukpa identity, made the Drukpa elites extremely uneasy. Propaganda about the destabilising role of the people of Nepali origin in the fall of the Chogyal, the ruler of Sikkim, and its merger with India, in 1975 fanned a phobia of the Lhotsampas destabilising the monarchy in Bhutan.

Like other South Asian nations, engaged in nation building, Bhutan has been facing the problems of national integration, arising out of sub-national conflicts. An insecure state leadership in Bhutan is facing growing demands for political participation by an emerging middle class. Democratic consciousness has been slow to reach Bhutan but incipient pressures are building up in support of the establishment of popular sovereignty and the rule of law.

The response of the state has been to create and exploit the religious and ethnic divide between the north and south. Now, it has started to divide the Buddhist population. The Nyingmapas, who historically co-existed with the Drukpa Kargyupas, are being discriminated against. The Nyingmapas are being seen with suspicion and the practice of their religion is subjected to state scrutiny. The Sarchops belong to the Nyingmapa sect. The arrest of Rongthong Kuenly Dorji in New Delhi in April 1997, at the behest of the Bhutan government, has focused attention on the increasing involvement of the Sarchop community in the democratic movement. Dorji is the chairman of the United Democratic Front working for the establishment of democratic rights in Bhutan. The heavy security presence in southern Bhutan is being extended to eastern Bhutan, where the Sarchop community is concentrated.

Since the inception of hereditary monarchy in 1907, institutionalization of dynastic rule has been a problem in Bhutan. Even the traditional legitimacy of the rule of Wangchuk dynasty has been questioned. The four Shabdrungs, the Dharma Rajas or the monk rulers from Tibet who unified Bhutan, were assassinated at the behest of Wangchuks. The present Shabdrung reincarnate lives in exile in India.

The north-south or Drukpa-Lhotsampas tension developed in the 1980s when the Bhutanese government initiated several policies which actively disadvantaged the Lhotsampa community which eventually led it to its revolt against the domination of Drukpa government.

Buddhist fundamentalism

The role of Buddhism in Bhutan has direct implication for Lhotsampas and other minorities. In Bhutan, the Buddhist religion and the state are inseparable. As per Buddhist tenets, the ruler is not only the manager of secular affairs of the state but also the guardian of the religion and the patron of the monastic bodies, the lamasaries and the religio-cultural traditions of the land.

Buddhism is the most important factor in Bhutanese society. The lamas, the clerics, hold positions of esteem and repute in Bhutan. Religion in Bhutan is not only a body of supernatural beliefs and practices but also a body of knowledge, science, art, medicine and astronomy. Social and economic life are integrally connected with religion. Drukpa and Sarchop societies revolve round the monastery. A good proportion of their manpower is involved in monastic affairs, whether they take up religion as profession or not. Buddhism is the state religion, but royal authority reigns supreme over ecclesiastical authority. Even the *je khempos* (chief abbot) is appointed by the king. Control of the monastic order was reinforced in 1969 when the government substituted the system by which monastic institutions used to collect land rent in kind from designated lands with direct state subsidies.

The monarchy used Buddhism to legitimise the rule of Druk Gyalpo and the political programme of ethnic cleansing. State sponsored revival of Buddhist fundamentalism led to communalisation of politics. The revival of political Drukpaisation and Buddhism shaped several Drukpa myths. The Drukpas came to be viewed as the defenders of the faith and the country against heathen encroachments from not only the Hindu Lhotsampas but also the Sarchops. The Lhotsampas were declared illegal immigrants and the Sarchops of Nyingmapa sect a threat to Drukpa Kargyupa Buddhism and the Drukpa value system. Drukpa Buddhism as the preserve of Druk Gyalpo has been used actively by the state both to consolidate control and to discredit the opposition. The Drukpaisation programme aims at preserving the feudal order in Bhutan against emerging democratic consciousness.

Drukpa ethnocentrism

The government is pursuing a programme to make Bhutan culturally homogenous through the policy of One Nation One People. This policy stresses the need for a distinct "national identity", but does not envisage forging this identity to encompass the diversity of national cultures.

The present political crisis in Bhutan owes its origin to Drukpa ethnocentrism which is determined to build a nation-state on Drukpa culture and values out of a multi-ethnic society. The policy of cultural purification consists of a series of laws passed in recent years, culminating in a national dress code, a national code of conduct and uniform language requirements.

Dress code

The Druk Gyalpo issued a royal decree (*kasho*) on January 6, 1989 implementing *driglam namza* to promote a distinct national identity in pursuit of a One Nation, One People theme. The *driglam namza* decree imposes the code of the Drukpas of the north upon the entire populace. It deals with how to eat, how to sit, how to speak, how to dress and how to bow down before authorities in true feudal style. The dress code which enjoins all to wear the dress of the northern

Drukpas, that is, *gho* for men and *kira* for women, is being strictly enforced with penalties. *Gho* and *kira* are the traditional costumes of the northern Drukpas and not at all suited to the warm climate of the southern Terai.

Failure to abide by the *driglam namza* is subjected to a week in prison or a fine. The royal decree states that "all persons not following this directive will be answerable to the concerned *dzongdas* (chief district administrators) who have been vested with full authority to implement this policy". This policy has led to widespread abuses. Even the king was obliged to remonstrate with his over zealous officials. "I told the southerners that they could wear what they liked, as long as it is distinct from the dress of neighbouring countries. We are a small nation between two giant neighbours. All we have is our cultural identity", the king explained.

Language policy

Under the *driglam namza*, the government made the Dzonkha language, the mother tongue of Drukpas, the sole national language. In February 1989, the teaching of Nepali language as part of the school curriculum in southern Bhutan was banned. Schools had been teaching Nepali language since the 1960s. Dzonkha was introduced in the school curriculum in the 1990s in southern Bhutan.

Earlier, all official correspondence in southern Bhutan was done in Nepali. Laws and even five year plan documents are written in Nepali. *Kuensel*, the official newspaper, was published in Nepali, Dzonkha and English. The government-controlled radio, Bhutan Broadcasting Service, broadcasts in four languages, including Nepali. The deliberations of Tshogdu were simultaneously translated into Nepali.

No objection certificate

In 1990, the government introduced a draconian rule requiring a no objection certificate (NOC) from the police and local administration in southern Bhutan. The government contends that "to ensure that all bona fide Bhutanese children received the first preference for admission in schools, a no objection certificate was made essential". However, NOC "would not be issued to those students who have been involved in anti-national activities or to the children of illegal immigrants." NOCs were also required "for the release of cheques to farmers for the sale of their cash corps". The certificate is denied to anyone whose relative is suspected of having participated in the peaceful demonstrations of September and October 1990. NOCs were virtually impossible for Lhotsampas to obtain.

This rule has effectively ensured that Lhotsampas are denied admissions to schools and colleges in Bhutan, excluded from getting scholarships to study abroad and promotion in government services. Moreover, the farmers are denied the sale proceeds from their cash crops. The rule is still in force despite official claims of abandoning it. The NOC is used to prevent Lhotsampas from taking jobs or educational seats in many districts of Bhutan

Marriage Act

The Marriage Act was forcefully implemented in 1988 targeting the Lhotsampas. The law denies promotion in government service, training and fellowships abroad, to all those who marry non-Bhutanese citizens. Lhotsampas who marry non-Bhutanese become ineligible for election to Tshogdu, for jobs in the Foreign Service or Armed Forces and for medical treatment abroad and for business and agricultural loans, state subsidised fertilizers and seeds. The

Lhotsampas are particularly hard-hit by this law as there is a tradition of choosing spouses of their own ethnic groups from Nepal and India.

Until the late 70s, the government did not allow Lhotsampas, Sarchops and other ethnic groups to buy land or property north of Chhimakothi, in Thimpu or in the north-western districts where Drukpas lived . Even for travel within the country, all ethnic groups except Drukpas needed prior approval of the Home Ministry. As a result there was little interaction among the various ethnic or religious groups. The absence of lateral and feeder roads linking different districts reinforced the isolation of the different communities.

Given the lack of communication infrastructure within Bhutan, it was easier to travel to a neighbouring country than to visit other districts of Bhutan. Bhutanese are required to travel through India to go from east to west in the south and from south to north and east to north-west. The expansion of development activities in Bhutan after the 1960s held out the prospect of jobs in government and business. Educated Lhotsampas looked for educated spouses of same ethnicity from neighbouring countries, who could work in the offices and start businesses. Darjeeling district in India is regarded as the best place for education in the entire region of Bhutan, Nepal and North-East India. Most of the Lhotsampas students married schoolmates who were from Darjeeling and Nepal.

Inter-community marriages in Bhutan are rare. In 1988, the government reported 11,442 marriages between Bhutanese and non-Bhutanese in the last 20 years. Today, marriage to a non-Bhutanese can result in the denial of citizenship rights. Refugees have denounced the Marriage Act 1988 as a grand design on the part of the state to harass the Lhotsampas and force them to leave the country. Moreover, the law is implemented in a discriminatory manner, very rigidly against the Lhotsampas and not at all against the Drukpas who may have Chinese, English, Italian or American wives.

Citizenship Act, 1985

The question of nationality and the method employed to determine citizenship is at the core of the refugee crisis in Bhutan. Bhutan's first attempt to define citizenship came with National Law of Bhutan, 1958. This Act was changed in 1977 and again in 1985. The government attaches great importance to these laws as forming a bulwark. It is all that stands between the survival of the distinct political and cultural identity of the people of Bhutan and overwhelming demographic pressures from outside.

The National Law of 1958 granted citizenship to anyone whose father was a Bhutanese citizen, who was born within Bhutan or who had lived there for ten years and owned agricultural land within the kingdom. The 1985 Citizenship Act codified a new basis for citizenship in Bhutan: a proof of residence in Bhutan before December 31, 1958. The new citizenship law required that both parents be Bhutanese citizens in order to transfer citizenship rights to their children.

Children born of a marriage between a Bhutanese and a non-Bhutanese are not entitled to Bhutanese citizenship by birth. The child can at the age of fifteen apply for naturalisation. Rigorous conditions have to be met to be eligible for naturalisation, including fluency in speaking, reading and writing the Drukpa mother tongue, Dzonkha. Few Lhotsampas and Sarchops pass the test. Most are illiterate even in their own mother tongues. Naturalised citizens must also prove prior residence in Bhutan of 15 to 20 years and be recorded with the Department of Immigration and Census and the Ministry of Home Affairs. The Council of Ministers including the Home Ministry was established only in 1968 and the Department of Immigration and Census, in the mid-80s. Moreover, such persons must have no record of having spoken or acted against king, country and the people of Bhutan. Even if all these requirements are fulfilled, the government reserves the right to reject any application for naturalisation without assigning any reason . Northerners do not have to prove anything at all to retain their nationality and citizenship.

Residents in the south, who could not prove that both parents were Bhutanese citizens were declared illegal immigrants, retroactively, even if they had been citizens under the National Law of 1958. These rules enable the government to claim that the most of the Lhotsampas are not Bhutanese citizens. International human rights groups have reported that the authorities confiscate and destroy whatever documentary evidence exists particularly citizenship identification cards, issued by the government.

The Citizenship Act, 1985 has great scope for creating statelessness. Under this law dissidents accused of speaking or criticising the king and government can be stripped of citizenship. Further, there are those who fled Bhutan to escape persecution, only to find that they have been stripped of their nationality, because fleeing amounts to disloyalty according to the Bhutanese authorities.

Census or eviction exercise

The Citizenship Act, 1985 came into force in 1988, when the government undertook a population census in southern Bhutan. The census set out to determine the citizenship status of Lhotsampas by categorising residents into seven groups: i) genuine Bhutanese, ii) returned migrants, iii) dropout cases of people who were not around at the time of the census, iv) a non-national woman married to a Bhutanese man v) a non-national man married to a Bhutanese woman, vi) adoption cases and vii) non-nationals, i.e. illegal immigrants.

Officially, the 1988 census implemented the Citizenship Act, 1985, with its three methods of attaining citizenship: by having two Bhutanese parents, by registration of residence since 1958 and by naturalisation. In practice, however, the census exercise provided justification to expel people who were no longer wanted.

The census rules mandated that the Lhotsampas provide proof of residence in the country during 1958, the cut-off year. The only valid document acceptable to the census team was the land tax paid receipts for 1958. Receipts issued before 1958 were not accepted on the pretext that the person could have migrated out of the country prior to 1958 and returned after the cut-off year. As a result several thousand were declared "illegal immigrants". For in-country migration, people were asked to produce a certificate of origin from the district authorities. Those who had lost their documents due to natural calamities were simply treated as illegal immigrants

The government has claimed that the level of illegal migration into southern Bhutan after 1958 has been as high as to comprise 20 percent of the total population. But these so-called illegal immigrants have lived in Bhutan for years, owned houses and properties, paid taxes to the government and contributed to the nation building of Bhutan. Some have served in government offices, the armed forces and police and received government scholarships to study abroad. They were bonafide citizens until 1987, but were made illegal immigrants in 1988 because southern Bhutan had to be depopulated to pre-empt any dissidence and demand for democratic reforms.

Following the census of 1981, all citizens were issued citizenship identity cards. The government claims that these cards are forged. Initially, the Bhutanese government claimed that any documentary evidence whatsoever, land ownership deeds, sale receipts, inheritance of land and tax receipts would prove residence in Bhutan in 1958 and thus conclusive proof of citizenship. But now the government contends that payment of property tax in itself is no proof as many illegal immigrants in Bhutan had acquired property.

The situation in southern Bhutan has been exacerbated by the government's failure to make known in advance what would happen to people in southern Bhutan once they were categorised as non-nationals. Since 1990, many of these people, some of whom were born in Bhutan and had lived there for years, were forced to quit Bhutan. Moreover, thousands of citizens have been forced to flee or asked to fill up voluntary migration forms under duress. Citizens who "voluntarily" migrated are not allowed to return to the country.

Census exercises are being used to target Lhotsampas. In May 1997, a census exercise took place in Samchi district in southern Bhutan, the sixth in less than 10 years. The census authorities revoked the citizenship of hundreds of Lhotsampas. As a result they cannot return to work in the capital Thimpu, nor can they stay at home.

Green belt policy

In March 1990 the government introduced a green belt policy creating a kilometre-wide belt of forests along the border in southern Bhutan. The area involved was not wasteland but some of the only available plains in the country, providing the most fertile paddy fields being cultivated by the Lhotsampas. Even where compensation was forthcoming, the Lhotsampas resisted being resettled in northern lands, unsuitable for agriculture and disruptive of their community. The programme has been quietly abandoned as ill conceived.

Unwanted peoples: resettlement and integration

In a bid to crush the democratic movement, the government has deftly crafted three strategies. The first is to discredit the democratic movement by projecting the Lhotsampas as illegal immigrants through "paper war" or propaganda. The propaganda machinery of the government is spreading the canard that the Nepali people who outnumber the indigenous Drukpas are determined to take over political power in Bhutan as they did in Sikkim.

The second strategy is to break the leadership of the democracy movement by getting Rongtong Kuenley Dorji of the UDF extradited to Bhutan. In April 1997, Dorji was arrested in Delhi at the behest of the Bhutanese government for fraud and non-payment of loans to the Bank of Bhutan and for political offences against the Bhutanese state. The Indo-Bhutan extradition treaty imposes restrictions on the extradition of political dissidents. However, to make the extradition case stronger and give it an abetment to terrorism dimension, an orchestrated media campaign has insinuated that Dorji collaborated with the Bodo and ULFA militants of Assam. Pro-democracy activities claim that it is the government of Bhutan, which has forged a covert alliance with the North-East insurgents providing them sanctuary in return for their muscle power in terrorising the Lhotsampas. The policy has come home to roost with the Indian government pressing the Bhutanese authorities to allow "hot pursuit" to flush out the ULFA and Bodo insurgents. Bhutan has so far refused.

The third strategy is an insidious move to resettle and integrate the Bhutanese refugees in India. Reports indicate that the Bhutanese government is lobbying with UNHCR to disband the refugee camps in Nepal. A plan to resettle 50,000 refugees in India, 50,000 in Nepal and to repatriate 15,000 to Bhutan is being tossed around.

Conclusion

Local or regional integration is not a solution. It legitimises the right of the state to disenfranchise their citizens. Moreover, in the long term it could encourage more population displacements. South Asia is the home of cross border migrations. Nepalis for one, are spread all over India and Bhutan, Bhutanese are settled in Nepal and India. Given the ethnic volatility of the region any move to regionally integrate the Bhutanese refugees, would create problems. There is no guarantee that the Bhutanese refugees will turn their backs on the oppression of the Lhotsampas in Bhutan.

The UNHCR proposal to send back the refugees in batches of 5,000 is devoid of political realism. If the refugees are sent back without affecting any political reform, the refugees are bound to come back. The plight of the Bhutanese refugees is a humanitarian issue. But any settlement of the refugee problem must extend beyond issues of human rights to political solutions. Moreover, the state's forceful assimilation of cultures has revived "lost identities". A significant politicisation of the refugees has taken place.

Bhutan's greatest challenge will be how to bring the alienated Lhotsampas back into the mainstream of Bhutanese participatory life. But there are deep-rooted suspicions among the Lhotsampas about the intentions of Thimphu regime. The seven rounds of Nepal-Bhutan ministerial level talks on the refugee crisis has only reinforced misgivings about the non-accommodative attitude of the Bhutanese government. Unless the king , who reigns supreme in Bhutan begins a dialogue with the leaders of the democratic movement and agrees to the repatriation of all the refugees without any preconditions, the refugee crisis will remain.

Bhutanese Refugees
Right to return

Ratan Gazmer

Bhutan's population of 600,000 comprises three major ethnic groups. The Drukpas inhabiting western Bhutan comprise 15 percent of the population, the Sarchops settled in the east are 33 percent and the Lhotsampas or the Nepali-speaking Bhutanese constitute 45 percent of the population and live predominantly in southern Bhutan. Bhutanese refugees in Nepal and India constitute 17 percent of the total population of Bhutan and are mostly southern Bhutanese.

Making of a stateless peoples

In 1988, the Royal Government of Bhutan (RGB) implemented the 1985 Citizenship Act and began to revoke the citizenship of tens of thousands of southern Bhutanese. Having revoked their citizenship, arbitrarily, the RGB declared Bhutanese, bona fide citizens under the 1958 Nationality Law and 1977 Citizenship Act of Bhutan, illegal immigrants.

On January 16, 1989, the RGB implemented the "One Nation One People" policy — encroaching upon the cultural sovereignty of southern Bhutanese and other ethnic groups in Bhutan by denying them the right to enjoy their own culture, wear their ethnic dress and learn their own language. Instead, the language, culture and dress of the ruling western Bhutanese elite was made mandatory and imposed on all Bhutanese. Failure to observe the policy entitled punishment.

On April 9, 1988, Tek Nath Rizal and B.P. Bhandari, the elected royal advisory councillors for southern Bhutan appealed to His Majesty King Jigme Singye Wangchuk to restore citizenship to those southern Bhutanese from whom it had been withdrawn. Tek Nath Rizal was arrested. After three days in prison, Rizal was released, his councillorship, terminated. As human rights abuses in Bhutan intensified, Rizal went into exile in Nepal from where he launched a campaign to protect human rights in Bhutan. Rizal was abducted in Nepal by the RGB on November 16, 1989 and thrown into a Bhutanese jail. Rizal continues to suffer arbitrary detention.

The southern Bhutanese people organised peaceful demonstrations in protest at the discriminatory citizenship laws and the racist One Nation One People Policy. The movement for human rights eventually transformed into a movement for democracy. But the RGB crushed the peaceful peoples movement, imposing military rule in southern Bhutan. There were hundreds of arbitrary arrests and detentions without trial. Harassment, torture and rape became routine. Confiscation of citizenship cards, loot, plunder and arson by the security forces was rampant.

In southern Bhutan, schools were closed down and turned into army barracks and prison-cum-torture centres. Restrictions were imposed on health, education and other welfare facilities. Movement of essential commodities like salt and kerosene was banned. No objection certificate (NOC) was introduced as a prerequisite for access to education, civil service jobs, and for sale of cash crops. Families with members suspected of involvement in the movement or participation in a demonstration, were denied NOCs.

During the 70th session of the National Assembly in 1991, the RGB resolved to evict anyone involved in the peaceful demonstration or anyone related to a supporter of the human rights movement. Eviction was legitimised with the RGB introducing the voluntary migration forms (VMF). Putting this plan into action, the RGB rounded up prominent citizens in schools which had been turned into detention cum torture centres and coerced them to leave the country. They were tortured until they agreed to sign the VMF. Once prominent citizens in southern Bhutan capitulated, the general population fell an easy prey. Today, the majority of the Bhutanese refugees in Nepal and in India are those who have been forced to sign the VMF under duress and forced into exile.

According to David Thronson, the state policy has been one of cultural cleansing. "The picture is not one of a sudden realisation, thirty years after the fact, that Bhutan was inhabited by a large number of illegal ethnic Nepalis, but rather a scenario of escalating concern over the failure to integrate this portion of the population into the politically dominant Drupka culture. The progression of citizenship laws, the policies on *driglam namza* (western Bhutanese traditional and cultural values) and language, and especially the events since 1988 reflect a growing assimilationist, and failing that exclusionist, mood," writes Thronson.[1]

The refugee crisis

In the face of government repression and fearing persecution, thousands of southern Bhutanese fled into India. As of September 30, 1996, there were 92,787 Bhutanese refugees in camps in east Nepal. Another 50,000 Bhutanese refugees are scattered in parts of Nepal and the north-eastern states of India.

A sample survey conducted by the Home Ministry of Nepal in February 1995 among 12,500 heads of households in the refugee camps, showed that 85 percent possess citizenship identity cards, 10 percent have land tax receipts, and three percent school certificates or other official documents. Only two percent have no certification, and many of them claim it was confiscated by the authorities before they left Bhutan.[2]

Both at the government level and at the people's level, there have been several initiatives to resolve the refugees crisis.

Bhutan-Nepal bilateral talks

The Bhutan-Nepal Joint Ministerial Level Committee (JMLC) was formed on July 17, 1993. Since then there have been seven rounds of bilateral negotiation between the governments of Bhutan and Nepal to solve the Bhutanese refugee problem but there has little progress towards solution.

Round One: Kathmandu, October 1993 : The JMLC agreed to classify Bhutanese refugees into four categories: i) bonafide Bhutanese citizens who have been forcibly evicted; ii) Bhutanese who have emigrated; iii) non-Bhutanese people and iv) Bhutanese who have committed criminal acts.

Round Two: Thimpu, February 1994: Nepal pressed for the involvement of a third party.

Round Three: Kathmandu, April 1994: Disagreement between Bhutan and Nepal on the four categories.

Round Four: Thimpu, June 1994: Disagreement between Bhutan and Nepal on their position on the four categories

Round Five: Kathmandu, February-March 1995: The JMLC held extensive discussions on their positions regarding the four categories.

Round Six: Thimpu, April 1995: The JMLC exchanged names of five members of the Joint Verification Team.

Round Seven: Kathmandu, April 1996: Unlike the other rounds of talk, the seventh round of dialogue between Bhutan and Nepal was held at the level of foreign ministers. Talks were resumed at the backdrop of a people peace march to Bhutan undertaken by Bhutanese refugees and the European Parliament's call on March 15, 1996 asking the Bhutanese government to take practical steps to prepare for a UNHCR supervised repatriation of the Bhutanese refugees.

Although the level of optimism prevailing before the seventh round of bilateral talks was high, the talks ended in a fiasco. The Bhutanese delegation remained adamant that refugee verification should be based *only* on citizenship and the emigration law of Bhutan. Bhutan would not take back people falling under category (ii) that is, those who were said to have emigrated. As for Nepal the then Foreign Minister, Dr. Prakash Chandra Lohani declared, "If they (Bhutan) can apply Bhutanese law, then Nepal too can apply its own law which does not provide Nepali citizenship to refugees. By law then, these refugees are stateless people. In essence, what this means is that if Bhutan refuses to take back all the refugees, then there will be thousands of stateless people which is a violation of UN Universal Declaration of Human Rights.... Our position is that the whole idea of voluntary immigration (by refugees) does not make sense. They were Bhutanese citizens before coming to the camps in Nepal and they should turn back home."

It is evident that a resolution of the problem through the bilateral negotiation is not possible. Unfortunately, the government of India which has the requisite leverage and influence to solve the problem has continued to remain silence on the issue.

Bhutanese refugees appeal movement

Disenchanted at the lack of progress in the Bhutan-Nepal bilateral talks and the diminishing international attention to their plight, Bhutanese refugees launched an appeal movement. Representatives from all the seven Bhutanese refugee camps in east Nepal and Bhutanese non-governmental organisations in exile, came together in September 1995 and set up Appeal Movement Coordination Council (AMCC). The objectives of the appeal movement are: i) the restoration of fundamental human rights in Bhutan. ii) the repatriation of Bhutanese refugees.

The AMCC sent a series of petition to His Majesty the King of Bhutan appealing to him to embrace national reconciliation to solve the problem. However, it failed to receive any positive response from the Royal government and launched Phase II of the movement. It began with a peaceful appeal march to Bhutan on January 14, 1996.

A hundred and fifty Bhutanese refugee volunteers from camps in east Nepal set off on a peace march to Bhutan in an assertion of their right to return to their country and the right of freedom of peaceful assembly and association as enshrined in Articles 13 and 20 of the UN Universal Declaration of Human Rights. Unfortunately, on January 17, the 150 peace marchers were stopped at the Indo-Nepal border on the Mechi bridge by the Indian police on the grounds that they were violating section 144 of the Indian Criminal Procedure Code prohibiting assembly.

The refugees, in fact, were returning along the same land route that they had taken while fleeing the Bhutanese government's persecution. Technically, India had been the first country of asylum. But the peace marchers were arrested by the Indian police and detained in the jails of Siliguri and Jalpaiguri, West Bengal.

Subsequent peace marches by batches of Bhutanese refugee volunteers have met the same fate at the Indo-Nepal border. They have been arrested and detained in the jails of Siliguri, Jalpaiguri and Berhampur. The first batch of peace marchers were unconditionally released on February 27 following an indefinite fast undertaken by 74 of them in the Jalpaiguri jail. The ruling by the Sub-Divisional Judicial Magistrate's Court declared the promulgation of section 144 of the Criminal Procedure Code baseless and hence their arrest illegal. Subsequently, by March 25, all other peace marchers were unconditionally released. Four batches, totaling 950 volunteers, including 157 women, participated in the first wave of peace marchers till March 12, 1996.

The second wave of peace marches took place in the district of Jalpaiguri after the peace marchers were unconditionally released by the Judicial Magistrate in Darjeeling. However, when 150 volunteers resumed the Peace March to Bhutan from their relief camp in Panchanadi, Siliguri, they were intercepted by the administration of Jalpaiguri district on March 17 and were arrested and detained in Indian jails. On March 19, another batch of 188 volunteers was severely lathi-charged by the Indian police at Shaheed Nagar in north of Siliguri in Jalpaiguri district. In this second wave five batches of 792 peace marchers including 128 women participated between March 17 to April 5, 1996. Although they were allowed to move into Darjeeling district, they were arrested as soon as they entered Jalpaiguri.

On three occasions, the peace marchers were brutally lathi-charged. In jail the conditions were appalling. One of the peace marchers Baburam Shengden died in Berhampur central jail. On July 5, the Calcutta High Court ordered the unconditional release of the peace marchers after they went on an indefinite fast in Berhampur jail.

In the third wave, 258 Bhutanese refugee volunteers including 44 women undertook a peace march to Bhutan between June 3-25. This time the Indian administration introduced a new twist in the tactics of interception and arrest. Peace marchers were picked up and the original 150 crossed the Indo-Bhutan border on August 15, 1996, only to be brutally thrown back on Indian soil by the Bhutanese police at night on August 16. The peace marchers were thrown out of running vehicles in the middle of right and left in dense jungles. The Indian authorities turned a blind eye to the whole situation despite the fact that this deportation of Bhutanese citizens onto Indian soil by Bhutanese forces was an outright violation of international law.

The AMCC has been repeatedly appealing to the Indian government and the world community about the plight of the Bhutanese refugees. The Indian administration's harassment of the Bhutanese refugee peace marchers is testimony of the negative attitude of the government of Indian towards the suffering the Bhutanese refugees.

On November 16, 1996 another batch of fifty Bhutanese peace marchers were arrested by the Indian police from the Indo-Bhutan border at Phuntsholing. The peace marchers were trying to enter the kingdom to appeal to the King in person, to solve the problem of Bhutanese refugees. But the Bhutan police barricaded the entry gate at Phuntsholing barring peace marchers from proceeding. The Indian police arrested them under the pretext of "apprehension of breach of peace" promulgating section 107 Criminal Procedure Code. The marchers were detained in Alipurduar jail, Jalpaiguri district of West Bengal, India.

The Bhutanese refugees are firm on their determination to return to Bhutan, their country of origin. The AMCC remains committed to work for a safe and honourable repatriation of the Bhutanese refugees.

Notes

1. David B Thronson, *Cultural Cleansing*, Inhured, Kathmandu, 1993.
2. Extract from *Refugees of the Peaceful Dragon*, by Lutheran World Service; see also Amnesty International, *Bhutan: Forcible Exile*, 1994 p1.

Tibetan Refugees in Nepal

Balancing humanitarian and security concerns

Angela Dietrich

A year after the emergence of the People's Republic of China (PRC) the Chinese occupation of Tibet began in 1950. Upon Mao Zedong's announcement that he would "liberate" Tibet by January 1950, the Dalai Lama dispatched envoys to Nepal, India, the US and the UK requesting assistance to maintain Tibet's sovereignty. Though India and Nepal were obliged by treaty to assist Tibet in the event of an invasion, neither of these countries was prepared to intervene at the crucial moment.

Nepal was bound by the Nepal-Tibet Treaty of 1856 to assist Tibet in the event of an attack. That Nepal had viewed Tibet as an independent state was evident as late as 1949 when, in an effort to strengthen its case for admission into the United Nations, Nepal emphasised that it entertained diplomatic relations with Tibet as an "independent state".

In May 1951, China pressurised Tibet into signing a 17-Point Agreement, which formalised the alleged "peaceful liberation of Tibet". The Chinese government pledged to recognise Tibet's autonomy, its system of self-government, the leadership of the Dalai Lama and the Panchen Lama, to respect Tibetans' religious freedom and to ensure the protection of monasteries and the maintenance of the education system of Tibet. The Chinese progressively retracted from most of the points of the Agreement.

Upon the Dalai Lama's dramatic escape to India on March 17, 1959, he was given a warm welcome by Prime Minister Jawaharlal Nehru. In the wake of the unrest which broke out in Lhasa after the Dalai Lama's flight, 87,000 Tibetans were reported to have been killed by Chinese security forces. Nehru stated in the Indian Parliament, "We have every sympathy for the people of Tibet, and we are greatly distressed at their helpless plight. We hope still that the authorities of China, in their wisdom, will not use their great strength against the Tibetans, but will win them to friendly cooperation in accordance with assurances they have themselves given about the autonomy of Tibet region. Above all, we hope that the fighting and killing will cease".[1]

The Dalai Lama formally repudiated the 17-point Agreement in April 1959 and formed the Tibetan Government in Exile or the Central Tibetan Administration (CTA), as the sole legitimate governmental authority for Tibetans, inside and outside Tibet. Soon, about 100,000 Tibetans were to flee Tibet and become refugees. By June, 1959, nearly 20,000 had made their way to Nepal, India and Bhutan. In their escape over treacherous mountain terrain, they ran the risk of death, disease and frostbite, but those who managed to survive, that is the first influx of Tibetans, were granted asylum in Nepal and India.

Following the Dalai Lama's departure from Tibet, the situation there rapidly deteriorated as revealed in a secret report on the situation in Tibet in 1962, recently released by the Tibet Information Network (TIN). The report is based on a 70,000 character petition supposedly made by the Panchen Lama to the Chinese government to review its policies in Tibet. In the report, the Panchen Lama, the most important religious leader in Tibet following the Dalai Lama's departure and the head of the Tibetan government there, apparently disclosed the existence of mass arrests, political executions and starvation in Tibet between 1959 and 1961.[2] According to the TIN release the Panchen Lama wrote, "In many parts of Tibet people have starved to death ... in some places whole families have perished and the death rate is very high .... In the past Tibet lived in a dark barbaric feudalism but there was never such a shortage of food, especially after Buddhism had spread." The Panchen Lama makes it clear that the deaths were the result of official policies, not of natural disasters, as Mao claimed to foreign visitors.

It revealed that starvation still existed in Quinghai in 1962. The TIN report appears to confirm the suspicion that China had concealed a man-made famine in the years after the Great Leap Forward. It substantiates the allegations made by Tibetan refugees at the time, which had been openly ridiculed in the West. The report supports the findings of the 1960 report by the International Commission of Jurists which concluded that there was *prima facie* evidence of genocide in Tibet. In the petition the Panchen Lama stated, "The population of Tibet has been seriously reduced ... (which) poses a grave danger to the very existence of the Tibetan race .... Of the 2,500 monasteries which had once existed only 70 were left and 93 percent of the monks and nuns had been forced out". This was four years before the Cultural Revolution which is usually blamed for the closure and destruction of the monasteries in Tibet.

According to the Office of Tibet, a branch of the CTA, approximately 1.2 million Tibetans, about a sixth of the total population, have died since 1949 as a result of political persecution, imprisonment, torture and famine. The TIN report interprets the Panchen Lama's 1962 petition as a plea to policy makers to respect the special characteristics of Tibet. Subsequently, this argument was central to Deng Xiaoping's policies in China during the 80s when the Panchen Lama was allowed to introduce some liberal concessions in Tibet. However, by early 1992, the Chinese Communist Party withdrew the 'special characteristics' concession. The recent efforts to limit religious worship, to appoint political loyalists to monastery committees and to restrict language teaching, has seen the reversal of the religious and cultural concessions.[3]

Model refugee resettlement

Tibetan refugees entered Nepal mainly through the passes of Humla, Dolpa, Mustang, Rasuwa, Tatopani and Khumbu. Though some remained behind with Tibetan-speaking populations, particularly in the Khumbu, Thakkola and Mustang regions, others made their way to the Kathmandu Valley. Toni Hagen, the representative of the International Conference of the Red Cross (ICRC) entrusted with refugee welfare, claimed that in the beginning, nearly 10,000 found shelter with relatives and Sherpas in the northern mountain regions. "Soon it became clear that most of them were in a bad condition and if left to their fate, would soon represent a major economic and political danger for the small and impoverished country of Nepal," observed Hagen.[4]

It was imperative that Nepali hospitality to the refugees not become an intolerable strain, especially as they had been granted the privilege of unconditional asylum and no restrictions were initially placed on the number accepted by Nepal. The then Nepali Prime Minister B.P. Koirala and the Home Minister Surya Prasad Upadhyaya agreed with Hagen that the Tibetan refugees should be integrated into the economic life of Nepal. Emergency and survival relief aid could only be temporary and not a long-term solution.

Moreover, the Nepali government was assured that international donors would care for the refugees. International donors, as Dawa Norbu, an authority on Tibet remarked, "often see aid to Tibetan refugees as humanitarian compensation for their states' political inability to help the Tibetan cause".[5] The response to the Tibetan refugee question has been shaped by the politics of the cold war. At the UN the Tibetan question was declared "an internal affair of China". The Tibetans who fled their country were not officially recognised as refugees. Under international law, they could be extradited to China but the Nepali government assured the refugees that it would not do so.

In fact, the government made its policy towards the Tibetans statutory by creating a National Refugee Committee consisting of the Defense Minister and Secretaries of the Foreign and Home Ministries, besides Toni Hagen. The UN resolution not to recognise the Tibetans as refugees, led to a curious situation whereby August Lindt, the UN High commissioner for Refugees, (UNHCR), despite his personal sympathy for their plight, could not divert UN funds directly for their aid. However, he issued a strong appeal to potential donors, which resulted in several organisations contributing funds, notably the Indo-German Social Service, the Oxford Famine Relief, the Australian National Commission for World Refugee Year and the British Council of Churches — all of which donated funds for Tibetan settlements in Nepal.

Eventually, it was decided that the ICRC, a politically 'neutral' organisation, would coordinate and supervise the resettlement of the Tibetans in specially designated refugee camps and assure their gradual integration into the Nepali economy. Within three decades, the Tibetans in Nepal have emerged as one of the most successful refugee communities.[6] They had become self-reliant and self-supporting.

The hospitality of the Nepalis towards the Tibetan refugees paid tremendous dividends to the Nepali economy. According to Hagen's account, it was through the introduction of the carpet industry amongst the refugee communities by a few concerned foreigners, that earnings from the carpet industry exceeded that of even the tourist industry otherwise the country's major foreign currency earner. By 1967, the carpet-weaving workshops initially established in the refugee camps were transformed into private companies with joint Tibetan and Nepali ownership. By 1990, around 110,000 jobs had been created, about five times the number of Tibetan refugees in Nepal. By 1992-93, the foreign currency earnings from the carpet industry amounted to US$ 169 million, three times that from tourism. Together with agriculture, the carpet industry has become the backbone of the Nepali economy.[7]

Besides the Tibetan refugees, poorer sections of Nepali society, especially in the Tibetan refugee settlement areas like Kathmandu Valley, Pokhara Valley, Mustang and Solukhumbu have benefited in the process.[8] There has been a rise in the general standard of living. Moreover, the cooperative attitude of the Tibetan refugees towards the Nepali community helped train Nepalis in the art of carpet weaving. Most of the official carpet manufacturing centres located in the refugee camps and Tibetan carpet exporting companies have been paying taxes to the Nepali government.

Nepalis residing in proximity to the camps have taken advantage of the schools, dispensaries and other facilities made available to the refugees. By 1968, four major settlements had been established in Nepal, with an infrastructure that included housing, primary schools and dispensaries, besides handicraft centres and cooperatives which could market the carpets, handicraft items and agricultural products of the settlements. The refugees were trained in trade and other skills like carpentry, metal work, weaving and masonry.

UNHCR invested about US$ 377,000 in their rehabilitation. It was a fraction of the total assistance received by international donors. In addition the Nepali government provided land and constructed housing for them in the settlements.[9]

According to information supplied by the Office of Tibet in Kathmandu, there are a total of 16 refugee settlement areas housing about half of the estimated 19,000 Tibetan refugees in Nepal today. The other half live independently, mostly in Kathmandu Valley, where they are engaged in a variety of professions, besides the carpet industry. These include the manufacture and sale of tourist goods like sweaters, scroll paintings *(thankas)* and jewellery. Some also run restaurants and hotels.

Unofficial figures, put the Tibetan population at about 100,000, a figure with which many xenophobic Nepalis find credible. But it is difficult to determine their exact numbers due to the presence of other Tibetan-speaking Nepali populations like Sherpas, with whom Tibetans have begun to intermarry. Besides, Tibetan refugees, especially of the second and third generations, are today very mobile. Many travel regularly to India, if not to other foreign countries. As a result there is considerable fluctuation in the actual number of Tibetan residents in Nepal.

Fresh influx of refugees

A report by Ludmilla Tueting indicates that after 1989 there has been a significant increase in the number of refugees entering Nepal, mainly in transit to India. Monthly, about 250 refugees mostly monks, nuns and children, escape from Tibet.[10] The revival of unrest in Tibet has seen a continuing escalation in the numbers of Tibetans escaping. A Tibetan language magazine, *Rangzen*, quoting Nepali immigration officials, claims that in 1995 alone, approximately 5,000 Tibetans entered Nepal. The *World Refugee Survey 1994* puts the figure at 2,076.[11] The higher figure of 5,000 would mean that the number fleeing Tibet is nearly 425 per week, which by all appearances, seems rather high. According to my own findings derived from interviews with personnel of the Tibet Office in Kathmandu, for 1995 and 1996, the number of refugees entering Nepal varies from 50 to 150 per week.

The fresh influx of refugees must be viewed against the background of the continuing if not escalating human rights violations in Tibet. According to the CTA publication *Striving against Surveillance*[12], 1995 witnessed a dramatic increase in arbitrary arrests and detentions, twice as many as reported for 1994. It is linked with an attendant increase in the number of demonstrations against the Chinese government's policies in Greater Tibet. This includes a steady transfer of ethnic Chinese population into Tibet, so that ethnic Tibetans are reduced to a minority. According to a report of the Tibet Office, demographically there are now 6 million ethnic Tibetans against 7.5 million ethnic Chinese, in addition to 2.5 million Chinese military personnel in Tibet.

In addition, there has been a curtailment of the right to religious freedom and anger at the government's interference in religious matters. A major source of grievance is Beijing's selection of the Panchen Lama's reincarnate, in opposition to the Dalai Lama's choice. The latter has been made to disappear. In fact, at seven years of age, he is the 'youngest political prisoner of the world'. 1994 also saw the banning of pubic display of photographs of the Dalai Lama and increased raids on monasteries and nunneries, resulting in mass arrests, detentions and expulsions of monks and nuns. Work teams have been instituted to "re-educate" them. Prisoners of Conscience have been tortured, and there are reports of deaths in custody.

The World Refugee Survey states that the Tibetans are "generally fleeing Chinese repression on pro-independence activism or seeking the opportunity to pursue traditional religious studies, which the Chinese government does not permit them to do freely in Tibet".[13] This accounts for the large number of child refugees.

In the face of these fresh waves of refugees, the Nepali government has to maintain a delicate balance, not antagonising China on the one hand, while yielding to international pressure to permit the refugees free passage, on the other. Nepal's policy has been to allow them to enter, without giving them de facto recognition as refugees and without permitting them to remain in Nepal. In practice, it is difficult for Tibetan refugees to enter Nepal safely. *Rangzen* quotes Nepali immigration officials claiming that "many refugees choose to stay on in Nepal itself, or return to Nepal after a brief visit to India".[14] It is a claim which serves to justify the arrest, imprisonment and finally, forced repatriation of the refugees. This is in contravention of the international protection regime for refugees which provides for asylum in the first country of arrival.

Corroborating the *World Refugee Survey* account, Tueting indicates that hundreds have been deported back to Tibet where they are subject to torture, imprisonment or enforced "re-education" in work camps which includes rigorous physical labour. As inducements for handing back the refugees to the Chinese side, high "capture rewards" are said to be paid to the Nepali soldiers for each person apprehended and returned to Chinese officials. Besides, the Nepal-China border is said to be kept under regular surveillance by armed Chinese paramilitary troops.

UNHCR, for its part, is attempting to counter this situation by deputing its Protection Officers to the border to encourage Nepali security personnel to adhere to human rights conventions and international refugee law which stipulates that Nepal, as the first country of passage, should desist from forced repatriation. Though Nepal is not a signatory to the international protection regime for refugees, it has largely upheld the humanitarian principle of *non-refoulement*.

UNHCR also offers economic incentives, by providing compensation to Nepali officials who escort the refugees from the border to the Department of Immigration in Kathmandu for registration. The refugees are then handed over to a UNHCR official who takes to an "unofficial" the Reception Centre run jointly by UNHCR and the Tibet Office.

As regards the allegation that the refugees stay on in Nepal, Tibetan sources are sceptical as they are immediately taken into custody as soon as they cross the border. At the Reception Centre, they are screened to determine their actual reasons for seeking asylum. They are kept in a transit camp near the Centre for up to a week and given medical attention, if necessary, before being taken in a chartered bus to the Indian border. Once there, they are transferred to another vehicle and taken to Dharamsala, where the CTA assumes full responsibility for their resettlement.

In contrast, the CTA's branch office in Kathmandu, does not facilitate their resettlement in Nepal in the established refugee camps nor does it facilitate access to an educational or monastic institution, as in India. This fact is impressed upon the minds of the new arrivals, who are made to realise that they would be considered 'undesirable aliens' in Nepal. In consequence, as the *World Refugee Survey* suggests, very few filter back to Nepal from India. Of the 2,076 Tibetan refugees who reached Kathmandu in 1995, the survey indicates, all were escorted to India where they were issued identity cards.[16] In Nepal, the practice of issuing identity cards was discontinued after the first wave of refugees.

Despite the initiatives adopted by the UNHCR Protection Officers, problems persist regarding the entry of Tibetan refugees into Nepal as, officially, the government does not recognise Tibetans to be 'bona fide refugees'. With Beijing weighing down on its northern border Nepal cannot afford to be seen encouraging dissenting Tibetans. So, while Nepal is pursuing its initial policy of clemency towards the new arrivals and following UNHCR's directives to ensure their safe passage to India, there are reports of refugees caught by Nepali border guards who have been immediately turned back or harassed. The harassment includes physical abuse, rape, extortion and internment in Nepal prisons according to *World Refugee Survey*. I have myself been told that the Nepali border guards harass the refugees by firing at them.

The few who do manage to resettle in Nepal as opposed to India, do not appear to have posed much of a problem for the Nepali government or society. It would appear that overall, the assimilation and integration of Tibetans into Nepali society and culture still continues to be assured due to the common cultural and religious bonds as manifest in the Himalayan region as a whole.

In Kathmandu Valley, in particular, a substantial Tibetan sub-culture has been successfully created. This has enabled the Tibetans to preserve their cultural identity. So remarkable has been the success of this refugee community in rebuilding its culture that the anthropologist Christoph von-Fuehrer Haimendorf has described it as a veritable renaissance of Tibetan civilisation in exile, articulated mainly through the religious sphere: "The ability of homeless and impoverished groups of refugees to build and fund in foreign lands numerous monasteries of a remarkably high architectural standard and their success in developing viable monastic communities similar to those of Tibet is one of the miracles of the twentieth century."[17]

In Nepal and India, the economic success of the refugees has been so conspicuous as to increase the tendency of "local politicians manipulating anti-Tibetan sentiments"[18] as occurred in Dharamsala in April of 1994 when Tibetan shops and people were attacked by local residents. In Nepal, xenophobic violence could be triggered off because of jealousy on the part of the Nepalis, many of whom are bitterly resentful about the popularity of Tibetans with foreigners and their continued support of the Tibetans, both economically and otherwise. Indigenous craftspeople and businessmen who must compete with Tibetans, lose sight of the reality that Nepal has gained much more from playing host to the Tibetans than they have lost. There is the economically beneficial spillover effect from the Tibetan refugee led growth in the carpet industry.

However the outbursts of violence against new arrivals indicates a potential flashpoint. Recently a group of Nepali youths armed with sticks and *khukris* (knives) attacked the refugees in the UNHCR maintained transit camp, causing injury and damage to property. However, because of their "illegal" status in Nepal, recourse to the police could not be effectively made, even though the incident was reported to the local authorities. The perpetrators were released soon from custody.

Resentment on the part of the Nepali youth is further fuelled by the conspicuous lifestyle of rich Tibetans who drive around in flashy cars and Pajero jeeps and build expensive houses especially in the Boudha area. It is easy to overlook that only a small percentage of the Tibetan population has prospered, so appreciably. But exceptions like the extremely wealthy lama, an authority on Tibetan medicine, in Jawalakhel refugee camp in Patan, have come to symbolise, the meteoric rise in the prosperity of the refugee community.

But the vast majority are not wealthy. Those staying outside the camps are considered lower middle class, but many within the camp, too, have a low standard of living. Moreover, the Tibetans have implanted in their recreated settlements, the feudal class divisions of Tibet, that is between the haves and have-nots. Dissatisfaction among the less well off refugees is further aggravated by the fact that traditionally the focus of charity has been the religious institutions and personages like the Rinpoches or reincarnate lamas, rather than the less prosperous members of the community.

It is the second and third generation refugees who are most restive with lot. As remarked by an official in the Office of Tibet, young refugees see their prospects of having secure and lucrative employment, constrained by their refugee status. Their aim is to migrate to 'greener pastures' in western countries, preferably to the US. The US State Department, though sympathetic to the plight of the Tibetans, has not accorded them a preferential status when it comes to immigration.

Tension between Nepalis and the refugee community is for the present no cause for worry for the people or the authorities. Pressure from Beijing to push back new arrivals, has so far been effectively countered by pressure from the international community to provide free passage through Nepal for Tibetan refugees seeking asylum in third countries. Recently, the European Union incorporated in its financial law for 1997,[19] a conditionality clause for funds for Nepal. Finances destined for Nepal must be guaranteed by non-expulsion of Tibetan refugees there, by the government. It obviously pertains to new arrivals, since there is no question of the expulsion of the settled refugees. Furthermore, funds for the Tibetan refugees have been increased to 2.6 million ECU.

The European Union also calls for the renewal of funding initiatives to verify respect for human rights and to promote collation of information on non-violent action in support of human rights and democracy in Tibet. This includes the funding of research programmes on Tibet by the International Institute on Research for Peace. It also provides for funding to sustain non-governmental organisations which are working for the defense of human rights in Tibet.

In the West, concern for the welfare of the Tibetan community, in and outside Tibet, has traditionally been strong, especially among non-governmental organisations. The fact that it is now becoming a legitimate concern of governments is evident in the initiative taken by the European Union.

NOTES

1. H.B. Jha, *Tibetans in Nepal*, Delhi 1992, p 13. See also The Dalai Lama, *My Land. My People: Memories of the Dalai Lama of Tibet*, New York, 1992.
2. Secret Report by the Panchen Lama Criticises China, Tibet Information Network (TIN) London, 1996.
3. ibid.
4. Toni Hagen, *Building Bridges to the Third World: Memories of Nepal 1950-1992*, Book Faith, New Delhi, 1994, p 205.
5. Dawa Norbu, *Tibetan Refugees in South Asia: A Case of Peaceful Adjustment, in Refugees and Regional Security in South Asia*, eds. Muni and Baral, New Delhi, 1996, p 78
6. ibid, p 84.
7. Hagen, p 289.
8. Jha, pp 17-27.
9. *Rangzen*, The Magazine of the Tibetan Youth Congress, Dharamsala, Vol.XXL, No.2, Summer, 1996, p16.
10. Ludmilla Tueting, "Abschiebung Tibetischer Fluchtlinge aus Nepal" (Expulsion of Tibetan Refugees out of Nepal), *Suedasien* (South Asia), 6/96, Germany, p 44.
11. *World Refugee Survey 1994*, US Committee for Immigration & Refugee Services. Washington DC, 1996, p 101.
12. *Striving Under Surveillance: A Brief Overview of the Human Rights Situation in Tibet 1994-1995*, Central Tibetan Administration, Dharamsala, 1996, p100.
13. *World Refugee Survey 1994,* p100.
14. *Rangzen.*
15. Tueting p44 and *World Refugee Survey 1994,* pp 100-101.
16. *World Refugee Survey 1994.*
17. Christoph Von Fuehrer, Haimendorf, *The Renaissance of Tibetan Civilisation*, Bombay, 1990, p398.
18. Norbu, opcit, p 93.
19. *Tibetan Refugees in Nepal*, Office of Tibet, Kathmandu, 1996 Strasbourg EU Parliament Financial Law of the European Union for 1997, October, 1996.

SECTION FIVE

The Unmixing of Peoples
Topographies of displacement in Sri Lanka

Darini Rajashingam

EELAM IS A KILLING FIELD
FOR OUR POLITICS
A BATTLE FIELD FOR INDIA
A GRAVE YARD
FOR OUR PEOPLE

Graffiti in University of Jaffna
Jaffna under Indian Peace Keeping Force 1989.

The mixing and unmixing of peoples, faiths and cultures through trade, migration, intermarriage and various colonizations is an old phenomenon in the island of Sri Lanka. The unmixing of peoples through ethnic cleansing and riots is not. Since 1983 when tension between the majority Sinhalas who number 74 percent and the dominant Tamil minority who number 17 percent of the Sri Lankan population, escalated into an outright war between the secessionist Liberation Tigers of Tamil Eelam (LTTE) and the Sri Lanka government, the social demography of the north and east and to a lesser extent in the south, has been transformed by forced migrations and the delinking of inter-communal ties. While the LTTE has practised ethnic cleansing in the northern areas they claim as their homeland, a slow but ever increasing exodus of Tamils has occurred from the Sinhala dominated south due to periodic anti-Tamil riots condoned by segments of the Sinhala dominated post-colonial state.

The ethnic unmixing of peoples in the south has been a gradual process with Tamils moving northward or overseas since the first anti-Tamil riots in 1958, ten years after Sri Lanka became independent. Ethnic unmixing in the north has been more recent, dramatic and systematic, beginning in 1983 and culminating with the LTTE's policy of ethnic cleansing when Sinhalas and Muslims who constituted minorities in the Tamil-dominated north were asked to leave their homes in 1990. With characteristic brutality the LTTE warned the departing Sinhalas and Muslim, "Do not even dream of coming back". The result is that today the Jaffna peninsula which is ravaged by war between the LTTE and Sri Lanka military is denuded of non-Tamils, and contains a depleted Tamil population traumatised by war and repeated displacements. The only non-Tamils in the north are Sri Lanka military personnel who effectively constitute an occupying force. In the south, many Tamils live under close surveillance by the military and fear of arbitrary search and arrest. The Tamil search for routes of migration overseas continues.

Post-colonial ethnic nationalism in Sri Lanka has undone much of the cultural mixing that has occurred in the wake of centuries of migration to and within this island. Sri Lanka is situated at the intersection of major sea routes from east and west. Historically, the south of Sri Lanka was dominated by Sinhalas speaking peoples including Muslims,

Christians, Tamils, Euro-Asian communities, as well as tiny Malay and Chinese communities. Despite past and present localized conflicts of a religious nature, ethnic co-existence and cultural hybridity was and still is a way of life along the coastal areas and in urban centres of Sri Lanka, but it is gradually being eroded. In the context of the proliferating nationalist myths that Sinhalas and Tamils have been in perennial conflict, and given the violence, suffering and displacement that has occurred among all communities in this island, it is both salutary and sobering[1] to remember that until relatively recently, native and foreign ethnographers almost routinely remarked on the peaceful co-existence of Sri Lanka's diverse and hybrid cultures.

It is then to the history of post-colonial nation building that we must turn to explain the ethnic violence that has turned Sri Lanka from a model democracy in the 60s and 70s into a land ravaged by ethnic conflict culminating in a fifteen-year-old fratricidal war which has displaced approximately ten percent of the population. Fifteen years of war has resulted in the militarization of the state and civil society. Restrictions on people's mobility from north to south and vice versa has seen the development of an ethnic enclave mentality, whereby local minorities are viewed by local majorities as security threats.

This paper focuses on forced migrations and attempts to expose the logic whereby people who cross cultural borders are perceived as security threats to local communities, the state and international actors. The movement of peoples, state-sponsored and otherwise, has both fuelled the conflict in Sri Lanka and been fuelled by it.

Building a Nation: Dividing peoples

At independence in 1948, social and economic inequality was squarely on the agenda for post-colonial nation building of both the United National Party (UNP) and the Sri Lanka Freedom Party (SLFP) — the two political parties which has dominated post-independence Sri Lankan electoral politics. The Marxist-Maoist youth led JVP insurrection of 1971 was read by the country's political elites as both a reminder and warning of the consequences of economic inequalities still to be addressed. The response to the perceived threat of southern Sinhala youth unrest (a mirror image of early Tamil youth unrest which culminated in the formation of Tamil militant groups) was a series of not very well coordinated liberal and socialist policies focused on impoverished Sinhala communities. And there was good reason for doing so. Given the prevailing electoral system, the logic of numbers meant that the Sinhala vote was preeminent. Thus the competitive elites of UNP and the SLFP upped the stakes in the anti-Other game in order to woo the Sinhala electorate.[2] The first to feel the effects of social engineering were the Burghers of Eurasian descent as well as the elite segments of the Tamil community who held a disproportionately high number of positions in the colonial civil service and administration. Ironically, attempts to strengthen democracy by development aimed at addressing the demands of marginalised communities for social justice, appear to have set in motion processes which caused subsequent displacement and conflict.

The two parties sought Sinhala votes and favour, through a set of social engineering policies whereby the ethnic minorities were sometimes intentionally and often inadvertently the losers. Coupled with the rise of anti-western Sinhala-Buddhist cultural nationalism, the result was the growing political and cultural tyranny of the Sinhala majority, and the breakdown of the contract between ethnic minorities and a state increasingly dominated by the majority Sinhalas. Post-colonial democracy and development then effectively meant that the Sinhala majority came to dominate an increasingly centralized welfare state, while chipping away at the economic and political privileges that some ethnic minorities had come to enjoy in certain spheres of national life under British rule.

It is possible to trace several moments which mark the rise of Sinhala Buddhist nationalism, the marginalisation of minorities and the concomitant politicization and militarization of the Tamils in this period :

i. Passage of the 1956 bill that made Sinhala, the language of the majority community, the only official language of the country. This Act effectively ended the two language formula which was accepted at one time by the Sri Lankan polity. At this point the Federal Party's call for a semi-autonomous Tamil state was met by Sinhala mob violence. The anti-Tamil riots of 1956 further polarized the country along ethnic lines.

ii. Disenfranchismement of a majority of Indian Tamil Plantation labourers who arrived in Sri Lanka during the 1830s.[3]

iii. Enactment of the first republican Constitution in 1972 which ended the dominion status of Sri Lanka. The constitution created a political structure that ensured the superiority of the legislature, with little regard for the demands of minorities in a Sinhala-dominated parliament. It removed previous minority safeguards and gave preeminence to Buddhism, the main religion of the majority Sinhalas. Representatives of the Tamil minority boycotted the proceeding of the Constituent Assembly which drafted the new Constitution.

iv. The widespread riots of 1983 when Tamil homes and businesses were attacked following the killing of 13 soldiers by the LTTE in the north and the escalation of Tamil youth resistance to the Sri Lanka army in the Tamil dominated northern Jaffna Peninsula in the form of armed conflict (It paralelled in many was the anti-state Sinhala JVP insurrection in the south).

v. The armed conflict between the LTTE and the Sri Lanka state which has been fought with periodic intermission through the late 1980s and 90s.

Yet it must be emphasized that Sri Lanka's post colonial ethnic conflict is more the outcome of attempts to engineer social class equality than a grand conspiracy by Sinhala nationalists. There was a haphazard quality about the progress of minority marginalisation. For while the disenfranchisement of the estate Tamils was explicitly racist, the imposition of quotas for university admission which effectively reduced the number of Tamil students who entered the university, was meant to benefit under privileged Sinhala groups. Likewise, it seems fair to say that the highly contested settlement of Sinhala peasants in lands that had been historically Tamil-controlled during the large development and colonization schemes in the north-central and eastern provinces often seemed more ethnicity blind that Machiavellian in intent. But certainly, they reflected the growing power of Sinhala politicians. However, the self-conscious projection Sinhala-Buddhist nationalists of the land colonization schemes, as a return to and a resurrection of the ancient Sinhala agricultural civilization of the Anuradhapura period when the great Sinhala kings waged war against Tamils, was highly provocative to the Tamils.

The rise of Sinhala-Buddhist nationalism and its entrenchement within the state, affected minority communities differently. Segments of the moderate Tamil elites, dug their heels in for a political battle that culminated in a demand for a separate state in the north of Sri Lanka where Tamils constitute a majority. On the other hand, the youth belonging to Tamil castes in the north who felt marginalised by the Colombo-based high caste Tamil leadership, became increasingly militarized. The culmination of that process has been the LTTE's brand of fanatic nationalism epitomized in the cult of martyrdom and suicide bombing.

At the same time the professional and skilled Tamil middle classes migrated overseas like the Burghers or the Eurasian population. The declining numbers of Burghers, most of whom found homes in Britain or the Old Commenwealth after 1948, is indicative of the fact that it was not just ethnic minority Tamils who felt marginalised by the rise of Sinhala-Buddhist nationalism in the post-colonial nation-state.

Arguably the segment of the Tamil population that has been most affected by anti-Tamil riots in the Sinhala dominated south is the Indian or plantation Tamils, who currently number 5.5 percent of the population. Many of them are stateless. These Tamils of Indian descent were brought to Sri Lanka to work on tea plantations in the central hill country in the 1830s. They have historically been treated by Sri Lankan Tamils as an undercaste. The Indian Tamils have remained, by and large, geographically, politically and culturally distinct from the Sri Lanka Tamils who are concentrated in the northern peninsula and in urban centers like Colombo. Sri Lanka's hill country Tamils have been consistently classified as Tamils of Indian descent in the successive censuses of the governments of Ceylon/Sri Lanka. Their relative isolation from the rest of society, whether Tamil or Sinhala, is partly explainable in geographical terms. The structure of the plantation economy, where social conditions were until recently very poor, also contributed significantly to the marginalisation of the hill country Tamils in national politics and culture. The political marginalisation of Tamils of Indian descent was evident in the ease with which the government disenfranchised them in 1956.

Attempts to argue that the Indian Tamils are migratory by nature, maintain their social connections with India and do not have an abiding interest in Sri Lanka, have a long history. Attempts by the Sri Lankan and Indian governments to negotiate the granting of citizenship to Sri-Lankan Indian Tamils also have a long history, largely of failure. It suffices to say here that since the entire Indian Tamil population was effectively disenfranchised in 1956, it was only after the Srimavo-Shastri pact in 1964 that the actual number of stateless persons was determined, and India agreed to accept the repatriation of 600,000 of the 975,000 Sri Lankan Indian Tamils. Though the agreement between the Indian and Sri Lankan governments came to an end 15 years later, the process of repatriation continued until 1984 when, at the request of the Sri Lanka government, it was brought to end with the close of the ferry service between Rameshwaram and Talaimannar. As it currently stands, according to the 1988 Granting of Citizenship to Stateless Persons (Special Provision) Act No. 39, a further 94,000 people were added to the figure, who had not applied for Indian citizenship or Sri Lankan citizenship. Moreover, the process of issuing certification of Sri Lankan citizenship was delayed and today there are at least 200,000 who are still awaiting the grant of Sri Lankan citizenship and another 150,000 reckoned as Indian citizens yet to be repatriated.

The present stalemate affects about 350,000 or approximately a third of the Sri Lankan-Indian Tamils. As a result, while some segments of the Sri Lankan-Indian Tamil community have become increasingly politicized, others have suffered multiple displacements following periodic anti-Tamil riots in the plantation areas. Yet a leader of the Sri Lankan-Indian Tamils, S. Thondaman, is currently in the extraordinary position of being simultaneously a cabinet member of the Peoples' Alliance Government and a Member of Parliament from the opposition United National Party. It indicates the extent of the bargaining power of the enfranchised hill-country Tamils, a situation that is a legacy of the proportionate representation system.

Topographies of displacement and the new border

In the north and south of Sri Lanka state repression has its mirror image in the enormous Tamil-separatist violence and ethnic cleansing. Civilians caught in the crossfire fled. The displaced in the war between the Sri Lanka government and the militant LTTE have swelled the ranks of refugees and internally displaced people the world over. Estimates are that 78 percent of the internally displaced are ethnically Tamils, 13 percent are Muslims, and 8 percent are Sinhalas. Many displaced people, Tamils, Muslims and Sinhalas, fled the Sri Lanka army at various points in the conflict.

At the end of December 1995 the Ministry of Rehabilitation and Reconstruction estimated that there were 1,017,181 internally displaced people in Sri Lanka while 140,000 were displaced overseas. Figures of displaced persons are however controversial. The University Teachers for Human Rights in 1993 estimated that half a million Tamils have become refugees overseas. The decennial census of Sri Lanka scheduled for 1991 has not taken place due to the conflict.

Over the course of 15 years of war, a new border has emerged with the displacement of peoples. Today refugee camps and military camps alternatively plot a new perimeter across the island. A majority of the internally displaced who are concentrated along the border area between the north where the fighting is concentrated and the Sinhala-dominated south, are residents of the north. Geographically, the new border stretches in a gentle arch from East to West, further south on the coast and further north inland. In some places it extends over miles traversing lush vegetation or the dusty plains and scrub jungle of the dry zone. The new border is the creation of fifteen years of war between successive Sri Lanka governments and the ethnic minority Tamil separatist, LTTE. It constitutes a broad swath of land between territory controlled by the Sri Lanka government and the LTTE. Culturally, the border is a space where war and peace resonate in curious ways. The border zone has its own political economy of cooperation and co-existence. The Sri Lanka army, LTTE cadres, villagers and other bit players in the conflict sometimes maintain here an uneasy truce. Enemies, at times, cooperate for the good of others — particularly refugees and civilians — and for personal profit. At other times it is in these zones that the war is most bitterly fought. It is in this swath of land that the bloodiest memories of massacres are rooted which perpetuate the logic of blood for blood. Yet economically, the space where the war is most bitterly fought, is also the point at which ethnic co-existence and detente is a necessity.

Administering the border

Parts of the border zones are overseen and sometimes administered by the Sri Lanka government and the LTTE. International agencies, including the United Nations High

Commission for Refugees (UNHCR), the International Committee of the Red Cross (ICRC), Save the Children (UK), Redd Barna, FORUT, CARE, MSF, OXFAM (UK) and other non-governmental relief and development organizations are also active, that is, with the support of the Sri Lanka government and the LTTE.

Through the years of conflict the government has provided food, medical and other basic services to the displaced, including those located in LTTE-controlled areas. The UNHCR has administered relief supplied by the international community and the government to refugees returning from India and internally displaced persons. It is often alleged that supplies are insufficient, but the government contends that supplies have been siphoned off by the LTTE for its cadres.

Sri Lanka is one of the countries where the mandate of the UNHCR has been extended from its original paramaters which pertain to the care and resettlement of refugees or people who have crossed international borders. UNHCR has since 1990 been using existing centres of relief distribution to provide a relatively safe environment for persons needing shelter. This operation was formalized in 1993. Security forces agreed not to intervene in the camps without previous consultation and the LTTE forces have generally respected this as an informal agreement.

A study of the situation of refugees and internally displaced people in Sri Lanka deemed the Sri Lanka relief programme one of the more successful refugee relief operations in ethnic conflict situations in the world. The US Committee for Refugees in its 1991 report on "Sri Lanka : Island of Refugees" comments: "Humanitarian assistance to internally displaced people in Sri Lanka can fairly be described as something of a model programme... Relief —

and to obviously varying degrees, protection — for displaced people is provided by a number of different players..." Perhaps this is the reason that internally displaced people in Sri Lanka have not hit the BBC headlines as have refugees in similar situations in Rwanda or Bosnia. Alongside cooperation for relief there has also developed a hidden economy around the transport of prohibited items. In Jaffna there are reliable reports that the LTTE uses Pajeros smuggled into the Jaffna Peninsula.

The freedom of movement of peoples displaced along this border, a freedom which is guaranteed by Article 13 (1) of the Universal Declaration of Human Rights and Article 12 (1) of the ICCPR which confirms the ability to move freely within a region or country and the right to set up residence in an area of one's choice, has been seriously restricted by the LTTE and the government of Sri Lanka's security regimes. The Sri Lankan government severely restricts the movement of Tamils displaced southward, the LTTE will not permit Sinhalas to move or settle in the north. In fact both the LTTE and the Sri Lanka government have used displaced persons as security shields or buffers.

Refugees and camps: A chain of displacement

In Puttalam the majority of refugees are Muslims who found succour among fellow Muslims. The emigrants were given a warm welcome and much sympathy when they first arrived and settled in the area. Now many of those who remain in the camps feel that they have overstayed their welcome. Many landlords who for five years did not charge them rent and allowed them the meagre produce of the land, want their lands back. When a fire broke out in one of the camps, it was rumoured that it had been ignited by the local landlord to hasten the departure of unwanted guests.

Some refugees who could afford to move out of camps rented houses, bought land and are trying to integrate into the local life and the economy. By most accounts, the economy and town of Puttalam has expanded over the past five years. Of course garment factories and prawn farms also account for this growth. Schools in areas of resettlement are overcrowded with the influx of refugee children.

Many of the inmates of camps in these areas have been displaced for over five years. For the under-five, home is a refugee camp. For the middle-aged and elderly home has become a space to be painfully forgotten. Without security, houses and fields, they say, are useless. Some refugees who have married into local families say that even after a durable peace has been worked out they would prefer to stay where they are now. Others, particularly farmers whose livelihood stems directly from the land wish only to return. Displacement affects those who live off the land most. Farmers, unlike those in the service sector or government workers, have found it most difficult to integrate into the local economy given the scarcity of land.

But, if it were possible, what would the refugees return to? Today the houses left behind by Puttalam's Muslim refugees in the Jaffna peninsula house Tamil refugees. The LTTE administration resettles Tamils displaced from the south and from the areas near the Sri Lanka army camps in the peninsula, where shelling and bombing is often severe, in the houses of the Muslims, Sinhalas and Tamils who have left. Repatriation, if and when peace returns, will mean a chain of displacements.

Hosts and guests on the border: Issue of (re)settlement

Among the army camps and refugees camps along the new border also exist scattered old and new settlement villages. Many of the residents of these villages have been repeatedly displaced during the 14 years of war. Those who return to their villages do so because they are tired of living on handouts in the camps. In 1994 when the Bandaranaike government came to power they returned to fields gone wild and homes ravaged by elephants but with the hope of peace and promises of resettlement allowances from the newly elected Peoples' Alliance government. The lucky ones are still waiting for a permanent peace and resettlement allowances, others have been hacked to death by the LTTE or caught in the crossfire between the LTTE and army.

While many border villages are ethnically homogenous some are ethnically diverse. In many of these villages the existence of Sri Lanka army camps are a problem even if less feared than the LTTE. The state of war does not permit villagers who are predominantly farmers to earn their living off their lands. For security reasons, the army prevents villagers from going to their fields at night and has banned the lighting of fires to keep away the elephants who destroy crops. Also, villagers may not carry torch lights at night. When the LTTE attacked and killed 11 army personnel at the nearby camp in 1993, the villagers were left alone. One villager died in the crossfire. Later the army ordered the villagers to leave since they could not guarantee their safety. In other parts of the border, the army trains a home guard force. Elsewhere refugee camps are used as a buffer against the LTTE. Along this border live those who have been repeatedly caught in crossfire, people who have been traumatized by war, people who have been made refugees more than once.

In Sri Lanka popular romanticization of the "home", in the construction of internally displaced people as victims (the Sinhala term - *anathagatha kattiya* - literally means the abandoned people, while the Tamil term *veedu attavargal* means people without a home), often obscures the realities of living at home. However, there is now strong evidence to suggest that despite the psycho-social traumas that displacement entails, long-term displacement has provided windows of opportunity for greater personal and group autonomy and experiments with identity and leadership for displaced people, particularly for women.[4] Certainly this has been the case for many displaced Tamil women, many of whom have lost husbands and sons in the conflicts.[5] It is time now for humanitarian relief efforts to be conceptualized in terms of i) sustainability, ii) maintenance of local balance of ethnic coexistence and empowerment between displaced people and their local hosts and iii) empowerment of women within a radically different conception of the family. In Sri Lanka this is particularly necessary if the ethnic conflict is not to spread to new areas where the displaced have found refuge and are often perceived to be in competition with poor local populations.

Displacement and implications for peace

The transformation of the social demography of the north and east through the displacement of people has implications on a number of different levels. Its most immediate impact will be felt in any peaceful political settlement of the conflict. Population shifts caused by the war, will have a long-term effect on the workings of the proportionate representation system as well as on addressing the real and imagined grievances of minority groups.

In any peace settlement the issue of displaced people whose movement south has shifted the de facto ethno-national border zones southward will be a compelling one. The northern territory is claimed by the LTTE as a Tamil homeland and will be regionally autonomous under any peace settlement with the Tamils. Will the government permit many of the displaced people, particularly Sinhalas and Muslims, to settle permanently in areas where they have found refuge? Will the LTTE accept those non-Tamil peoples whose exit it ordered in twenty-four hours, five years ago?[6] In the words of a Muslim refugee, the LTTE cadres had said, "Do not even dream of coming back". Many a Muslim and Sinhala refugee has done precisely that — given up the dream of return.

Ten years of ethnic conflict, displacement and resettlement, has upset pre-war ethnic balances and this could pose a major challenge to the electoral process based on proportionate representation in Sri Lanka. In this scenario, the return of internally displaced people is a cynical necessity which is ironically dictated by the democratic process. If and when bargains for peace are struck, and the acceptable criteria is ethnic quotas tied to land guarantees on the one hand and a federal system of power sharing on the other, will they be expected to stay where they are now or to return?[7] The question remains: will the longed-for peace entail an unwelcome settlement for many internally displaced people in Sri Lanka? Will a peace settlement be a cause for renewed conflict?

Historical myths and mythical identities

History repeats itself but not always as Marx anticipated in *The Eighteenth Brumiere*. The emergent boundary appears to replace an ancient one in the island. It seems to traverse an ancient border, for according to received readings of the ancient Buddhist chronicles — the *Pali-vamsas* — conflict between Sinhala Buddhists and Tamils for control of the island in the border zones is hardly a recent phenomenon.

Have not conflicts between the Sinhalas and Tamils been recorded from the second century onwards? Yet the new border rents what had appeared to most natives and colonial administrators, since early this century, as the natural, that is territorial and geographic unity and sovereignty of the island of Sri Lanka.

The purpose of a potted history of past conflicts is to establish that the *recording* of internal ethno-political boundaries in the island of Sri Lanka, Ceylon, Serendip, (the borders often shifted with the name and perspective), is not new. Four and a half centuries of Portuguese, Dutch, and British rule, not to mention pre-European political feuding among the island's principalities, or what anthropologist Tambiah terms "galactic polities", has meant the periodic shift and reconstitution of internal geo-political units and boundaries. Rather, it is the character of the boundary now emergent, since Britain conquered and unified the island after six hundred years in 1815, that is noteworthy.

Unlike pre-independence and pre-British boundaries, which were geo-political, the current boundary is ethno-national in character. The British after all rewrote the map of Ceylon by uniting the Kandian highlands whose king was incidentally of Tamil descent, with the far more ethnically mixed lowlands. Contrary then to what LTTE homelands propaganda and Sinhala nationalists claim, the north-south axis of conflict in the island was not always ethno-religious in character. The new border has been forced upon the people of Sri Lanka by the LTTE which, itself, was in response to another shift that was begun with development and land colonization schemes undertaken by Sinhala nationalist governments in post-colonial Sri Lanka. The best know of these schemes is the Mahaveli river diversion and resettlement scheme. This process of resettlement which reconstituted Sri Lanka's ethnic map through the settlement of a large number of Sinhalas in hitherto Tamil dominated lands, was a major the cause of the present conflict.

In this context, it is noteworthy that in his letter to President Chandrika Kumaranatunge, one of the reasons that the LTTE leader gave for withdrawing from the peace process of 1995 was the resettlement of internally displaced persons without LTTE consent in the contested border areas during the ceasefire. The government had embarked on a process of resettling refugees, with much pomp and ceremony north of Trincomalee during the ceasefire. The government, action may be understandable given the plight of displaced people and the hope of peace and security raised by the peace process. We might also question the violence with which the LTTE broke the ceasefire. But the fact remains that (re)settlement is not a politically innocent process. Resettlement in these areas must and can only take place with the sanction of all players in the conflict, if displaced people are not to become yet again pawns in war.

Rather than seeing the shift and consolidation of present borders as the enactment of an ancient feud between Tamils and Sinhalas from the time of Duttugemunu and the Elara in the third century BC, it is more relevant to view the border as an invention of modern ethno-national schisms in a historically diverse, multi-ethnic, society. Yet, in another sense, the border is old, porous and diverse space.

The existence of the border and long-term displacement has real implications for how any political solution to Sri Lanka's ethnic conflict is worked out. Along this border villages have appeared and disappeared, forests have turned into villages and returned to wilderness, place names have been transformed overnight to suit political and ethnic interests as is the case with Manal Aru, now called Welli

Oya. It is not a coincidence that some of the bloodiest battles between the LTTE and army have been fought along the border zone. It is at the border that the cultural geographies of the nation are most apparent because contested.

The emergent border — the result of war — challenges many of the dreams and certainties to which the nationalists in Sri Lanka cling to. Yet many in the south remain oblivious to its existence. Until recently, those whose job it was to know and explain the state of the nation to the Sinhala public in the south, denied the emergent border. The new border is arguably a more powerful symbolic challenge than the LTTE to Sinhala dreams of dominance over the island of Sri Lanka. The graffiti by the University Teachers for Human Rights, Jaffna quoted in the beginning of this essay, highlights another of the wages of war. Eelam is a dream turned nightmare for most Sri Lankan Tamils.

Involuntary displacement and de facto settlement in territories of refuge is a continuum in long-term, armed, ethnic conflicts. Coping with displacement entails constructing new homes, identities and "imagined communities". Many internally displaced people have given up the dream of return. But they are in the paradoxical position of being materially and psychologically displaced by the very human rights and humanitarian instruments, discourses and practices, that define them as victims who need to be returned to their original homelands for their own protection and for the restoration of national and international order and peace. In war-torn Sri Lanka, where over a tenth of the population is displaced, the assumption of return evident in NGO, state and international policies, vis-a-vis internally displaced people, might actually be contributing to prolonging the conflict.

Displacement and nationalism

Recently, on the principle of state sovereignty which orders the international system and state-centric nationalism, James Rosenau commented, "psychic needs for territoriality and independence are sufficiently powerful to enable states to retain their prerogatives..."[8] Rosenau is probably right that sovereignty, however besieged by cross-border flows of people, capital, and culture, as well as, internal conflicts, will continue to be a defining principle of the international order, but not for the reasons adduced.

The idea that people are rooted to land pervades international systems thinking, and the concomitant view that uprootedness is disorder, has been naturalized and universalized in Rosneau's formulation of "psychic needs for territoriality and independence", meaning attachment to a territorially-defined nation-state. It presumes humankind knows only one form of belonging. Such universalisation against a diversity of refugee, immigrant and diaspora experiences of "homelands", negates non-territorialised conceptions of belonging, and reaffirms the logic of the nation-state. It is this logic that makes refugees and immigrants a source of new world disorder which the international system then purports to manage in the form of humanitarian protection for people it defines as "displaced".

Non-refoulement, the core of refugee law, seems the exception that proves the rule of sovereignty. Since the 1951 Refugee Charter and its 1967 protocol, the principle of *non-refoulement* which prevents a person from being forcibly repatriated to a country where his/her life or fundamental freedoms are in danger, has constituted an attempt to balance the competing claims of security, order, and justice. The principle of *non-refoulement* protects against repatriation, only if life or fundamental rights are endangered. The presumption is that the displaced are rooted to homelands within the framework of states of origin in all other cases. There is no comparable principle for internally displaced people.

If international law has recognized and defined some types and forms of human displacement because they disrupt the order and borders of nation-states, conceptualized as communities, anthropologists until relatively recently, marginalized displaced peoples for the same reasons. Immigrants, refugees, people-in-between cultures, rarely entered the anthropological frame or ethnography, while those who did usually represent were outside historical time, a characteristic of colonial forms of representing "other" cultures.[9] While the heritage of colonial forms of representing bounded communities continues to resonate in post colonial nationalism throughout South Asia[10] increasingly anthropologists are coming to terms with the discipline's colonial past in the study of colonial encounters, crossing of cultures, peoples, and histories and the process whereby borders between "self" and "other" are made and marked.

Displacement, sovereignty, order and peace

Peace, as Rajni Kothari has noted "means different things to different people".[11] Kothari speaks of peace in two senses: i) peace as a just order, free of inequity, exploitation and violence, that is, a shifting and fluid arrangement, and ii) peace as a congealing of present structures.

Since the crisis in the former Yugoslavia, where unprecedented ethnic cleansing has been practised for all the world to see, the international community has been concerned to define the right of civilian minorities to remain in situations of conflict as a fundamental human right. This was the thrust of the UN High Commissioner for Refugees,

Sadako Ogata's address to the Human Rights Commission in 1993. While the right to remain is an attempt to address the issue of displacement at the "root cause" level,[12] and certainly warranted in this context, it says little about those who do not wish to and cannot return. Women who bear the children of ethnically motivated rape are high in the category of displaced peoples who feel they cannot return.[13]

In Sri Lanka, the presumption that displaced people will and must return, which structures the types of assistance that the government and humanitarian agencies provide, has kept many dependent on relief hand-outs, rather than helping them to sustain themselves. Ironically, assistance has prevented rather than helped displaced people who are trying to construct new lives and recover from the traumas of displacement. Others have been forcibly resettled by the government, and many have been repeatedly displaced during cycles of war and detente between the government and LTTE.[14]

International public law, including human rights and humanitarian law and policy, despite going a long way to break the borders of sovereignty, retain a romantic, nostalgic and potentially damaging attachment to original homelands. The idea that people are rooted to places to which they will return might serve to contain conflicts within nation-states, but promotes attachments to a primordial homeland or origin point.

It is also arguably the root cause of many ethnic conflicts including between the government and the LTTE, as well as being the cause of a new trauma for "displaced" people who are trying to start new lives in new places. The fetishism of home and territoriality in human rights and humanitarian law perspectives and practice might sometimes cause more harm that good and even contribute to prolonging war. What we need is subtle and nuanced legal structures which are sensitive to the changing dynamics of personal and group identities.

Non-refoulment for IDPs

By and large internally displaced people, though they outnumber refugees, have been ignored in international law. The absence of protection for refugees is partly explainable by the fact that international public law has historically been limited to arrangements between states, rather than within states. Thus refugees who disrupt international borders have become the focus of international human rights and humanitarian interventions while internally displaced people who remain within national borders have been marginal to this perspective. The Report of the representative on Internally Displaced People of the UN Secretary General to the Commission on Human Rights has however come close to recommending the formulation of a "quasi *non-refoulement* principle" for Sri Lanka.[15]

International law differentiates between refugees or those who have crossed international borders because of the well-founded fear of persecution, and internally displaced people who have had to flee their homes for similar reasons, but remain within the domestic jurisdiction of their home state, even when they are fleeing state violence. The time has come to develop a principle similar to and yet different from *non-refoulement* for the protection of internally displaced peoples living in a situation of long term ethnic conflict, a principle which will promote their security and peace of mind.

Notes

1. Jane Russell in an authoritative study of communal politics observed that "since independence Sri Lanka has been a model third world country" was not exceptional. See Jane Russel, *Communal Politics under the Donoughmore Constitution 1931-1947*, Dehiwela Tissara Prakasakyo, Colombo,1982.
2. With the provision for territorial representation, the Sinhalas, particularly the low country Sinhalas, were placed in an unassailable majority in the state Council. Thus despite the fact that the Sinhalas were fragmented into sub-groups, they constituted an entrenched majority. Additionally, long standing cleavages between the hill country Kandian Sinhalas and the low-country Sinhala elites had been more or less bridged by S.W.R.D. Bandaranaike's espousal of the Kandian cause at independence which opened the way for the emergence of a pan-Sinhala-Buddhist nationalism. It effectively ensured the cultural subordination of all other communities.
3. This action by the Sinhala dominated government gave cause to Tamil elite parties to organize against Sinhala hegemony. Yet differences between the Tamils of Indian origin and the Sri Lanka Tamils remained a political reality. In fact, the leadership of the plantation Tamils has supported successively chauvinistic Sinhala nationalist governments for its own political ends and remains more or less autonomous from the Sri Lanka Tamil political leadership.
4. See S. Sachethanandam, Participatory Approaches to Development Urdu Civil War Conditions: The Experience in Batticawa, Sri Lanka 1991-95. Paper presented at the workshop on "Participatory Approach to Development," organised by Intermidate Technology Development Group, Sri Lanka. Colombo, Nov. 1995.
5. My preliminary research among internally displaced Muslim women however indicates a similar yet different pattern. Depending on the location of camps and the resources that families had, some women feel they have gained autonomy in their new situations while others complain of greater segregation.
6. A large number of Sinhalas and Muslims were settled in the border areas by Sinhala nationalist governments

after independence in 1948 in the course of large development and land settlement projects. Many of the worst massacres in the conflict have occurred in these settlement areas.

7. The question of return for some Sinhalas and Muslims is complicated by the fact that some of them are recent settlers under the government-sponsored irrigation and land settlement schemes in the post-war period, which resulted in ethnically skewed settlements. The Tamils claim Mahaveli settlement lands as their traditional area. Since ethnically screwed settlement is one of the main reasons that the LTTE cites as the original cause of its war against the government, resettlement in these areas must and can only take place with the sanction of the older residents of the area, and now, perhaps with that of the LTTE.
8. See James Rosenau, "Sovereignty in a Turbulent World, Beyond Westphalia" in *State Sovereignity and International Intervention* edited by G. Lyons and M. Mastanduno. John Hopkins University Press, Baltimore, 1995.
9. Edward Said, *Orientalism,* Fontana, New York 1976.
10. See P. Chatterjee, *Nationalist Thought and the Colonial World*, United Nations University, Oxford University Press. 1986. Richard Gombrige and G Obeyesekere, *Buddhism Transformed: Religions Change in Sri Lanka*, Princeton University Press, Princeton, 1988. *Sri Lanka: History and the Roots of Conflict* edited by J Spencee and E. Nessan, Oxford University Press, 1990.
11. Rajni Kothari, *Peace in an Age of Transformation in Culture, Ideology and World Order*, Westview Press, Boulder, 1984.
12. A Zolberg, *Escape from Violence: Conflict and the Refugee Crises in the Developing World*, Oxford University Press, 1989.
13. UNHCR "Don't Let the Sun Go Down", *Refugees* December 1993.
14. Francis Deng, Report of the Representative of the Secretary General, Mr. Francis Deng submitted pursuant to Commission on Human Rights Resolution 1993/95. Profiles in Displacement: Sri Lanka E/CN. 4/ 1994/44 add. 1 (Jan. 25, 1994.
15. Ibid.

Internally Displaced Persons in Sri Lanka

Joe William

Thousands of people forced into nomadic existence, fleeing areas of active conflict in search of a more secure and settled existence, is the untold history of Sri Lanka since 1983 when armed conflict broke out between the Sri Lankan security forces and the Tamil militant groups. But even before anti-Tamil conflicts in the southern parts of Sri Lanka in 1958, 1977 and 1978 pressurised is many Tamil people to leave their homes in the Sinhala-dominated parts of the country and move to the north and east.

The bombing of the Central Bank building in the heart of Colombo, as well as the bombing of a commuter train in Colombo in 1996, are grim reminders that the war is not confined to the north alone. Degrading harassment of Tamil civilians follow these atrocities. Loss of life including that of the breadwinner, severe and permanent disability, destruction of personal and productive assets, loss of income and psychological trauma, accompanied by alienation, along with an enduring sense of uncertainty are the scars of this war.

According to official figures, over 50,000 persons have lost their lives due to the civil war. The number of displaced persons as of December 31, 1996 is estimated to be 782,706. Children under five number 75,000. The number of displaced in Jaffna peninsula is 199,000, in Vanni 429,000 and in the east 56,000. The other large concentration of displaced persons are Muslims, 52,500 in Puttalam. Some persons have now spent more than six years of their lives as displaced persons, living in extremely difficult, stressful and inhuman conditions. The question of Internally Displaced Persons (IDPs) in Sri Lanka is one of the main challenges for humanitarian and human rights communities.

Categories of IDPs in Sri Lanka

i. IDPs in government-controlled areas in the north and the east;

ii. Internally displaced Tamils in north and east territories held by militants;

iii. Internally displaced Muslims from the north;

iv. IDPs in border areas between the government and LTTE-controlled areas

v. IDPs living with friends and relatives.

IDPs in government-controlled north and east:

a. Jaffna Peninsula

The war in the north and east, in its third phase, escalated to unprecedented levels after April, 1995. The intensified military operation against the LTTE saw government forces capture Jaffna town in December 1995 and establish their control over an area considered to be at the heart of the separatist movement. It resulted in the most serious displacement of persons from Jaffna town and its environs.

It was a huge and largely unacknowledged crisis for the northern Tamils. Other areas under LTTE control in the Jaffna peninsula were brought under the sway of the security forces in 1996.

The population of Jaffna had been about 850,000. Current estimates put the population between 450,000 to 500,000 of which nearly 200,000 persons are IDPs. The strength of the security forces in the peninsula is estimated to be between 38,000 to 40,000 which includes 330 women and 2,300 policemen. Visitors to the peninsula regard their presence as an armed encampment with military fortifications and extensive military and police checkpoints.

The Jaffna peninsula can be divided into three areas from a military standpoint, namely, security zones, cleared areas and uncleared areas. Civilian movement into the security zones is prohibited while travel between cleared and uncleared areas is permitted during the day, subject to intensive security screenings at checkpoints which may be located a hundred meters from one another. A daily curfew is imposed between 2100 hours to 0600 hours the next day. People make their way back early to ensure that they make it home, through the several check posts, before dark.

The civilian population including the IDPs lives in a situation of constant personal insecurity and physical and psychological isolation from the rest of the country. On top of that there is the lack of essential supplies, electricity and the breakdown of even the existing infrastructure. A demographic shift has taken place with the upper and middle classes abandoning the peninsula. Most of the productive work force between the age group of 18 to 40 years has left the peninsula as well. There are periodic attacks by LTTE cadres operating in the peninsula. The security measures taken to counter-attacks has deepened civilian resentment towards all parties involved in the conflict.

Moreover, there is serious concern about violence against women and the extra legal activities of the security forces, particularly "disappearances". Travel in and out of Jaffna is restricted by the extensive requirements for a travel clearance and further limited by air and ship capacity.

b. The East

The strategic and political importance of the east has meant large scale militarization of the area which in 1990 saw the dislodging of the LTTE from towns and major trunk roads. The east is a shifting patchwork of "cleared" and "uncleared" areas where the general situation is very unstable. Belying the belief that the LTTE was a weakened force after the loss of Jaffna and other areas in the north, the LTTE continues to be strong and effective in the east and controls most of the territory north of Trincomalee to the south of Batticaloa. The area is so large that the armed forces are stretched to protect the roads during the day. With the LTTE no longer obliged to defend its positions, it is free to be an effective guerrilla force again.

The other factor which distinguishes the conflict in the east is its ethnic mix. The eastern province, particularly Batticaloa continues to be extremely volatile, with tensions running high between the LTTE, Tamil civilians and the Muslim community. Civilians continue to suffer from bombing and shelling and are caught in a crossfire in the event of direct confrontation. The people in the East are subjected to frequent round-ups and security checks. The military are barricaded in virtual prisons every couple of kilometers along the road to Batticaloa. These encampments are situated in the middle of the road causing all traffic to be diverted around the camp. This offers an excellent opportunity for the military to harass civilians and extort money. The military controls the roads by day and remain in their camps at night. The LTTE roams free in the countryside.

c. Vavuniya: The gateway to the north

With the capture of Jaffna and Kilinochchi and the link up to Mannar from Vavuniya, the town of Vavuniya, the gateway to the north, has become a hub of activity. Civilians leaving LTTE-controlled areas of Mullaitivu and Kilinochchi, to travel to Jaffna or other parts of the island have to go through Vavuniya. People are leaving the LTTE controlled areas and moving into "secured areas" with Vavuniya becoming a key transit point. The areas under LTTE-control are shrinking. The inability of the militants to provide the basic needs of food, medicines and adequate shelter, has paved the way for people to move away from LTTE held territory, more easily than it was thought possible. Coming into Vavuniya, the IDPs face the second phase of their ordeal in their journey away from the theatre of conflict.

Civilian life in the Vavuniya district continues to be hampered by the ongoing war. There has been a permanent displaced population of nearly 55,000 persons since 1990. In addition, thousands of civilians have crossed over from militant-held areas to Vavuniya since the military operation in 1995-96 and have been 'interned' in transit camps. They live in overcrowded camps on a daily dole of US $ 0.88 per adult and US $ 0.50 per child. At present there are over 16,000 persons who are held up in Vavuniya, some of them for over three months. There are no restrictions placed on those who want to travel to Jaffna. They are transported free of cost overland to Trincomalee and from there by boat to Jaffna.

As for the others, four categories of persons are permitted to leave the transit camps. They are:

i) those seeking medical treatment not available at the Vavuniya Base Hospital,

ii) government servants returning from Jaffna,

iii) those holding documentary evidence for travel abroad for jobs, or a guarantee from an immediate member of the family living in the south who can provide a valid reason for a visit, and

iv) undergraduates who wish to pursue further studies.

Those who have crossed over to Vavuniya are not all destitutes. Many are people with a means of livelihood. But everyone is made to suffer indignities. They want freedom to move to the home of their relatives in Vavuniya or to proceed to places like Colombo. Their fundamental freedom of movement is violated. As Sri Lankans, the only wrong they have done is to have been born Tamils.

Tight security measures adopted by the military have led to physical checks at several barrier points, frequent combing operations, round ups, arbitrary and unfair arrests and disappearances of youth. Regulations which prevent free movement of civilians out of war-affected areas or war zones go against international humanitarian law.

IDPs in militant-held territories

In the Vanni and other contested areas in the north and east, described by the Sri Lankan military as "uncleared areas", the government maintains a skeleton administration and provides basic services. The LTTE has established a de facto parallel administration which organizes and controls civil and economic life.

The civilian population in LTTE controlled areas has endured seven years of economic blockade, briefly lifted during the peace talks in late 1994 and early 1995 but re-imposed by the present government after the breakdown of talks on April 19, 1995. The lack of regular and efficient transport facilities in these areas coupled with the restriction on fuel, medicines, building materials and other necessary amenities of life, imposes a severe burden on this category of displaced population. The economic embargo and the lack of electricity have seriously affected education and employment opportunities. Many skilled labourers like masons, carpenters, welders and painters have neither raw materials nor work.

Towns like Vavuniya and Batticaloa are heavily fortified with bunkers, barricades and sentry posts. The scene 10 kilometers away in LTTE-held territory is entirely different. In LTTE controlled areas, civilians move about freely even late at night. Farming goes on, despite the ban on fertilizers, with people making maximum use of the daylight hours. The recent capture of the land route from Medawachchiya and Vavuniya to Mannar, just before what would have been a successful paddy harvest, has meant a substantial financial loss to the farmers who cultivated their fields under very difficult circumstances. An estimated 20,000 persons within the LTTE controlled territory in Vanni have been displaced.

Internally displaced Muslims

The Muslims of the northern province have also suffered as a result of the conflict in the region. They were thought to be in a neutral position. However, in October 1990, the LTTE forced the Muslims living in the north to leave within forty-eight hours. Many of them continue to live in welfare centres in the adjoining districts of the north in Puttalam, Anuradhapura and Kurunegala even after six years.

IDPs from border villages

The rise of Tamil nationalism has had its impact on the border areas. The vulnerability of the border areas made them easy targets during the early phase of militancy. The Sinhalese living in the border villages, although small in numbers, became victims of ethnic violence and the LTTE. The border villages in the east and north western provinces were claimed by the LTTE as a part of Tamil Eelam. The Sinhalese fled in fear when some of these villages were attacked. The LTTE massacred civilians including children in several border villages heightening tensions in the non-conflict areas. The Sinhalese too found themselves internally displaced. However, compared to other internally displaced persons, they are in a better position because they are living in areas that have a regular system of transport and communication.

Returnees from India

The situation in Sri Lanka illustrates the blurred distinction between refugees and IDPs. The only difference is that the refugees/returnees managed to make their way to Tamil Nadu while the IDPs did not have adequate resources to do so. Returnees and IDPs often return to the same village and face similar problems in starting a new life. UNHCR has, therefore, extended its mandate to assist IDPs. They comprise the majority of beneficiaries under the micro-project programme which targets communities where returnees are resettling, rather than individuals themselves.

Its obverse is the continuing trickle of refugees making the hazardous night crossing to India. These include some who were repatriated by UNHCR on two previous occasions. The fresh influx of refugees has further added to the nearly 60,000 Sri Lankan refugees living in India. No significant flow of refugees has been reported since the drowning in 1997 of over 100 persons when an overcrowded trawler with refugees bound for India, capsized off the coast of Mannar.

Scarcity of food, non-availability of medical supplies, violation of human rights and harassment are some of the main complaints of the refugees who have recently fled to

India. In the middle of this never ending saga a large number of Tamils have been forced into a nomadic existence and face an uncertain future to say the least.

IDPs outside welfare centres

Local and international attention is largely focused on displaced persons living in welfare centres. Less attention is paid to 60 percent of the IDPs who rely on the hospitality of relatives and friends. This constitutes a major relief operation undertaken by the communities themselves. However, the restrictions on providing accommodation for Tamils from the north and east in Colombo and other urban areas, security checks and other forms of intimidation under the guise of emergency regulations like the Prevention of Terrorism Act, have eroded the traditional hospitality towards displaced civilians.

Vulnerable groups

In the uncleared areas, basic services and institutions, the provision of food security, water, medical assistance, employment and education have practically collapsed. The population of the north-east has suffered widespread psychological debility, physical illness and other war-related injuries. Specially vulnerable groups are children, women, the old and the infirm.

Children stand out as the most vulnerable, most powerless and most innocent victims of war. Fifty percent or more of the victims of the Sri Lankan conflict are children. Bombing and shelling does not distinguish between civilians and combatants. Unrestrained attacks on communities provoke huge flights of survivors in search of security inside and outside the country. The majority of victims are children.

Among the displaced, one comes across children, who for ten years of their lives — a lifetime for many of them — have not known a settled existence, a home, a family, a village or a community. They feel no sense of belonging to a community or an area. There is insufficient capacity to cater to the educational needs of displaced children. The widespread recruitment of young people under 18 years of age as LTTE cadres for frontline duty appears to be a common practice endorsed by the movement's leadership.

Internally displaced women are also particularly vulnerable. Many have suffered sexual violence and carry the scars of psychological and physical trauma. They have witnessed killings and lost their family members. A large number of female headed households exist in the north and east. Such families are economically and psychologically vulnerable even in normal times. But in times of conflict, the reduction in the few economic opportunities available, less paddy to harvest and less fish to process and the slippage of the social safety net, causes extreme hardship to women.

As for internally displaced men, the adverse impact of the war on the two major economic activities, farming and fishing, especially the restrictions on fertilizer inputs in LTTE held areas and the inaccessibility to farming lands in government controlled areas, has meant that many males have no jobs. The ban on fishing in the north-east coast, has left thousands of fishermen and their families virtually destitute. A few who ventured to sail beyond the permitted distance from the coast, have paid for it with their lives.

After the military takeover of the Jaffna peninsula, the handicapped, the sick and the elderly stayed behind in areas occupied by the armed forces in the northern coastal belt and small islands in the north. While they get assistance from the government in the cleared areas, their day to day needs are often looked after by church-related organizations. In LTTE held areas, the plight of the sick and the infirm is more difficult as they have to move from place to place along with other fleeing civilians. The displaced, especially the sick and infirm, who are most in need of regular medical care, are frequently denied such assistance.

But there appears to be general unwillingness to provide supplies to medical institutions in the north and east to cope with injury, disease and sickness in accordance with internationally accepted standards of competence and compassion. This issue should be addressed more from a medical angle rather than a security one.

Third Eelam war since 1995

The government of Sri Lanka is following a twin strategy of weakening the LTTE militarily and limiting humanitarian supplies to civilians to dangerously low levels. The LTTE on the other hand has been carrying out its attacks on two fronts, military and economic. But the strategy of the government to weaken the LTTE and to force them to the negotiating table does not seem to be working and the bloodshed continues. The war has turned out to be more destructive than ever before with the likelihood of it becoming even more brutal and protracted. The mounting number of human casualties and the enormous suffering of the displaced people calls for a reassessment of the government's strategy of seeking to impose a political settlement through military means.

The international community is well aware that the government is confronted with an armed guerrilla force which unilaterally broke the cease-fire agreement and is capable of unleashing terror among the civilians like the bombing of the Central Bank in Colombo, seen by television viewers throughout the world. What is not seen by them, however, is the extent of destruction and civilian suffering resulting from the military operations in the north.

The IDPs are at the receiving end of battles to take and hold territory by both parties, not only in the north but in the east as well. There is a heavy LTTE presence in the east. Armed clashes with the army are routine. Attacks on border villages result in the killing of innocent civilians. The suffering of the civilian population in and near the areas of military operations continues to increase, frustrating the efforts of humanitarian agencies to bring some degree of security and dignity to the lives of displaced persons. While the number of displaced persons is on the increase every day, humanitarian assistance and the commitment of the government to meaningfully address their needs is decreasing. The gap between need and the availability of essential supplies is widening, at least in the short term.

Protecting IDPs

IDPs, like refugees, have been forced to leave their homes and find themselves in refugee-like situations. But the fact that they remain in their own countries means that the international refugee protection regime is not applicable. However, the provisions of international humanitarian law are applicable to internally displaced civilians living in a situation of armed conflict. International Humanitarian Law seeks to protect the victims of armed conflict. Once an armed conflict exists inside a country, the provisions of humanitarian law becomes applicable.

Situations of non-international armed conflict are governed by some of the most central principles of humanitarian law and many international human rights guarantees. Human rights law is applicable, although rights and guarantees are increasingly subject to restriction and in extreme cases, even derogation. Nevertheless, human rights law and humanitarian law reinforce each other in internal armed conflict situations. Human rights law generally restrains the abusive practices of only one party to the conflict, namely the government and its agents. The state has an obligation to guarantee human rights. That non-state actors, also, should be internationally accountable for human rights abuses, has gained ground in recent years.

The crux of the problem for IDPs lies in how internationally accepted human rights and humanitarian safeguards can be enforced under a hostile domestic environment in which the state apparatus is one of the major actors. They are vulnerable to round ups, arbitrary arrests and forcible resettlement. IDPs risk forcible conscription and sexual assault. They may be deprived of food and health services. At the same time their access to international protection and assistance which is guaranteed by international law and convention to refugees, is constrained by the condition of national sovereignty. More than ever before, warring parties are ready to use humanitarian access, life saving assistance and even civilians themselves as weapons in their political-military struggles.

The IDPs are victims of a lacunae in the international protection regime. At present there is no clear formulation of the legal principles applicable to IDPs. Both UNHCR and humanitarian agencies have stressed the importance of having a legal framework which can be used as the basis for discussions with state authorities. A consensus has now developed in support of compiling existing norms and evaluating them to assess the adequacy of protective coverage. But implementing norms remains the main challenge.

IDPs are particularly vulnerable in situations which are below the threshold for the application of humanitarian law. At the same time, while human rights guarantees may be enshrined in state constitution, they are legitimately derogated or restricted in the interests of public order or security. Emergency regulations restrict the enjoyment of fundamental rights provided in constitution other than the right to life and freedom from torture which are non-derogable. Moreover when there are racial, ethnic or religious overtones to the conflict, there is often hostility between the controlling authority, usually the military, and the affected civilian population.

Sri Lanka is a party to several international legal instruments which provide a standard of norms which could be applied in respect of IDPs. Regardless of the particular circumstances faced by the state, international norms and institutional frameworks should be seen as imposing obligations on states. The primary responsibility for the welfare and protection of IDPs lies with the state.

UNHCR on several occasions has been called upon to provide protection and assistance to internally displaced persons. A basic criteria for legitimising their involvement is the existence of a link with a refugee situation, that is, UNHCR's efforts on behalf of IDPs are permitted in so far as it acts to prevent IDPs from crossing the border and becoming refugees. UNHCR has assisted IDPs in returnee areas, in refugee areas, in cross-border operations and in situations where assistance may alleviate the need to move across borders. NGOs and UNHCR should increase their cooperation to strengthen their common commitment to the needs of IDPs.

Based on the Geneva Conventions and Protocols, the International Committee of the Red Cross (ICRC) monitors the implementation of international humanitarian law. It gives protection and assistance to victims of armed conflicts. Being a neutral, impartial and independent intermediary, it contributes significantly to the protection and assistance of internally displaced persons. NGOs need to learn from the ICRC a lesson in understanding the concepts of neutrality, impartiality and being independent intermediaries. This would not only help in obtaining humanitarian access to IDPs but also create space for dialogue with parties to the conflict.

Children in situations of armed conflict must be treated as a distinct and priority concern in all humanitarian interventions. Whenever sanctions are imposed they should provide for humanitarian child-focused exemptions. The concept of humanitarian assistance must be broadened to include measures that protect a child's psycho-social well-being and education. Education in emergency situations can give structure to children's lives, instill community values, and promote respect for human rights. Long-term community based approaches are essential in rebuilding families. A campaign should be launched to stop the recruitment of children under 18 for combat duties. This will need to take into account situations that drive children to combat duties, specifically prolonged life in welfare centres and as continuously displaced persons.

Every effort must be made to reach those in need of protection and assistance on all sides of the conflict. It is obvious that any initiative to assist the victims of war can be meaningful only if attempts are made within an overall movement towards peace and reconciliation and after a cessation of hostilities. In the meantime, initiatives to improve the quality of life of civilians, particularly the displaced, should be put in place. Regional efforts at conflict resolution are also essential because in the long run, this is the most effective way to find solutions for displacement. This can only be achieved if the root causes are addressed and political solutions found.

As the problem of IDPs is common to the countries of South Asia, a study of the situation at the national and regional levels should be undertaken with the aim of developing a regional mechanism which would provide a code of conduct for all countries in the region. While the onus of formulating a normative framework falls squarely on the shoulders of governments, NGOs must make meaningful attempts to institutionalize the rights of IDPs at national and regional levels. The poorest and dispossessed layers of society rarely have access to the judicial system. In view of the large numbers of IDPs involved, NGOs need to consider these issues as worth seizing upon and challenging in courts.

We cannot ignore the rights of the IDPs just because the legal framework to address their protection and survival needs has not been developed.

Politics of the Refugee Crisis in Sri Lanka

Ajith Rupasinghe

In discussing the question of refugees, migrants and stateless persons, it is important to focus on the character of the modern nation-state. The state is the dominant institutional concentration of political power which articulates and perpetuates the system of social relations in a given society. It is a system of social and productive relations maintained and reproduced by the structure of state power which fundamentally accounts for and generates civil conflict.

In the case of Sri Lanka, the modern state was constructed by the British colonial administration in league with the dominant Sinhala political elites. The result was a majoritarian form of hegemonic parliamentary rule that entrenched the power and privilege of the Sinhala Buddhist majority over that of all other ethnic, religious and national minorities.

The first act of the new state was to disenfranchise the entire Indian Tamil population, that is, the plantation workers brought in by the British colonial administration from south India as bonded labour. This was achieved by denying them their right of citizenship through a majority vote in parliament.

From there followed a systematic policy of discrimination, violent repression and subjugation carried out against the Tamil nation in the north-east. This policy was intensified by all successive governments. Discrimination was intensified with a vengeance in all spheres including language, religion, education, employment, land alienation, and in development policy.

The armed Tamil national liberation movement arose as a result of the failure of the Tamil parliamentary representatives to win any concessions decades of peaceful, constitutional struggle and in the face of mounting armed state repression.

Whatever the weaknesses and distortions in the line and vision of the leadership in the strategy, programmes and the forms of struggle of the armed national liberation movement, the clear fact is that the state is fundamentally accountable and responsible for having generated and intensified this crisis.

This is why it is important to address the character of the nation-state in dealing with question of refugees, migrants and stateless persons.

Magnitude of the refugee crisis

The latest government figures published by the Ministry of Shipping, Ports, Rehabilitation and Reconstruction indicate that there is a total population of 785,187 persons displaced as of October 30, 1996. Out of this total, 691,618 are from the north-east provinces and 60,668 are from the bordering districts. As this entire region is engulfed in a civil conflict, it has resulted in about 752,286 persons being internally displaced and rendered destitute. The worst-affected areas are in the Northern Province accounting for some 628,293 internally displaced persons.

The official government figures are misleading in that they are based on the issue of dry rations/cash and World Food Programme (WFP) assistance. A much greater number of people have been deprived of any form of sustainable livelihood who do not have access to government assistance in the north.

This raises the question of how we define refugees. It is misleading to limit the definition to those who have been compelled to leave their homes due to political violence. The fact is that the entire population of the north and a majority of the population in the east and in the border villages, have been deprived of any form of sustainable livelihood and have been reduced to a subhuman level of survival. They too are refugees held hostage by political processes beyond their control.

For our purposes, we should define refugees as those who have been compelled to abandon their homes as a consequence of social and political processes beyond their control and have no sustainable means of livelihood.

Hundreds of thousands of internally displaced persons in the Vanni, the heartland of the north virtually live under trees without adequate shelter, food, water, medical supplies or sanitation facilities. Given the onset of the north-east monsoon, it is expected that there will be widespread epidemics, including hepatitis, meningitis, typhoid, cholera, dysentery, malaria and other diseases Along with this, some of the existing vital infrastructure has been destroyed by incessant and indiscriminate bombing and shelling, including the Killinochchi hospital.

The people of this entire region have suffered the brutal consequences of this civil war for some 14 years. Most have been displaced more than once, some for several years at a time. Many had sought refugee in south India. Some have returned only to be caught up once again in a cycle of war. Some have begun to return to India. But they are now being interdicted on the high seas by the combined efforts of the Indian and Sri Lankan navies. Those who sought refuge outside South Asia, now find themselves being hounded, harassed and forced to return to the waiting security agencies. Wherever they seek refuge, they meet with callous indifference, enforced means of subsistence and political harassment, based on a denial of the most elementary human and democratic rights.

Even before the resumption of hostilities in 1995, the plight of the refugees both within and outside Sri Lanka was pathetic. Apart from the subhuman conditions prevailing in the camps, they were subjected to other forms of abuse. Some were forcibly resettled although the security conditions were not stable, simply for the propaganda value of claiming that these areas were under government control. Some were resettled in areas they did not like and where conditions were deplorable. Powerful politicians and bureaucrats accumulated vast sums of money by their control over the relief, rehabilitation and reconstruction programs. The refugee population had no effective voice, no political power to have their grievances heard, let alone addressed.

With the outbreak of the third stage of the Eelam War, the refugee situation has reached unprecedented dimensions, constituting a spiraling mass scale humanitarian crisis. At the same time, there does not seem to be any immediate prospects for a negotiated political settlement. The indictments brought against the Liberation Tigers of Tamil Eelam (LTTE) on some 720 counts, including mass murder, constitute unparalleled legal and political barriers against opening lines of communication, let alone negotiations. The indictments are meant to delegitimise and criminalise the

LTTE. This would have the most profound consequences, militarily and politically. It appears that the government is committed to dragging out the war with the objective of gaining a final and decisive military victory over the LTTE. This can only mean a further militarisation and internationalisation of the conflict and more intensive destruction. These developments are bound to further magnify and compound the refugee crisis.

This immense suffering, this colossal human degradation and the repeated cycle of brutal and destructive civil war, which has plunged the whole of society into an abysmal economic, political, social and moral crisis, is fundamentally the result of the inability of the Sri Lankan state to address the issue of the right of national self-determination of the Tamil people in the region.

Both the Sri Lankan state and the LTTE have used the refugee crisis for political advantage. The state has used the denial of emergency aid and assistance to the people as a political weapon to coerce the population into submission, justifying it on the grounds of denial of supplies to the LTTE. Similarly, the LTTE has used the crisis to expose the government, to harden attitudes against the state and to increase recruitment. Both have restricted the free movement of the civilian population.

While it is a truism, that in a state of war it is expected that each side will strive to use everything possible for its own advantage, the denial of emergency relief by a state to its own population, reduced to subhuman struggle for survival by a political logic beyond their control, is unacceptable and intolerable by any standards.

At the same time, there is virtual censorship. Humanitarian agencies, peace activists and journalists are restricted from visiting the area, which prevents the world from knowing the reality of the situation. Truly, the refugees are a hostage population caught in a vicious logic of escalating political victimisation beyond their control.

Most seriously, the entire international community has remained either ineffective or silent about this humanitarian crisis. Foreign governments have, in effect, fallen in line with the decisions and policies of the Sri Lankan state. Some, particularly those which are most strident in crusading against international terrorism, have even provided the funds, the weapons and the diplomatic support to perpetuate the crisis.

The fact is that the killing fields all over the world have become hunting grounds for major regional and international powers to carve out their own strategic terrain regardless of the cost in human lives and the suffering inflicted upon masses of innocent people.

All these events demonstrate the stark fact that refugees do not possess any form of effective political power. They are one of the most disempowered and vulnerable of all social groups in the modern world. And their numbers will magnify a thousandfold since all signs indicate that the so-called new world order is characterised by more intense, violent cataclysmic political upheavals than anything we have yet known in the South Asian region

In this context, the effort to draw up a regional charter of rights for refugees in the form of a protocol is timely and urgent. Yet it must not be confined to a policy of advocacy. The existing international agencies, including the UNHCR, have been pathetically ineffective in dealing with the current crisis. The major international and regional powers are providing material and diplomatic support to the Sri Lankan state in prolonging the civil war. Along with the effort to establish a protocol, we must strive to build organisational forms and mechanisms to effectively empower the refugees, migrants and displaced people in South Asia so that they may articulate, fight for and defend their fundamental human and democratic rights as an independent political force.

We must combine all our efforts by networking and mobilising all our resources and constituencies so that we can become a force for democratic transformation throughout South Asia, so that the problem of refugees, migrants and displaced persons will be relegated to the dustbin of history. If we have the vision, the courage and the determination to unite as the people of South Asia, we can begin to have some real political leverage. Then we can define a people-based, human-centered strategy for collective struggle to ensure that our protocol is indeed respected and implemented, otherwise, we too may become unwitting pawns in the prevailing game of international, regional and domestic politics.

SECTION SIX

Economic Migration
A traditional right

Sadeq Khan

Migratory population movements have been a regular feature and a motive force in the development of human order out of the cauldron of civilisations. From prehistory, migrations have led to conflicts followed by conciliation or subjugation, oppressive or otherwise. Population invasions, apart from the ravages of conflicts, often drove out, the original occupants of a land into more difficult terrains, causing maladjustment and annihilation of sections of affected tribes, clans and societies. The process continued along the fringes of civilisation and in particular, amongst nomadic tribes through out the Middle Ages. Fresh eruptions of this process have taken place of late in Africa and in the Caucasus after the end of the cold war.

Ancient empires have absorbed population movements and migratory pressures. With the rise of the maritime powers, the colonisation process elbowed out indigenous populations from the new territories they invaded. Until the late 19th century, a system of passports and visas to restrict population movements did not exist. Closed markets preceded closed state frontiers of this century, as the ugly face of nineteenth century capitalism began to overwhelm human accommodations of the feudal kind.

Political upheavals and territorial partitions in the 20th century, surpassed population displacements in terms of sheer size, pushing upwards to a million plus as in the case of the White Russian exodus in the 20s, the exodus of Spanish loyalists from Franco's Spain in the 30s, the Chinese exodus from the mainland after the PLA victory and Palestinian partition victims in the 40s. Nearer home in our own subcontinent, the biggest exodus of contemporary human history took place during the partition of British India, with some 18 million people turned refugees on both sides. The Bangladesh war alone caused a temporary exodus of over half that number in 1971. The Afghan civil war still has millions of refugees to take back home from across its borders with Pakistan. Nepali refugees from Bhutan, Rohingya refugees from Myanmar and Chakma refugees from Bangladesh are all victims of political situations, as in a reverse sense are the many settlers of Bangladeshi origin in India who are subjected to a push-back programme from time to time across the border into Bangladesh.

But my concern is to focus not on the political dimension of the refugee problem, but the economic dimension. Indeed, throughout the millennia, economic expectations have been the principal driving force behind migratory pressures. It is strange to observe how in the 20th century, under the pretension of upholding human rights, political persecution is accepted as the only valid ground for migration and the economic immigrant, has become a dirty word, a permissible target of community persecution on the rebound. It is ironical how the benign face of 20th century capitalism, in welfare states and command economies alike, has been shutting out the natural flow of economic refugees, in the name of protecting the interests of its working population and the inertia of its social equilibrium and selectively letting in only the political fugitive.

Human rights and the human dignity of the economic migrant are being trampled upon at will by the governments of host communities. He is exploited as slave labour by employment rackets, despised by alien neighbours, ill-treated by malcontents, hunted by police and generally pushed around, if not pushed back across hostile frontiers. Whether he languishes in a foreign jail without legal aid or in a refugee camp on meagre dole, the economic migrants' lot today is pitiable. It should not be since in capitalist terms, he is but an entrepreneur with labour, skilled or unskilled, as his capital. His situation in life is not of his own making. How is it that the opportunity he is making for himself by suffering the odds of migration, an age-old traditional opportunity, is sought to be denied him by the frontiers of nation-states in the late 20th century.

At the threshold of the 21st century, we are talking about shared earth and environment, about global freedom and capital flows, a global capital market and about the World Trade Organisation's regime of free competition in the marketing of products. Why is it then that we are severely restricting the free movement labour ? Albeit there is a case for the qualified protection of class privileges in a given socio-political system, for peaceful evolution in the flux of changing realities, but that should accommodate rather than exclude external migratory pressures. Unmanageable situations arising from unrestricted migratory pressures are not desirable, but neither can exclusive islands of human order be sustainable in a shared earth.

One of the late realisations of the 20th century has been the issue of the protection of indigenous people. But that has not restricted in any significant way the fundamental right of citizens to internal migration. Article 13 of the Universal Declaration of Human Rights clearly stipulates that (a) everyone has a right to freely travel and to settle within one's state boundaries, and (b) everyone has a right to travel freely leaving his own country or any other country and to return to one's own country. The international dimension of the right of free movement and domicile certainly needs to be more elaborately addressed in the light of current realities.

International development thinkers and development agencies are toying with the idea of spatial and temporal planning for regional resource management in cross-border flows and interactions. Indeed, projected economic growth areas of the 21st century in Asia in particular, are hardly cognisant of the restraints of state frontiers. Such restraints are absent or minimal in the European Union embracing the area of the NATO alliance, as well as in the North American Free Trade Area. ASEAN leads the way in Asia in the beginning of meaningful regional cooperation. Should SAARC be far behind ?

On the other hand, it is precisely the utter lack of spatial and temporal management of regional resources and their natural cycles that has been the cause of many a human catastrophe, particularly, affecting Bangladesh, the drainage outlet of three mighty eastern rivers at the foot of the Himalaya. Farakka vividly illustrates the example of regional mismanagement of a perennial natural resource which has led to widespread desertification of the Ganges basin in Bangladesh. It has had an enormous consequence with substantial fallout on migration. Lost lands from river erosion in the active delta region and spoilt lands from flash floods in the table lands of the Himalayas, are two major causes of internal migratory pressures in Bangladesh, only a trickle of which spills over into the restricted avenues of external emigration.

External migratory pressures from Bangladesh cannot but increase, and legitimately so, if its land-man ratio, already intolerably adverse, is further destabilised by a sea-level rise from global warming on the one hand and the undermining of food security in relation with projected population growth, on the other hand.

Spatial and temporal planning for the management of regional resources must therefore include human resources and regional stress of population flux in the region. The SAARC region could provide a possible framework or it could be within a broader regional context, including Afghanistan and Myanmar, or a narrower one involving Myanmar, Bangladesh, eastern India, Bhutan, Nepal and north-eastern India, identified as a potential growth triangle. Within the context, it may be worthwhile to set up intergovernmental committees to attend exclusively to the needs and problems of migratory pressures.

In a speech to the United Nations General Assembly in 1996, Bangladesh Prime Minister Sheikh Hasina made an appeal to the international community to address the problem of economic migration in a meaningful manner, lest it become a major problem in the future. The Bangladesh prime minister emphasised that "migratory flows of peoples over the globe today, are, to be very candid, inspired more by economic motivations than any other factor"

The Bangladesh prime minister drew attention to the fact that according to some estimates, as many as 125 million people live outside their countries, with more than half of them moving from developing country to developing country.

As many of them are also in violation of the immigration laws of their host countries, they are often the victims of exploitation and abuse. They do not receive the benefits and protection of the laws and conventions that apply to those fleeing political persecution, she said. For the international community to tackle the issue could mean "rules and regulations at the international level and certainly also measures to remove or redress the root causes of such migratory flows. It is a social issue, an economic issue and also a humanitarian issue that impinges on human security," Sheikh Hasina said.

No migration, in a sense, is voluntary. It is all involuntary. Where there is an adverse land-man ratio, people will migrate. It is a traditional right for people to migrate. In international fora, arguments are made in favour of unrestricted global flows of capital, trade and also services. An equally persuasive case can be made for more deregulated movements of labour. History tends to corroborate the view that immigrants have enriched and enhanced, rather than impoverished, countries, where they have gone in search of a better living.

Bangladeshi Immigrants in Sindh

Haroon Ahmed

More than a million[1] Bangladeshis are to be found hidden in the lanes and bylanes of the Sindh province of Pakistan. They are de facto stateless people, victims of human rights abuses and police harassment, treated as illegal immigrants in Pakistan and disowned by Bangladesh as citizens. The "illegal status" of the Bangladeshis migrants and Burmese refugees spawns a cross-border network of Pakistani, Indian and Bangladeshi underworld touts and agents who feed off their desperation. Within Sindh, the local population tends to view them as straining their meagre resources, industrialists view them as a source of cheap and compliant labour, while the government regards them as an internal security threat.

Also in Pakistan's largest province, Sindh, are to be found Bihari, Burmese, Afghan and Iranian refugees. Political turmoil in the Arakan state of Myanmar drove Burmese Muslims, the Rohingyas, across the border to Bangladesh and from there to Pakistan. The Burmese refugees are treated as illegal migrants although they fled ethnic persecution, generalised violence and economic underdevelopment.

Biharis are the Urdu-speaking, ethnically non-Bengali, "stranded Pakistanis" in Bangladesh who colluded with the Pakistan army in the 1971 war. Over the last 25 years, about 161,000 Biharis have been repatriated to Pakistan but 238,000 are still left in Bangladesh, unwanted by Pakistan and Bangladesh. The issue of "stranded Pakistanis" complicates any initiative to bring within some kind of a legal framework the more than one million Bangladeshi migrants in Karachi, and rescue them from the clutches of the underworld and the police.

Bengali migrants

Migration of Bengalis from the then East Pakistan to West Pakistan was encouraged as a matter of state policy in the late 1960s by President General Ayub Khan. In the name of national integration, peasants from East Pakistan were brought over and resettled in rural Sindh. They were given agricultural land and encouraged to bring their families over. However, the wetland rice culture of East Pakistan was very different from dry land farming in Sindh. With little support to adapt themselves to a different style of farming, most of their farms withered away. The government took no responsibility for them. The Bengalis soon migrated to Karachi, Pakistan's largest city, in search of work.

Thereafter, Bengalis on their own initiative, driven by abject poverty, landlessness and floods, were drawn to Pakistan to fill an expanding job market. Once they found jobs, they sent for their families and settled down permanently. In Karachi they settled in Rehmanabad which was a *kachi-abadi* (unauthorised squatter settlements) but has since been regularized. Although this group of Bengali migrants from then East Pakistan settled in West Pakistan when it was one country, the authorities make no distinction between the more recent Bangladeshi migrants and them. Overnight, these citizens of Pakistan, became stateless.

Domicile documents are dismissed as fake if the local police, in league with the network of underworld touts, are not bribed. Documents like national identity cards, passports, ration cards or inclusion in a registered voters list, have been sharply devalued as proof because of the flourishing racket in fake IDs. An informal survey by the Human Rights Commission of Pakistan (HRCP), among the residents in the migrants area of Ali Akbar Shah Goth, revealed that most of them had domicile documents and ration cards dating back to the 70s.[2] But with fake IDs available for Rs 2,000 to 4,000, proof has become a matter of money, not fact.

During the 1971 war with East Pakistan and following the break-up of Pakistan, there was an exodus of Bengalis back to then East Pakistan. A growing sense of insecurity in West Pakistan, discrimination and even dismissal from the workplace and the prospect of a better life in a new country, drove many to return to Bangladesh. However, famine conditions in Bangladesh, soon after independence, pushed many to migrate back to Pakistan.

Hidden people

Most of the present day migrant workers arrived after 1971 and are treated as illegal immigrants. Their status is dealt with under the Foreigner's Act 1946, which makes crossing the border illegal.

In Karachi, a recent report based on a 1995 police survey, shows that there are one million undocumented Bangladeshis and over 200,000 Burmese. The migration began in the mid-70s, as a consequence, a large proportion of the children have been born in Pakistan.

Moreover, many of the Bengalis are not migrants at all. A very large number, especially children and women are victims of trafficking, smuggled in to meet the demand for child labour and the flesh trade. A 1993 survey by the Lawyers for Human Rights and Legal Aid (LHRLA), estimated that practically every day 100-150 Bangladeshi women and children are smuggled into Pakistan, primarily to Karachi. About 2,000 Bangladeshi women are languishing in various jails. A survey of jails in Sindh has revealed the presence of a large number of Burmese women and children. The majority of Bangladeshi and Burmese women in jail have been charged under the Foreigners Act, 1946 and/or the Hudood Ordinance.[3]

From the mid-70s a highly organized network of *dalals* (agents), spread over Bangladesh, India and Pakistan have been running waves of Bangladeshi economic migrants. Karachi is not always the last destination. Some move on to the Gulf. Bangladeshi migrants form the cheapest labour force and there are reports of resentment from the local labour force, especially in the fishing sector. In one incident in the village of Ibrahim Hyderi, a local organisation launched an anti-immigrant campaign against Bangladeshi and Burmese migrants working in the fishing industry.[4]

Most Bangladeshi migrants work in the export sector, like carpet and fish industries. Women and children are largely engaged in the shrimp or carpet industries. Others work as domestic servants and cooks in restaurants. And then of course there is the flesh trade.

Bonded child labour in the carpet industry is provided by migrant workers' children in Karachi. Children even as young as seven are offered as collateral to a carpet contractor who lends money to a migrant family for a house or a passport.

Bangladeshi migrants are settled in 60 to 70 unauthorized *bagali-paras* (slum settlements) and pay regular *bhatta* (protection money). On top of that is the daily extortion by *dalals*, the local mafia, the police and minor government functionaries. Their illegal status makes them easy prey to every kind of abuse by the local police, petty officials, underworld touts and unscrupulous employers.

Even those who have been living in Karachi for over a decade, can be easily identified by their accent and vulnerability to blackmail. They have no documents and even if they have authentic identity cards or a passport procured by bribery, they still have to pay a bribe if they want to visit Bangladesh or if they are picked up by the police. Virtually, a million Bangladeshi will be exposed as stateless, if the police stops taking bribes and enforces the Foreigners Act.

Every time there is an outburst of violence in Karachi, there is a tendency to round up the Bengalis and throw them in jail. In 1995, following the carnage in Karachi, the Federal Minister of the Interior, Naseerullah Babar ordered a crackdown on Bengali immigrants. Crossing the border was made a non-bailable offence by amending the Foreigners Act. Hundreds were rounded up arrested and some even deported.[5]

But Deportation is no solution, for each time the authorities in Pakistan decide to deport a plane load of "illegal migrants", the Bangladeshi authorities disown all responsibility, asserting that they are Pakistani citizens and their documentary claims to be Bangladeshi citizens are false. Over the last couple of decades only 1,689 Bengalis have been deported or repatriated. Most end up like a football, tossed back and forth by the Pakistani and Bangladeshi authorities, neither of them wanting to claim any responsibility for the Bangladeshi migrants.

Complicating the deportation issue is the dead weight legacy of the 1971 war, namely the "stranded Pakistanis", the Biharis, who the Bangladesh government wants to get rid of but Pakistan does not want for fear of upsetting the highly fragile demographic balance in Sindh.

Bihari immigrants in Sindh

In Pakistan, Biharis were those who migrated from the Indian state of Bihar to East or West Pakistan, after Partition. But now, they have been politically transformed into Urdu-speaking people who have re-migrated to Pakistan from Bangladesh. Unlike Bangladeshi migrants, the Biharis do not stick out as "foreigners". They speak Urdu and have Bihari relatives who migrated to West Pakistan after 1947.

A recent survey by Anwer Rashid of the Orangi Pilot Project of Ghaziabad, a *mohallah* (neighbourhood) of Orangi, shows the situation of the Bihari refugees who have been repatriated from Bangladesh. The majority of the people in Ghaziabad, are Biharis who migrated from Bangladesh after 1981. There is also a small percentage of ethnic Baluchis and Christians. It is a *kachi abadi* comprising 3,336 households. About 80 percent of the people are self-employed. No water or electricity is provided by the local civic authorities. Water has to be purchased from a tanker and for electric supply they are dependent on a generator. As there are no government-backed health facilities or schools, private schools and dispensaries have come up in the neighbourhood.

In brief, it was found that the Biharis are enterprising, more educated than their neighbours and eager to solve their problem themselves. However, Anwer Rashid, in his survey of Ghaziabad felt that, "because of the background of Civil War and their experience as prisoners of war, the leaders lack confidence when dealing with powerful political groups. They cannot respond to political pressure of any sort and withdraw, submissively. As they do not support any political party or group they are denied political patronage, which is vital for survival at the grassroots level.

"In Karachi, a city which does not support the Pakistan Peoples Party (PPP), one of the three National Assembly members is from Orangi, the other two are from, a suburban Sindhi dominated area and from Lyari. The elected member from Orangi is a Bihari who migrated from Bangladesh. Although he is with the PPP, which twice has been the ruling party, he has no clout nor has he been able to provide any 'political patronage' to his constituents."

Legitimate status for migrant workers

A 1995 police report on migrants in Karachi as well as activists working for migrants welfare, recommended the need for some kind of work permit. By regulating migrant workers, a work permit system would save migrant workers from exploitation by underworld agents, the police and employers and free them from perpetual fear and insecurity. It would of course require the governments of Bangladesh and Pakistan to acknowledge responsibility for their citizens, namely the Biharis by Pakistan and the Bangladeshis by Bangladesh. A regional framework could help in addressing the reality of unauthorised cross-border migration of peoples divided by the creation of nation-state borders. Movements of peoples driven by the "pull-push" factor will not stop. The alternative is a growing army of vulnerable stateless people.

Notes

1. See Nafisa Shah, " A Long way from home: A case study of migrant workers in Karachi", *Liberal Times*, vol 5 no 1, 1997, pp 4-8. She suggests that the migrant population in Sindh is 2.5 million.
2. Shah, p. 6.
3. Lawyers for Human Rights and Legal Aid, (LHRLA) Flesh Trade Report 1996, Karachi.
4. In one action, the local organisation, Anumane Samaj e Behbood of Ibrahim Huderi village, a thousand Bengalis residing in the area were thrown out. See Shah op. cit. p. 8.
5. Shah, ibid p. 5.

Bangladeshis in India

The numbers game

Gautam Navlakha

The all-India politicisation of the issue of Bangladeshi migrants peaked in the early 90s. All through the 80s the northeastern states of India, bordering Bangladesh, had been fired by a surge of xenophobia which targeted the "foreigner"—essentially illegal Bengali migrants. The communal frenzy whipped up in the wake of the Babri Masjid controversy also homed in on what was projected as a flood of Bangladeshi Muslim infiltrators swamping the demographic balance in the border states of India. There were official and unofficial raids or threats of raids on colonies of Bengali Muslims even in metropolitan centres and a zealous campaign to push back of "illegal Bangladeshi migrants". Of the national parties, the Bharatiya Janata Party (BJP) made it an integral part of its political campaign. The BJP is banking on public ignorance of the real dimensions of Bangladeshi immigration, in order to whip up its hate campaign.

At its national executive meeting, in April 1993, the BJP openly discriminated between Bangladeshi Hindus whom they accept as refugees, and Bangladeshi Muslims who were branded as infiltrators, to be summarily deported. Strangely, the party's estimate of "infiltrators" in Delhi remains constant. It claims that there are 300,000 Bangladeshis illegally residing in Delhi.

The party propaganda apparatus maintains that there are more than 20 million Bangladeshis in India. Of course, illegal immigrants by definition are not legally recorded, therefore it is impossible to provide a precise estimate of such immigration. But there is evidence to show that this estimate is a gross exaggeration. It is popularly accepted that there has been a disproportionately large increase in the population in the districts bordering Bangladesh. But as the census figures tabulated by demographer Prof Ashish Bose, shows, this is simply not true.

TABLE 1: District-wise Population Growth during 1971-91 (in percentage)

Dhubri	+55.77	Marigaon	+51.07
Kokrajjhar	+75.94	Naogaon	+51.17
Bongaigaon	+64.43	Golaghat	+53.09
Barpeta	+42.71	Jorhat	+32.68
Nalgari	+48.72	Sibsagar	+36.80
Kamrup	+64.69	Dibrugarh	+37.20
Darrang	+54.17	Tinsukia	+47.16
Sonitpur	+56.49	Karbi Anglong	+72.79
Dhemaji	+104.48	Kailakandi	+47.76
Cachar	+47.65	All India	+54.45

The figures show that population growth in the districts in Assam bordering Bangladesh is generally lower that the national average, except in district with high tribal population concentrations like Dhemaji, Kokrajhar, Karbi Anglong and the North Cachar Hills.

Table 2 : State-wise population growth during 1971-91

States	Population growth % during 1971-91
Arunachal	+84.93
Assam	+53.26
Bihar	+53.27
Manipur	+71.26
Mizoram	+107.51
Nagaland	+134.20
Tripura	+77.16
West Bengal	+53.63
Meghalaya	+75.43
All India	+54.45

The population growth rates in some border districts in West Bengal do indicate a substantial influx. Over the last two decades between 1971 to 1991 the population in Maldah, Murshidabad and South 24-Parganas shows a definite increase over the national average. That is, between 1997-81 it increased by +26 percent in Maldah, +29.63 percent in Murshidabad and +25.49 percent in South 24-Parganas. And for 1981 to 1991, the increase was +28.04 percent, +19.42

percent and +30.08 percent respectively. However, the growth rate in other bordering districts like Cooch Behar and Jalpaiguri was no greater than the national average.

If the state-wise population growth figures are examined, they reveal trends which belie the communal propaganda.

These figures show that the two states of Assam and West Bengal which are understood to have been most affected by migration from Bangladesh, actually have a population growth rate lower than the national average. The substantially above average growth rate in the small state of Tripura is the result of Bangladeshi migration. But these are essentially Hindus, Muslims, and Chakma tribals fleeing Bangladeshi government repression. Similarly, the abnormal population increase in the states of Nagaland, Mizoram and Arunachal is the result of both internal migration of unskilled and semi-skilled labour, as well as cross-border migration from Nepal, and Bangladesh.

In the state of Bihar, the districts of Purnea and Kishanganj are alleged to have been swamped by Bangladeshi immigrants. Their population growth rates for 1971 to 1981 are +227.42 percent for Purnea and 23.58 percent for Kishanganj, and from 1981 to 1991, they are 30.15 percent and +22.52 percent respectively. The figures reveal that the population growth rates in these two districts was much higher in the decade 1971-81 and dropped substantially in the following decade 1981-91. The population growth rate in Purnea for 1981-91 is only slightly higher than the national average, and that for Kishanganj is actually below the national average. This suggests that migration from Bangladesh to these two districts since 1971-81, has declined.

The district and state population growth figures recorded in the 1971, 1981 and 1991 censuses clearly show that the BJP's estimates of Bangladeshi immigration are greatly exaggerated. Moreover, international estimates of migration into India are much lower than those alleged by communal elements. According to the UNHCR as on December 31, 1995 there were 320,000 refugees, 780,000 "people of concern" but not recognised as refugees and 250,000 internally displaced people. This does not include Bangladeshis who came to India prior to 1970. According to the Union Home Ministry of India between 1948 to 1961, some 3.1 million migrants from the East Pakistan, settled in India. However, the Ministry is conspicuously silent about the numbers after 1971. The 1995-96 annual report of the home ministry merely notes, "The Bangladesh authorities have been sensitised about our security concerns as well as the problem being caused by large-scale infiltration by Bangladeshi nationals."

The use by political parties of the illegal immigrants issue has the explosive potential of pitching one group of people in India against another. There is already in India a strong feeling against "outsiders". If it is Bangladeshis in Assam, it is Chakmas in Arunachal who arouse xenophobic passion. There is no official confirmation of Operation Pushback under which innocent citizens have been taken away from their homes in the dead of night, their heads shaven, driven to the Indo-Bangladesh border under humiliating conditions and then "pushed" across without any proof of illegal migration or any agreement with the Bangladesh government. Stopping the movement of people or deportation campaigns like Operation Pushback against alleged Bangladeshis, are no solutions.

A disturbing feature of the current situation is the virtual silence and even complicity, of the Indian government. No official effort has been made to demystify the greatly exaggerated figures of Bangladeshi migration. Instead, alleged Bangladeshis have been summarily deprived of ration cards, struck off electoral rolls and threatened with deportation, apart from harassment by the police and communal elements in the lower levels of the bureaucracy. In many of the cases which were investigated, those so harassed, were found to be bona fide Indian citizens. This blatant violation of the laws of the land is continuing despite protests in Parliament, and official assurances to the contrary. Moreover, those whipping up communal passions on this issue are not being proceeded against despite the laws prohibiting this.

What is particularly distressing is that BJP activists have been acting as guides and informers. A resolution adopted by the BJP national executive at Calcutta on April 10, 1993 boasted, that "recently through the efforts of the BJP in Delhi about 1.5 lakh voters were deleted from the electoral rolls of 13 Assembly constituencies having large clusters of Bangladeshi infiltrators."

The confusion caused by the political manipulation of numbers was evident in the case of the Assam election in 1993. The then Chief Election Commissioner of India, T.N. Seshan stated that there were eight lakh "foreigners" in Assam. The Assam government however, flouted the EC's directions. The state government of Assam claimed that under the Foreigners Act of 1936, 1,800 illegal citizens had been detected and another 871 persons had been identified till January 1993. The Assam government pointed out that the available records did not justify the declaration of any area as "having substantial presence of foreign nationals". In fact, it reminded the EC that its directive which lays the "onus of proof" of citizenship on the claimant "to the satisfaction of the electoral registration officer" contravenes an earlier EC report from 1983 which stated that "the names of persons ... cannot be removed arbitrarily and under summary proceedings connected with the preparations or revision of electoral rolls .... The agency for undertaking the task of identifying such (foreign) names is not ... the election machinery as that cannot decide the question of citizenship".

In order to remove the sense of insecurity among people it is necessary for the government of India to go public on the debate on "foreign nationals". Since the number of foreign nationals varies between 0.5 to 25 million it is necessary to look into the matter of numbers and determine where they come from, that is Bangladesh, Nepal, Sri Lanka or Burma.

Brooding Over the Open Border

A personal view of Indian migrants in Nepal

Basanta Thapa

Let me begin with an anecdote. Last week, I was in the company of a group of American tourists flying from Chitwan to Kathmandu. At Kathmandu airport, I met another tourist who looked Italian but turned out to be from London. She asked me, "Where are you from ?" I said, "From Nepal." "Oh really ! I thought you were a Tibetan." That comment gave me a big jolt. To a person who has always considered his face to be a typical Nepali face and one who belongs to a social group now categorised as a *janajati* (Nepal's janajati leaders claim that 70 percent of the Nepali population are janajatis), it was profoundly distressing to find I no longer looked like a Nepali.

But now, in retrospect, I think the Italian-looking lady from London was correct. These days, wherever you look in the streets of Kathmandu, you see Indian immigrants in all forms — *paanwalas*, vendors, traders, shopkeepers, lodge-owners and construction workers. Their numbers are growing. Naturally, for an uninitiated visitor who has come to Nepal for the first time and who may be ignorant of the Gorkha glory, a very Nepali face may seem non-Nepali.

Why does Kathmandu seem flooded with Indian immigrants? This is particularly so after the political changes of 1990. After the democratic interim government came to power, one of the first things it did, was to start broadcasting news in Hindi on the radio and lift the regulation that required Indian workers to obtain work permits in Nepal. As a result, over the years, the influx of Indian immigrants has increased manifold. They are everywhere. Nobody knows for sure how many Indian immigrants are in Kathmandu or in Nepal. According to one estimates there are 300,000 Indian immigrants working and living in Kathmandu alone. That is quite a sizeable number in a valley of about 1.5 million people. They come, day in and day out, in search of a better living, in search of jobs and before long, they settle down here as permanent residents. They pick up the Nepali language in no time as it is very easy for Hindi-speakers to learn Nepali. There is a constitutional provision that after fifteen years of continuous stay in Nepal, one can apply to be a naturalised citizen.

Why is this happening? The only reason can be that the open border we have between the two countries encourages this flow from our southern neighbour. No doubt there are people from Nepal who are also going to India across the open border to seek jobs and a better standard of living. In that case, too, nobody knows how many Nepali people go to India every year.

There has been no study of this cross-border movement. There has been no study done on Indian immigrants coming to Nepal and neither on how much money Indian immigrants have been remitting back to India every year. We simply brush aside the issue of immigration and the problem of open border saying that this has been a traditional practice; that it has been like this since time immemorial; that we are blood brothers; that we are too close; that we share the same history, the same culture, the same religion and possibly the same destiny.

We cannot continue to live in history. We might have a shared history but it must be understood that we do not live in historical times. We cannot make assumptions saying that if 500,000 persons come from India to Nepal, as many people also go from Nepal to India. This is just an assumption. You cannot make plans on the basis of assumptions which could be dangerously incorrect.

I wonder, how our planners make plans and implement them. Nepal is reeling under a tremendous population growth. The rate of increase is about 2.6 percent, which means every year we have nearly half a million more mouths to feed. If you add the number of immigrants who come in every day, the figures will be mind boggling. Nepal is a resource-starved country. It is ill-prepared to handle this situation of high population pressure. This is why even 13 years after the Gurung Report was first published, the document still remains relevant. I would say it is of even greater significance now.

We have to look back at the situation in 1983 to understand what prompted our government to commission the study. When the Gurung Report came out, it was brutally criticised. Some people even demanded that Dr Harka Gurung be hanged.

The Gurung Report covered many aspects like international boundaries, industry, trade, citizenship, labour and employment, immigration and population policy. The Gurung Committee made seventy recommendations. Prominent among them were the recommendations that points of entry and between Nepal and India should be specified and people's movement should be regulated by registering the names of people who cross the border at the specified entry and exit points. It recommended that a multi-entry permit be issued to residents living within 10 kilometers of the border and the permit to be renewed every year. Finally, the report proposed that at an opportune time, the government introduce a regular passport system. Other recommendations were Indian nationals visiting Nepal be encompassed within the immigration recommendation policy and work permits be imposed on Indian citizens. The second was implemented, only to be lifted after the advent of democracy in 1990.

I feel that even after so many years these recommendations have not lost their relevance. Rather they have become more relevant. The problems existed then and they exist now and if they are not addressed soon, they will become insurmountable. There is a danger that the relationship between Nepal and India may sour, as a result.

Let's look at what is happening because of the open border. Smuggling of all kinds is taking place. Kidnapping in the border areas has become big business. Newspapers are full of stories about persons being kidnapped for ransom. Hordes of Nepali girls end up in the brothels of India. If the open border was regulated perhaps half of them would be stopped right at the border.

This open border between Nepal and India is unique in the whole of South Asia. Borders between India and other countries like Bangladesh and Pakistan, are also porous but they are not open like ours. Ours is not only porous, it is legally open as well. This is because of the treaty that the last Rana despot, Mohan Shamsher, signed with India in 1950. It is called the Nepal-India Friendship Treaty. Personally, I feel, the treaty has out lived its usefulness.

The treaty may have facilitated the movement of Nepalis earlier. We had no road links linking Kathmandu with other areas of Nepal. You had to come all the way to Raxaul to travel to Kathmandu from any part of the country. But things have changed. It was another time, another situation. Now we should look again at this issue and if the treaty comes in the way of regulating our border, let us review it and, if need be, abrogate it.

India is a big country and regulating its border with Nepal is not a priority. Besides, it gives room for its ever-growing population to stretch its legs. In Nepal, the problems with the open border are not faced because our rulers live under a psychosis of fear. There is a widespread belief that governments in Nepal are made and unmade by India. That is why our leaders, do not have the courage to bring up this matter and talk it over. We should be able to call a spade a spade. If we have a problem we should be able to point it out. I believe that even the problem of Bhutanese refugee would not have arisen if we had a regulated border. The Bhutanese refugees who crossed over first to India could not have crossed the border from India into Nepal. But they were shown the way to Nepal and told, "There is your homeland. Go there."

At one time, it may have been a boon to have an open border with a prosperous neighbour. But not any more. To say that Nepal is India-locked has become a cliché but behind that saying lies a larger truth that is not so explicit. We are surrounded by India, no doubt, but a closer look at the states of India around us is more revealing of what being India-locked means. There is U.P., the most populous state of India, Bihar the most backward state and also the resource-starved state of West Bengal. If you add the populations of these three Indian states, it will come roughly to about 300 million or more. If 10 percent, or even 5 percent of this 300 million decides to cross over and live in Nepal, can you imagine what will happen to the demographic profile of Nepal which has a population of 22 million?

The time has come to face this issue. Why do we want the border regulated? Because we want to have a better relationship with India. We cannot do without India. Our destiny is linked to India's by geography and by history. But we want a relationship based on mutual trust and mutual respect. That is why we need the border to be regulated.

In the end, I would like to say that even if my face has ceased to be a Nepali face, I am sure what I have expressed here is representative of the feelings of most Nepalis.

APPENDIX A

Model National Law on Refugees*

1. Purpose of the Act

The purpose of this Act is to establish a procedure for granting of refugee status to asylum seekers, to guarantee to them fair treatment, and to establish the requisite machinery therefor For the purposes of this Act the grant of refugee status shall be considered a peaceful and humanitarian act, shall not be regarded as an unfriendly act and does not imply any judgement on the country of origin of the refugee.

2.Terminology

In this Act, unless the context otherwise requires :

i. 'Asylum seeker' means a foreigner who seeks recognition and protection as a refugee.

ii. 'Refugee' means a 'refugee' defined in Section 4 and includes dependants of persons determined to be refugees.

iii. 'Country of origin' means the refugee's country of nationality, or if he or she has no nationality, his or her country of former habitual residence.

iv. 'Commissioner' means the 'Commissioner for Refugees', an executive officer, referred to in Section 8 of this Act.

iv. "Commissioner' means the 'Commissioner for Refugees', an executive officer, referred to in Section 8 of this Act.

v. 'Refugee Committee' means the 'Committee' established as an appellate tribunal by the Government under Section 8 of thisAct.

3. Non-Obstante Clause

The provisions of this Act shall have effect notwithstanding the provisions of any other law including *The Foreigners Act.*

4. Definition of Refugee

A refugee is :

a. any person who is outside his or her country of origin, and who is unable or unwilling to return to, and is unable or unwilling to avail himself or herself of the protection of that country because of a well-founded fear of persecution on account of race, religion, sex, na-

*This Model National Law on Refugees was adopted at the 4th Regional Consultation on Refugees and Migratory Movements in South Asia, held in Dhaka on 10-11 November 1997.

tionality, ethnic identity membership of a particular social group or political opinion,[1] or,

b. any person who owing to external aggression, occupation, foreign domination, serious violation of human rights or other events seriously disrupting public order in either part or whole of his or her country of origin, is compelled to leave his or her place of habitual residence in order to seek refuge in another place outside his or her country of origin[2].

5. Persons who shall be excluded from refugee status

A person shall be excluded from refugee status for the purpose of this Act if:

a. he or she has committed a crime against peace, a war crime or a crime against humanity, as defined in the international instruments drawn up to make provision in respect of such crimes;

b. he or she has committed a serious non-political crime outside the country of asylum prior to his or her admission into this country as a refugee[3].

6. Principle of Non-Refoulement

a. No refugee or asylum seeker shall be expelled or returned in any manner whatsoever to a place where there are reasons to believe his or her life or freedom would be threatened on account of any of the reasons set out in sub-sections (a) or (b) of Section 4.

b. The benefit of the present provision may not, however, be claimed by a refugee or asylum seeker where there are reasonable grounds for regarding him or her as a danger to the security of the country or who has been convicted by a final judgement of a serious crime and constitutes a danger to the community.

7. Application

a. Where an asylum seeker requests to be recognised as a refugee either at the point of entry or subsequently, the country concerned shall act in accordance with the principle laid down in Section 6 and refer the case to the Commissioner of Refugees for disposal.

b. Where an application is made by an asylum seeker for determination of his or her status as a refugee, pending determination of such status, no restrictions shall be imposed on the asylum seeker save and except those that are necessary in the interests of sovereignty and integrity of the State or public order.

8. Constitution of the Authorities

In order to implement the provisions of this Act the Government shall appoint:

a. Commissioners for Refugees; and

b. A Refugee Committee as the appellate authority.

9. a. A Commissioner for Refugees shall receive and consider applications for refugee status and make decisions.

b. The Commissioners for Refugees shall be of a rank not less than that of an Administrative Head of a District.

10. a. The Refugee Committee shall be the appellate authority and receive and consider applications for refugee status *suo moto*, or those made by the asylum seekers in appeal against the decision of the Commissioner.

b. The Refugee Committee shall consist of the following three members:

i. a sitting or retired High Court Judge designated by the Government in consultation with the Chief Justice of the Supreme Court as Chairperson,

ii. two independent members conversant with refugee matters.

11. Finality of Order

Every order of the Refugee Committee shall be final.

12. Determination of Refugee Status [4]

a. An asylum seeker who wishes to claim refugee status under the terms of this Act shall be heard by a Commissioner for Refugees before the determination of his or her status.

b. During the Refugee determination interview, the asylum seeker shall be given necessary facilities including the services of a competent interpreter where required, and a reasonable opportunity to present evidence in support of his or her case.

c. The asylum seeker, if he or she wishes, shall be given an opportunity, of which he or she could be duly informed, to contact a representative of UNHCR.

d. The Asylum seeker, if he or she wishes, shall be entitled to be assisted in the determination of the status by a person of his or her choice including a legal practitioner.

e. Where an application by the asylum seeker is rejected, the Commissioner for Refugees shall give reasons for the order in writing and furnish a copy of it to the asylum seeker.

f. If the asylum seeker is not recognised as a refugee, he or she could be given a reasonable time to appeal to the Refugee Committee as the appellate authority for reconsideration of decision.

g. If the asylum seeker is recognised as a refugee, he or she shall be informed accordingly and issued with documentation certifying his or her refugee status.

13. Persons who shall Cease to be Refugees

A person shall cease to be a refugee for the purpose of thisAct if:

a. he or she voluntarily re-avails himself or herself of the protection of the country of his or her origin; or

b. he or she has become a citizen of the country of asylum; or he or she has acquired the nationality of some other country and enjoys the protection of that country, or

d. he or she has voluntarily re-established himself or herself in the country which he or she left or outside which he or she remained owing to fear of persecution; or

e. he or she can no longer, because the circumstances in connec tion with which he or she was recognised as a refugee, have ceased to exist, continue to refuse to avail himself or herself of the protection of the country of his or her nationality.

14. Rights and Duties of Refugees

a. Every refugee so long as he or she remains within this country shall have the right to:

i. fair and due treatment, without discrimination on grounds of race, religion, sex, nationality, ethnic identity, membership of a particular social group or political opinion.

ii. receive the same treatment as is generally accorded to aliens under the Constitution or any other laws and privileges as may be granted by the Central or State Governments.

iii. receive sympathetic consideration by the country of asylum with a view to ensuring basic human entitlements.

iv. be given special consideration to their protection and material well-being in the case of refugee women and children.

v. choose his or her place of residence and move freely within the territory of the country of asylum, subject to any regulations applicable to aliens generally in the same circumstances.

vi. be issued identity documents.

vii. be issued travel documents for the purpose of travel outside and back to the territory of the country of asylum unless compelling reasons of national security or public order otherwise require.

b. Every refugee shall be bound by the laws and regulations of the country of asylum.

15.Situations of Mass Influx

a. The Government may, in appropriate cases where there is large-scale influx of asylum seekers, issue an order permitting them to reside in the country without requiring their individual status to be determined under Section 12 of this Act, until such time as the reasons for departure from the country of origin have ceased to exist, or the government decides that their status should be determined on an individual basis under this Act.

b. In the case of asylum seekers who have been permitted to reside in the country under this provision, they may be subject to reasonable restrictions with respect to their location and movement, but will otherwise be granted normally the same rights as refugees under this Act.

16.Refugees Unlawfully in the Country of Refuge

The Government shall not impose penalties, on account of their illegal entry, or presence, on refugees who, coming directly from a place where their life or freedom was threatened in the sense of Section 4, enter or are present in the country of asylum without authorisation, provided they present themselves without delay to the authorities and show good cause for their illegal entry or presence.

17.Voluntary Repatriation [5]

The repatriation of refugees shall take place at their free volition expressed in writing or other appropriate means which must be clearly expressed. The voluntary and individual character of repatriation of refugees and the need for it to be carried out under conditions of safety to the country of origin shall be respected.

18.Rules and regulations

The Government may frame rules and regulations, from time to time, to give effect to the provisions of this Act.

NOTES

1. This part of the definition is based onArticle 1 (A) (2) of the 1951 Convention on Refugees, which has universal approval for the refugee definition. However, taking note of the fact today's conflicts are linked to inter ethnic violence also, ethnic identity is added in the definition as given in the 1951 Convention on Refugees. It is also understood that membership of a particular social group includes gender based persecution.
2. This part of the definition is based on a border definition incorporated in Article 1 (2) of the 1969 OAU Convention. Remembering that promotion of human rights throughout the world of one of the purpose of the United Nations, and realising that in practice there are massive violations of human rights in many parts of the world, and also finding that the Cartagena Declaration on Refugees in 1984 incorporates massive violation of the human rights as a ground for treating asylum seekers as refugees, the same is incorporated in this part of the definition.
3. This provision does not mean that persons having committed political crimes are automatically to be considered as refugees. On the contrary, when there are serious reasons to believe that the asylum-seeker has committed a politically-motivated crime to endanger the right to life or physical integrity of another person, this asylum-seeker would normally not be recognised as a refugee, unless the punishment for such crime is expected to be discriminatory or disproportionate.
4. This Article is based on UNHCR ExCom Conclusion No. 8 (XXVII) - 1977 on 'Determination of Refugee Status'.
5. This provision is derived from UNHCR ExCom Conclusion 40 (XXXV) - 1985 on 'Voluntary Repatriation', at para (b).

APPENDIX B

Recommendations of the Seminar on Refugees, Migrants, Internally Displaced and Stateless Persons in South Asia: Need for a Regional Protocol

The participants of the Kathmandu seminar on Refugees, Migrants and Stateless Persons in South Asia : Need for a Regional Protocol, November 18 - 22, 1996,

Considering that South Asia has the fourth largest refugee population in the world, not taking into account the millions of internally displaced persons and environmental refugees;

Noting that in the region of South Asia, governments by arbitrarily changing their citizenship laws and introducing severe restrictions to retaining, acquiring or re-acquiring citizenship have created millions of stateless persons;

Cognisant of the peculiar process of colonial and post-colonial border making between India, Pakistan, Bangladesh and Nepal which has divided several trans-border communities disrupting their economy, society and family, and that it has also affected trans-border communities between Bangladesh, India and Myanmar on the eastern side and between Afghanistan, Iran and Pakistan on the western side;

Recognising that sometimes states do not accept refugees from another country for fear of incurring the displeasure of the refugee creating state;

Concerned that the situation of the refugees and displaced persons in South Asia has evolved in recent years to the point at which it demands special attention and action, call upon the South Asian states to develop and adopt a Regional Charter and a Protocol for the protection of refugees and displaced persons.

The Participants call upon the states to accede to and ratify the 1951 UN Convention on the Status of refugees and the 1967 Protocol, without reservation.

A Regional Charter/ Protocol must make it incumbent on the states to receive refugees on humanitarian ground and the regional charter should provide for a mechanism to support the refugee receiving country in such instances.

While recognising the right of a state to refuse permanent asylum to a refugee, the regional mechanism must ensure that the states grant temporary asylum and protection to the refugee till the person finds another country willing to accept her/him;

Underlining that states have a responsibility to prevent incitement of racial, religious and other hatred against refugees, migrants and displaced persons;

The Regional Charter/Protocol should ensure that any repatriation of refugees is voluntary and is declared to be so on an individual basis, and is carried out in an atmosphere of transparency with the cooperation of UNHCR and NGOs working in the area of relief and protection.

The Participants demand that the Regional Charter/Protocol must ensure that no person or community can be deprived of the right to citizenship, habitat, language, religion and culture arbitrarily by states/ governments or be made stateless. Citizenship must not be taken away because of marriage. There should be no gender discrimination on grant of citizenship including all rights flowing therefrom. States must ensure that all citizens enjoy the right to freedom of movement and residence within their borders. The states individually and the regional governments collectively must agree to protect these basic rights of the people of the South Asian region.

Aware that the definition of Refugees in the 1951 Convention is restrictive and that it applies only to persons who are outside their country,— "owing to well founded fear of being persecuted for reasons of race, religion, nationality, membership of a particular social group or opinion"—and that the definition does not provide protection to those who have been forced to flee or have been internally displaced because of ethnic strife, civil disturbance, breakdown of law and order, denial of human rights and insecurity of food, land and water caused by forces beyond their control;

Bearing in mind that the 1969 OAU Convention Governing the Specific Aspects of Refugee Problems in Africa, while retaining the definition of refugee contained in the 1951 UN Convention , expanded it by adding,

> "the term refugee shall also apply to every person who, owing to external aggression, occupation, foreign domination or events seriously disturbing public order in either part or the whole of his country of origin or nationality is compelled to leave his place of habitual residence..."

Observing that the Cartagena Declaration on refugees adopted by the Central American governments in 1984 further expanded the definition of refugees to include

> "persons who have fled their country because their lives, safety or freedom have been threatened by generalised violence, foreign aggression, internal conflicts, massive violation of human rights or other circumstances which have seriously disturbed public order..."

The participants call upon the states of South Asia to expand the definition of refugees along the lines of the OAU Convention and the Cartagena Declaration and also taking into consideration the following:

Victims of forced eviction, man-made and natural disasters and environmental refugees

Noting that some policies pursued by South Asian governments have impoverished vast sections of their peoples, particularly those belonging to minority communities and economically backward sections and that some of these development projects have adversely impacted the economy and livelihood of peoples across the border forcing them to be uprooted and some of them have crossed international borders to become "refugee/migrants";

Concerned that millions of people have been uprooted by such development projects and by natural environmental disasters to become internally displaced;

Regretting that the failure of governments to provide the security of food, shelter, land and water has caused mass migration of their peoples across borders in search of livelihood and shelter;

Observing that the integration of the economies of SouthAsia into the global economy has intensified the free flow of capital and goods, the participants urge the states to adopt a policy of developing an integrated labour market in the region of SouthAsia. This is essential to prevent the exploitation of migrants and displaced persons by unscrupulous employers in "sweat shops".

Recognising thatmigrant women and children are the worst affected, the states are called upon to make special efforts to protect their rights.

The participants further recommend that the SouthAsian Charter/ Protocol on refugees, migrants, internally displaced and stateless persons should recognise all such persons who have been displaced by natural and/or man made disasters and the denial of food, land and water security as Persons of Concern.

The states have an obligation to protect the rights of its citizen to remain in their habitat. The states shall endeavour not to create a situation which compels citizens to be displaced. States shall be responsible for the rehabilitation of all internally displaced persons in a dignified and secure manner. The participants are of the opinion that the states shall be held accountable for the displacement of their citizens to other countries.

However, when such displaced persons seek refuge in another state, the host state should respect the principle of *non-refoulement*.

Accepting that it is important to retain the distinction between people who flee because of political, ethnic and cultural persecution, discrimination, violation of human rights and the disruption of law and order and those who leave their homes because of insecurity of food and shelter;

But noting that the migration is complicated by the fact that governments and or majority groups are systematically denying relief and violating the human rights of affected communities, the participants urge caution in matters of classification of refugees and displaced persons as "economic refugees or migrants".

The assumption that migrants cause economic hardship to the poorer sections of the host country population by competing for lower wage jobs may not necessarily be correct. There is a need for research on this in South Asia.

Governments and NGOs should take up the task of developing a detailed status report on cross border population movements. Existing policies are based on assumptions and conjecture. The Nepal-India case is a telling example.

Minimum standards

Understanding that the South Asian states can not be called upon to provide for high standards of relief and support to refugees, stateless and displaced persons as envisaged in the 1951 UN Convention and the 1967 Protocol, it is necessary that minimum standards be maintained, otherwise the act of granting temporary asylum or residence permit becomes meaningless. This should be ensured through a regional standard setting exercise which must be enforceable. A regional fund and responsibility sharing mechanism need to be created to help smaller and poorer states.

In this regard the OAU Convention and the Cartagena Declaration can serve as models.

States should provide access and support to UNHCR, international and national aid and relief agencies to fulfil their obligations.

UNHCR and regional mechanism

While appreciating that UNHCR is expanding its mandate to cover internally displaced persons, there is concern that it has been diluting its protection mandate for refugees. This trend needs to be arrested. Anxiety is being expressed at the tendency of UNHCR to support "imposed repatriation" of refugees to home countries under "less than desirable conditions".

UNHCR has been decreasing its financial support for refugees in South Asia. This needs to be checked. The refugee determination process should be transparent. The process of status determination followed by UNHCR is not open to scrutiny. It is recommended that in the region of South Asia refugee status determination should be done jointly by the states and UNHCR under a Regional Charter/Protocol. This process should be open to judicial scrutiny and appeal.

Kathmandu,
November 22, 1996

CONTRIBUTORS

MR. AJITH RUPASINGHE, political activist, National Organiser, National Peace Council of Sri Lanka, Colombo.

MS. ANGELA DIETRICH, researcher in anthropology, Tribhuvan University, Kathmandu.

PROF. BARUN DE, eminent historian, Maulana Abul Kalam Azad Institute of Asian Studies, Calcutta.

MR. BASANTA THAPA, writer and commentator, Editor, Himal Magazine (Nepali), Kathmandu.

FR. C. AMALRAJ, human rights activist, Coordinator, South Asia regional office, Jesuit Refugee Service, Bangalore.

DR. DARINI RAJASHINGAM, academic, Senior Fellow, International Centre for Ethnic Studies, Colombo.

MR. GAUTAM NAVLAKHA, human rights activist, Associate Editor, Economic & Political Weekly, New Delhi.

MR. HARI PHUYAL, academic and lawyer, associated with Nepal Law Campus, Tribhuvan University and Supreme Court of Nepal.

DR. HAROON AHMED, eminent psychologist and human rights activist, Director, Psychology Centre, Karachi.

MR. JOE WILLIAM, human rights activist, Executive Director, National Peace Council of Sri Lanka, Colombo.

MS. MALIKA BASU, environmentalist and researcher, Multi Action Research Group, New Delhi.

DR. MEGHNA GUHATHAKURTA, academic and human rights activist, Department of International Relations, Dhaka University, Dhaka.

MUHAMMAD NUR KHAN, human rights activist and researcher, Director, Adhikar, Dhaka.

PROF. PARTHA GHOSH, academic, Director, Indian Council of Social Sciences Research, New Delhi.

PROF. RANABIR SAMADDAR, academic and human rights activist, Maulana Abul Kalam Azad Institute of Asian Studies, Calcutta.

MR. RAKESH CHHETRI, Bhutanese political refugee exiled in Nepal, Chairman, Centre for Bhutanese Studies, Kathmandu.

MR. RATAN GAZMER, Bhutanese political refugee exiled in Nepal, Coordinator, Appeal Movement Coordination Committee, Damak, Jhapa.

MR. RAVI NAIR, human rights activist, Executive Director, South Asia Human Rights Documentation Centre, New Delhi.

MS. RITA MANCHANDA, freelance writer and TV journalist, New Delhi.

MR. SADEQ KHAN, eminent columnist, Dhaka.

MR. TAPAN K. BOSE, filmmaker and human rights activist, South Asia Forum for Human Rights, Kathmandu.

78